Lecture Notes in Computer Science 9030

Commenced Publication in 1973
Founding and Former Series Editors:
Gerhard Goos, Juris Hartmanis, and Jan van Leeuwen

Editorial Board

David Hutchison
  Lancaster University, Lancaster, UK
Takeo Kanade
  Carnegie Mellon University, Pittsburgh, PA, USA
Josef Kittler
  University of Surrey, Guildford, UK
Jon M. Kleinberg
  Cornell University, Ithaca, NY, USA
Friedemann Mattern
  ETH Zurich, Zürich, Switzerland
John C. Mitchell
  Stanford University, Stanford, CA, USA
Moni Naor
  Weizmann Institute of Science, Rehovot, Israel
C. Pandu Rangan
  Indian Institute of Technology, Madras, India
Bernhard Steffen
  TU Dortmund University, Dortmund, Germany
Demetri Terzopoulos
  University of California, Los Angeles, CA, USA
Doug Tygar
  University of California, Berkeley, CA, USA
Gerhard Weikum
  Max Planck Institute for Informatics, Saarbrücken, Germany

More information about this series at http://www.springer.com/series/8183

Marina L. Gavrilova · C.J. Kenneth Tan
Khalid Saeed · Nabendu Chaki
Soharab Hossain Shaikh (Eds.)

Transactions on Computational Science XXV

Springer

Editors-in-Chief

Marina L. Gavrilova
University of Calgary
Calgary, AB
Canada

C.J. Kenneth Tan
Sardina Systems OÜ
Tallinn
Estonia

Guest Editors

Khalid Saeed
Bialystok University of Technology
Bialystok
Poland

Soharab Hossain Shaikh
NIIT University
Neemrana
India

Nabendu Chaki
University of Calcutta
Kolkata
India

ISSN 0302-9743 ISSN 1611-3349 (electronic)
Lecture Notes in Computer Science
ISBN 978-3-662-47073-2 ISBN 978-3-662-47074-9 (eBook)
DOI 10.1007/978-3-662-47074-9

Springer Heidelberg New York Dordrecht London
© Springer-Verlag Berlin Heidelberg 2015
This work is subject to copyright. All rights are reserved by the Publisher, whether the whole or part of the material is concerned, specifically the rights of translation, reprinting, reuse of illustrations, recitation, broadcasting, reproduction on microfilms or in any other physical way, and transmission or information storage and retrieval, electronic adaptation, computer software, or by similar or dissimilar methodology now known or hereafter developed.
The use of general descriptive names, registered names, trademarks, service marks, etc. in this publication does not imply, even in the absence of a specific statement, that such names are exempt from the relevant protective laws and regulations and therefore free for general use.
The publisher, the authors and the editors are safe to assume that the advice and information in this book are believed to be true and accurate at the date of publication. Neither the publisher nor the authors or the editors give a warranty, express or implied, with respect to the material contained herein or for any errors or omissions that may have been made.

Printed on acid-free paper

Springer-Verlag GmbH Berlin Heidelberg is part of Springer Science+Business Media
(www.springer.com)

LNCS Transactions on Computational Science

Computational science, an emerging and increasingly vital field, is now widely recognized as an integral part of scientific and technical investigations, affecting researchers and practitioners in areas ranging from aerospace and automotive research to biochemistry, electronics, geosciences, mathematics, and physics. Computer systems research and the exploitation of applied research naturally complement each other. The increased complexity of many challenges in computational science demands the use of supercomputing, parallel processing, sophisticated algorithms, and advanced system software and architecture. It is therefore invaluable to have input by systems research experts in applied computational science research.

Transactions on Computational Science focuses on original high-quality research in the realm of computational science in parallel and distributed environments, also encompassing the underlying theoretical foundations and the applications of large-scale computation.

The journal offers practitioners and researchers the opportunity to share computational techniques and solutions in this area, to identify new issues, and to shape future directions for research, and it enables industrial users to apply leading-edge, large-scale, high-performance computational methods.

In addition to addressing various research and application issues, the journal aims to present material that is validated – crucial to the application and advancement of the research conducted in academic and industrial settings. In this spirit, the journal focuses on publications that present results and computational techniques that are verifiable.

Scope

The scope of the journal includes, but is not limited to, the following computational methods and applications:

- Aeronautics and Aerospace
- Astrophysics
- Big Data Analytics
- Bioinformatics
- Biometric Technologies
- Climate and Weather Modeling
- Communication and Data Networks
- Compilers and Operating Systems
- Computer Graphics
- Computational Biology
- Computational Chemistry
- Computational Finance and Econometrics

- Computational Fluid Dynamics
- Computational Geometry
- Computational Number Theory
- Data Representation and Storage
- Data Mining and Data Warehousing
- Information and On-line Security
- Grid Computing
- Hardware/Software Co-design
- High-Performance Computing
- Image and Video Processing
- Information Systems
- Information Retrieval
- Modeling and Simulations
- Mobile Computing
- Numerical and Scientific Computing
- Parallel and Distributed Computing
- Robotics and Navigation
- Supercomputing
- System-on-Chip Design and Engineering
- Virtual Reality and Cyberworlds
- Visualization

Editorial

The Transactions on Computational Science journal is part of the Springer series *Lecture Notes in Computer Science*, and is devoted to the gamut of computational science issues, from theoretical aspects to application-dependent studies and the validation of emerging technologies.

The journal focuses on original high-quality research in the realm of computational science in parallel and distributed environments, encompassing the facilitating theoretical foundations and the applications of large-scale computations and massive data processing. Practitioners and researchers share computational techniques and solutions in the area, identify new issues, and shape future directions for research, as well as enable industrial users to apply the presented techniques.

The current issue consists of two parts. Part I is a Special Issue on Computer Vision/Image Processing Techniques and Applications edited by Prof. Khalid Saeed, Prof. Nabendu Chaki, and Associate Prof. Soharab Hossain Shaikh. Part II is devoted to Optimization and Networks, and covers a range of topics in social context-based computing, clustering, risk analysis, array restructuring, wireless sensor networks, and feed forward neural networks.

Part I is comprised of six papers, spanning areas of computer vision, image processing for biometric security, information fusion, and KINECT activity recognition. The full description of contributions and impact of those papers can be found in the Guest Editors' Foreword.

Part II is comprised of five papers united by the theme of optimization through novel methods for data fusion, clustering in WSN, fault-tolerance, probability, weight assignment, and risk analysis. These papers cover the topics of context-based social analysis for gait recognition, cluster head selection using weight and rank in WSN, multiple weight-and-neuron-fault-tolerance in feedforward neural networks, and optimization through coded and space-time cooperation with multiple relays in Nakagami-m fading. In addition, a new circuit for restructuring mesh-connected processor arrays is proposed and an urban railway operation plan is studied. The first article of Part II was initially submitted to the Special Issue on Advances in Autonomic Computing: Formal and Practical Aspects of Context-Aware Systems, while all other articles were submitted as regular papers.

We would like to extend our sincere appreciation, first and foremost, to the Special Issue Guest Editors Khalid Saeed, Nabendu Chaki, and Soharab Hossain Shaikh who assembled a fine collection of papers after a rigorous multistage refereeing process and who have demonstrated a high degree of professionalism and dedication to excellence. We also would like to thank all renewed members of the TCS Editorial Board for over five years of their service. We acknowledge the contribution of the external reviewers and thank them for their diligence and critical comments in preparing this issue. Last, but not least, we would also like to thank all of the authors for submitting their papers to the Journal. We are very grateful to the LNCS editorial staff of Springer, who supported us at every stage of the project.

We hope that this issue will be a valuable resource for Transactions on Computational Science readers and will stimulate further research into the vibrant area of computational science applications, including image processing, biometric security, and network optimization.

March 2015

Marina L. Gavrilova
C.J. Kenneth Tan

Guest Editors' Preface
Special Issue on Computer Vision/Image Processing Techniques and Applications

Over the last few decades, image processing and computer vision communities have been one of the dominant contributors in the field of research in Computer Science. The primary focus of the researchers concentrated on developing novel techniques for computer vision and image processing problems; emerging and innovative applications of computer-vision-based applications as well as theoretical contributions that are relevant to computer vision and image processing.

Papers submitted to this Special Issue of Springer's Transactions on Computational Science focusing on "Computer Vision/Image Processing Techniques and Applications" aimed at providing a comprehensive understanding of the fundamentals as well as the cutting-edge technologies and innovative applications of computer vision and image processing techniques.

There were several rounds in the review process for selecting the papers for the final publication. This Special Issue contains six selected papers out of more than 12 initial submissions.

Infrared imaging has attracted the attention of researchers for the last few years. Infrared devices capture only the heat-emitting objects. Visualization of the IR images is very poor due to low contrast of the images. Improvement in quality is required for a given IR image toward better perception and visualization. The first paper uses the concepts of fuzzy sets for visualization and enhancement of infrared images. Experimental verification on a standard benchmark database shows the efficacy of the presented method.

The second paper provides a fresh perspective on the technique of dance composition. Dance composers are commonly required to ensure a smooth flow of inter-gesture dance transitions. This paper presents an approach by incorporating the differential evolution algorithm to compose interesting dance patterns from a set of dance sequences. Authors make use of the Microsoft Kinect sensor for generating a skeletal image of the subjects.

A framework for moving object segmentation in maritime surveillance is presented in the third paper. This paper also considers the issue of dynamic changes in the background of the images.

A novel technique of feature extraction for content-based image identification is presented in the fourth paper. The new technique is named Sorted Block Truncation Coding (SBTC). The experimental results on the benchmark dataset prove the effectiveness of the proposed methodology. The SBTC feature extraction technique has also shown consistent performance in a compressed domain without having any significant degradation in classification performance.

The subjective evaluation method of usability is costly and time-consuming, and sometimes produces more unreliable data than the objective evaluation method because of the subjective view. On the other hand, the objective evaluation method is traditionally useful and reliable, but expensive. The fifth paper presents a method for objective evaluation of usability using parameters of user's fingertip movements.

The last paper addresses the importance of using image fusion techniques in the context of medical image processing. This paper uses Daubechies Complex Wavelet and the concept of Near Set for fusing medical images.

Let us take this opportunity to thank all the authors who submitted their manuscripts to this Special Issue and all the reviewers for their invaluable contributions to the reviewing process. We express our special appreciation and deep regards for Prof. Marina Gavrilova, the Editor-in-Chief of Springer's Transactions on Computational Science, for her untiring encouragement and support.

This Special Issue on "Computer Vision/Image Processing Techniques and Applications" provides the reader with interesting new insights into contemporary research with a focus on quantitative performance analysis from multiple aspects of computer vision ranging from image fusion to newer approaches to methodologies for dance composition. All six of the papers make valuable contributions and we hope that the readers of TCS journals will enjoy this Special Issue.

March 2015

Khalid Saeed
Nabendu Chaki
Soharab Hossain Shaikh

LNCS Transactions on Computational Science – Editorial Board

Tetsuo Asano	JAIST, Japan
Alexander V. Bogdanov	Institute for High Performance Computing and Data Bases, Russia
Martin Buecker	RWTH Aachen University, Germany
Tamal Dey	Ohio State University, USA
Osvaldo Gervasi	Università degli Studi di Perugia, Italy
Christopher Gold	University of Glamorgan, UK
Rodolfo Haber	Council for Scientific Research, Spain
Andres Iglesias	University of Cantabria, Spain
Deok-Soo Kim	Hanyang University, South Korea
Stanislav Klimenko	Institute of Computing for Physics and Technology, Russia
Ivana Kolingerova	University of West Bohemia, Czech Republic
Vipin Kumar	Army High Performance Computing Research Center, USA
Antonio Lagana	Università degli Studi di Perugia, Italy
D.T. Lee	Institute of Information Science, Academia Sinica, Taiwan
Laurence Liew	Platform Computing, Singapore
Nikolai Medvedev	Novosibirsk Russian Academy of Sciences, Russia
Graham M. Megson	University of Reading, UK
Edward D. Moreno	UEA – University of Amazonas State, Brazil
Dimitri Plemenos	Université de Limoges, France
Viktor K. Prasanna	University of Southern California, USA
Muhammad Sarfraz	KFUPM, Saudi Arabia
Dale Shires	Army Research Laboratory, USA
Alexei Sourin	Nanyang Technological University, Singapore
David Taniar	Monash University, Australia
Athanasios Vasilakos	University of Western Macedonia, Greece
Chee Yap	New York University, USA
Igor Zacharov	SGI Europe, Switzerland
Zahari Zlatev	National Environmental Research Institute, Denmark

Contents

Special Issue on Computer Vision/Image Processing Techniques and Applications

Perceptual Visualization Enhancement of Infrared Images Using Fuzzy Sets 3
    Rajkumar Soundrapandiyan and Chandra Mouli P.V.S.S.R.

Dance Composition Using Microsoft Kinect 20
    Reshma Kar, Amit Konar, and Aruna Chakraborty

A Framework of Moving Object Segmentation in Maritime Surveillance Inside a Dynamic Background 35
    Alok Kumar Singh Kushwaha and Rajeev Srivastava

Novel Technique in Block Truncation Coding Based Feature Extraction for Content Based Image Identification 55
    Sudeep Thepade, Rik Das, and Saurav Ghosh

Objective Evaluation Method of Usability Using Parameters of User's Fingertip Movement 77
    Nobuyuki Nishiuchi and Yutaka Takahashi

Medical Image Fusion Using Daubechies Complex Wavelet and Near Set . . . 90
    Pubali Chatterjee, Somoballi Ghoshal, Biswajit Biswas,
    Amlan Chakrabarti, and Kashi Nath Dey

Optimization and Networks

A Hybrid Method for Context-Based Gait Recognition Based on Behavioral and Social Traits 115
    Shermin Bazazian and Marina Gavrilova

Cluster Head Selection Heuristic Using Weight and Rank in WSN 135
    Gunjan Jain, S.R. Biradar, and Brijesh Kumar Chaurasia

An FPGA-Based Multiple-Weight-and-Neuron-Fault Tolerant Digital Multilayer Perceptron (Full Version) 148
    Tadayoshi Horita, Itsuo Takanami, Masakazu Akiba, Mina Terauchi,
    and Tsuneo Kanno

Performance Analysis of Coded Cooperation and Space Time Cooperation
with Multiple Relays in Nakagami-*m* Fading 172
   Sindhu Hak Gupta, R.K. Singh, and S.N. Sharan

Urban Railway Operation Plan Subject to Disruption.................. 186
   Amin Jamili

Author Index 201

Special Issue on Computer Vision/Image Processing Techniques and Applications

Perceptual Visualization Enhancement of Infrared Images Using Fuzzy Sets

Rajkumar Soundrapandiyan and Chandra Mouli P.V.S.S.R.(✉)

School of Computing Science and Engineering, VIT University,
Vellore 632014, Tamil Nadu, India
{rajkumars,chandramouli}@vit.ac.in

Abstract. Enhancement of infrared (IR) images is a perplexing task. Infrared imaging finds its applications in military and defense related problems. Since IR devices capture only the heat emitting objects, the visualization of the IR images is very poor. To improve the quality of the given IR image for better perception, suitable enhancement routines are required such that contrast can be improved that suits well for human visual system. To accomplish the task, a fuzzy set based enhancement of IR images is proposed in this paper. The proposed method is adaptive in nature since the required parameters are calculated based on the image characteristics. Experiments are carried out on standard benchmark database and the results show the efficacy of the proposed method.

Keywords: Image enhancement · Perceptual visualization · Fuzzy sets · Fuzzy enhancement · Adaptive image enhancement

1 Introduction

The incessant development of infrared (IR) imaging technology finds its applications predominantly in military field such as in long range surveillance, target detection etc. Target detection in IR images is the key problem in defense applications [1].

Infrared images are, in general, low contrast images. Human visual system can easily discriminate the content in visible images than in IR images. Heat emitting objects or warm objects are captured by the IR sensors such that the images in general appear as low contrast images. This results in poor visualization of the objects and hence detection and recognition of objects becomes very difficult. Low spatial frequency is a major drawback that affects the quality of IR images. This is caused by the diffraction effects induced by the IR optical system, which cause the spatial frequency of IR images to be not as high as that of visual images [2]. The edge and texture information about the objects in IR images are unclear than those in visual images and hence the enhancement of IR images is required. This is essential in long-range surveillance based applications. The problem is difficult because the objects of interest are much smaller than the background in the long-range surveillance [2]. For better understanding of the objects and for improved object detection and recognition, contrast enhancement is a mandatory step.

The contrast enhancement methods can be either a model of contrast stretching mechanism [3–5] or based on histogram equalization (HE) [6]. A transformation operation for elevation of intensity values is defined in the former category. Redistribution of the intensity values resulting in a uniform spread is the objective of the latter category.

The contrast stretching techniques are restricted by transformation function and hence cannot be adaptive to the image. HE [6] is often used in image enhancement but this is not suitable for infrared imagery because it often enhances the background portion than the foreground part. The foreground portion or the target area occupy few pixels in area since the images are captured from a long range and hence they generally look smaller in size compared to the non-heat emitting objects.

A self adaptive contrast enhancement algorithm using plateau based is proposed in [7]. In this method, threshold was selected with the local minima in the histogram of image but it is suitable for continuous probability distribution histogram but not for discrete case. A double plateau by adding a suitable lower and upper threshold values is proposed in [8]. In this method, upper threshold is used to suppress the background and lower threshold is used to improve the contrast of the image. The two thresholds may overlap the target and the background pixels occasionally, resulting in poor enhancement. Chih-Lung Lin [2] proposed an approach for IR image enhancement based on adaptive and a high boost filter. The background and foreground separation depends on the initial threshold value. If initial threshold is set to the mean of image, the method works good but when objects are small compared to background then one group of pixels will dominate histogram and in this case the mean of the input image as initial threshold value fails. Liang et al. [9] proposed an adaptive algorithm based on double plateau where the upper and lower threshold values are calculated at run time based on gray level distribution.

In addition, literature reveals some non-histogram based enhancement algorithms using filters. The simplest enhancement is done using max-median filter [10] but it fails when small target is surrounded by heavy clutter background. Highnam and Brady [11] developed two filters — spatial homomorphic filter and spatio-temporal homomorphic filter for enhancement of far IR images. Tang et al. [12] proposed adaptive spatio-temporal homomorphic filtering approach and is extended to far IR image sequences. These models require prior information about input IR image before processing.

Many researchers [13–16] proposed different algorithms to enhance the image by modifying the pixel values too. A complete adaptive approach that caters the IR images, captured at different illumination conditions, irrespective of the size of the target and the underlying background is the difficult task.

General visible images contain ambiguity and uncertainty of pixel values that arise during sampling and quantization. The IR images is no exceptional to this. Fuzzy domain [17] is the best domain for reducing the ambiguity and uncertainty. In this paper, the enhancement of IR images is done in fuzzy domain. In the proposed method there is no need of any prior information of input image.

The image under study is transformed into fuzzy domain. Modification of the fuzzified gray levels is done followed by defuzzification process. The proposed method with fully adaptive calculation of the parameters proves the efficacy of the method and the subjective and objective evaluation proves the same.

1. The goal of the paper is to enhance the IR images automatically for better visualization.
2. Novelty of the method is the adaptive calculation of parameters required for enhancement in fuzzy domain.
3. To the best of our knowledge, fuzzy based enhancement in IR images is not attempted by researchers.
4. Robustness testing on enhancement results.

The rest of the paper is organized as follows. The proposed methodology is discussed in Sect. 2. The standard evaluation measures used for statistical analysis are discussed in Sect. 3. Experimental results and performance analysis is given in Sect. 4. Section 5 concludes the work.

2 Proposed Methodology

An image X of size $M \times N$ with L gray levels can be considered as an array of fuzzy singletons, each having a value of membership denoting its degree of brightness relative to some brightness level l where $l = 0, 1, 2, \ldots, L - 1$. The fuzzy set of an image [18] is defined in Eq. (1).

$$X = \bigcup_{i=1}^{M} \bigcup_{j=1}^{N} \frac{\mu_{ij}}{x_{ij}} \qquad (1)$$

where μ_{ij} is the membership value of each intensity value at i, j and x_{ij} is the pixel intensity value. The membership function characterizes a suitable property of image such as edge, darkness, brightness, homogeneity, textural property and can be defined globally for the whole image or locally for its segments.

The block diagram of the proposed methodology is shown in Fig. 1. The steps involved in the proposed approach are as follows:

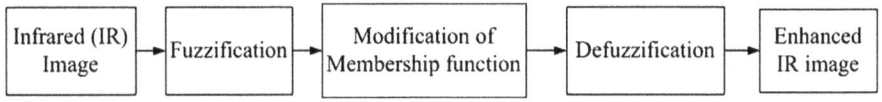

Fig. 1. The block diagram of the proposed method

1. Read the given IR image (x).
2. Fuzzification of x using Eq. (2).
3. Modification of fuzzified data using Eq. (3).
4. Defuzzification of modified fuzzified data using Eq. (6).

2.1 Fuzzification

The image in spatial domain is converted to fuzzy domain [18] using the Eq. (2).

$$\mu_{ij} = T(x_{ij}) = \left[1 + \frac{x_{max} - x_{ij}}{F_d}\right]^{-F_e} \quad (2)$$

where x_{max} is the maximum intensity level in the given image, F_e and F_d denote the exponential and denominational fuzzifiers. When $x_{max} = x_{ij}$ then, $\mu_{ij} = 1$ indicating the maximum brightness.

2.2 Contrast Intensification and Enhancement Operator

Contrast intensification operator (INT) [18] on a fuzzy set μ_{ij} modifies the membership value and is defined in Eq. (3). x_c is the cross over point determined such that the values of $\mu'_{ij} \lessgtr x_c$. The intensification operator monotonically increases the value of μ_{ij} for increasing values of x_c from 0 to 1. The value of x_c is 0.5.

$$\mu'_{ij} = \begin{cases} 2[\mu_{ij}]^2 & 0 \leq \mu_{ij} \leq x_c \\ 1 - 2[1 - \mu_{ij}]^2 & x_c \leq \mu_{ij} \leq 1 \end{cases} \quad (3)$$

The INT operator depends on the membership function. Iteratively the INT operator should be applied on the fuzzified image for the desired image enhancement. If the INT operator is repeatedly applied on the image then it introduces wide gaps between successive intensified curves - the plot between the fuzzified values and the modified fuzzified values. Researchers focused on the improvement of INT operator to reduce the gap. In this work, an attempt is made in automatic fuzzification of the given image. In this work, the values of the fuzzifiers are determined adaptively.

2.3 Fuzzifiers

The significance of fuzzifiers defined in Eq. (2) is that they are used to reduce the ambiguity in the image. For $F_e > 1$, the value of μ_{ij} decreases by a small amount. With further increase of F_e value, the reduction increases by a relatively smaller amount. The value for the exponential fuzzifier is taken as 2 by many researchers [18–22] and the value of the denominational fuzzifier is calculated using Eq. (5) by keeping the values of μ_{ij} and F_e as 0.5 and 2 respectively. The denomination fuzzifier reduces the fuzzified values and increases the values in the range $[0, 1]$.

Adaptive Calculation of Fuzzifiers. The values of the fuzzifiers are determined adaptively and is described here. Instead of static value assignment to F_e, various experiments are conducted for the adaptive calculation of the same. The experiments include max intensity value, min intensity value, standard deviation of the image, variance of the image, first and second order moments etc. Since the basic characterization of the images in the study are infrared i.e., low illumination images, these general trials could not achieve good results. On comparison with these mentioned experiments, it is observed that the value of F_e is calculated using sigmoid [23] function defined in Eq. (4). The mean intensity value of the image is passed as the parameter to the sigmoid function to determine the value of the exponential fuzzifier. It is represented mathematically in Eq. (4).

$$F_e = 1/(1 + exp(-m)) \qquad (4)$$

where m represents the mean of the input image.

The value of the denomination fuzzifier is determined using Eq. (5).

$$F_d = \frac{x_{max} - x_{min}}{0.5^{\frac{-1}{F_e}} - 1} \qquad (5)$$

2.4 Defuzzification

Defuzzification is the process of converting the data from fuzzy domain to the spatial domain by applying inverse transformation defined in Eq. (6).

$$E_{ij} = x'_{ij} = T^{-1}(\mu'_{ij}) = x_{max} - F_d \times \left(\left(\mu'_{ij} \right)^{\frac{-1}{F_e}} \right) + F_d \qquad (6)$$

3 Evaluation Measures

The different evaluation measures used for proving the results obtained statistically are discussed in this section. The quality of the enhanced image is measured through the measures namely Peak Signal to Noise Ratio (PSNR), Mean Absolute Error (MAE), Structural Content Calculation (SCC), Structural Similarity (SSIM), Normalized Correlation Coefficient (NCC) and Universal Image Quality Index (UIQI). In all the metrics defined here, I_{ij} and E_{ij} refers to the intensity value of the original image and the enhanced image at i, j respectively and P, Q represents the width and height of the image.

3.1 Peak Signal to Noise Ratio (*PSNR*)

PSNR [24] is a statistical measure defined as the ratio between the maximum possible power of a signal and the power of corrupting noise that affects the fidelity of its representation and is defined in Eqs. (7) and (8). This metric is used to assess the quality improvement between the original image and enhanced image.

$$\text{MSE} = \frac{\sum_{i=1}^{P} \sum_{j=1}^{Q} (E_{i,j} - I_{i,j})^2}{PQ} \qquad (7)$$

$$\text{PSNR} = 10 \log \frac{\text{MAX}^2}{\text{MSE}} \qquad (8)$$

where MAX is the maximum value in an image. The higher the PSNR value the better the quality of the enhanced image is.

3.2 Mean Absolute Error (MAE)

MAE [25] is a statistical quantity measure that shows the closeness of the enhanced image with the original image. MAE is defined in Eq. (9). Lower MAE value indicates the high similarity between original and enhanced image and vice versa.

$$\text{MAE} = \frac{\sum_{i=1}^{P}\sum_{j=1}^{Q} |(E_{i,j} - I_{i,j})|}{PQ} \qquad (9)$$

3.3 Structural Content Calculation (SCC)

SCC is a measure used to calculate the quality of the enhanced image with respect to the original image. SCC is calculated in Eq. (10) using ratio of sum of pixels in original image to sum of pixels in enhanced image.

$$\text{SCC} = \sum_{i=1}^{P}\sum_{j=1}^{Q} I_{i,j} / \sum_{i=1}^{P}\sum_{j=1}^{Q} E_{i,j} \qquad (10)$$

3.4 Structural Similarity ($SSIM$)

The structural similarity [26] of two images can be measured using Eq. (11).

$$\text{SSIM} = \frac{(2\mu_I \mu_E + C_1)(2\sigma_{IE} + C_2)}{(\mu_I^2 + \mu_E^2 + C_1)(\sigma_I^2 + \sigma_E^2 + C_2)} \qquad (11)$$

where μ_I - Average of I, μ_E - Average of E, σ_I^2 Variance of I, σ_E^2 Variance of E, σ_{IE} - Covariance of IE, $C_1 = k_1 L^2$ - Constant to avoid instability when $\mu_I^2 + \mu_E^2$ is close to zero; $k_1 = 0.01$, $L = 255$ and $C_2 = k_2 L^2$ - Constant to avoid instability when $\sigma_I^2 + \sigma_E^2$ is close to zero; $k_2 = 0.03$, $L = 255$. The value of SSIM index varies from -1 to 1. The value 1 indicates that the two images are identical in all aspects.

3.5 Normalized Correlation Coefficient (NCC)

NCC [27] is another metric for objective evaluation. It is defined in Eq. (12). The NCC value ranges between 0 to 1. NCC value closer to 1 indicates high similarity between the images and 0 indicates no similarity exists between the two images.

$$\text{NCC} = \frac{\sum_{i=1}^{P}\sum_{j=1}^{Q} I_{i,j} * E_{i,j}}{\sqrt{\sum_{i=1}^{P}\sum_{j=1}^{Q} E_{i,j}^{2}} \sqrt{\sum_{i=1}^{P}\sum_{j=1}^{Q} I_{i,j}^{2}}} \quad (12)$$

3.6 Universal Image Quality Index (*UIQI*)

UIQI [25] defined in Eq. (13) models image distortion as a combination of three factors namely loss of correlation, luminance distortion, and contrast distortion.

$$\text{UIQI} = \frac{(4 * \sigma_{IE})(\mu_I + \mu_E)}{(\mu_I^2 + \mu_E^2)(\sigma_I^2 + \sigma_E^2)} \quad (13)$$

where σ_{IE} - Covariance of IE, μ_I - Average of I, μ_E - Average of E σ_I^2 Variance of I and σ_E^2 Variance of E. The range of UIQI value between -1 to 1. If I and E are similar then the UIQI value is 1 and -1 indicates the dissimilarity.

4 Experimental Results and Performance Analysis

The experimental results obtained and performance analysis to prove the efficacy of the proposed method is discussed in this section.

4.1 Input Images

The proposed work is implemented on Intel Core 2 Duo processor with 2 GB RAM. In order to evaluate the proposed method, the standard OTCBVS [28] infrared image database is used. The database contains collection of 10 classes of pedestrian images namely from 00001 to 00010 with 284 images and 984 pedestrian objects. The dimensions of the image are 360 × 240 pixels captured under different environmental conditions such as light rain, partly cloudy, mostly cloudy, haze etc. To make the enhancement and detection challenging, the pedestrians have many complicated appearances such as walking, standing still with

Table 1. OSU Thermal pedestrian database details

Collection #	No. of images	Collection #	No. of images
1	31	6	18
2	28	7	22
3	23	8	24
4	18	9	73
5	23	10	24

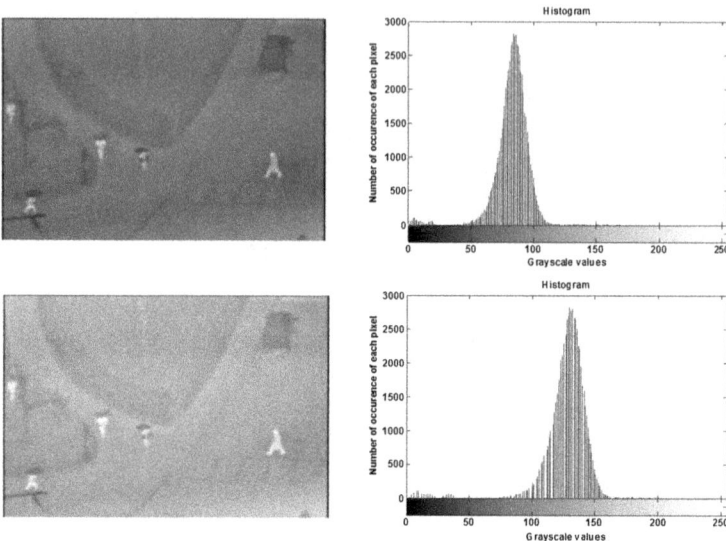

Fig. 2. Sample IR image and the enhanced IR image with corresponding histograms

backpack, umbrella, raincoat, running and so on. Each pixel in the data set is represented by 8 bits (i.e.) 256 gray-levels. The details of each collection are shown in Table 1. In order to detect the pedestrians accurately, the enhancement of IR images as a pre-processing step is mandatory.

4.2 Subjective Evaluation of Results Obtained

Figure 2 shows two columns wherein the first column shows a sample IR image and the enhanced image obtained from the proposed method. This image shows pedestrians on a rainy day. The second column of Fig. 2 represents the corresponding histograms. Bin shifting in Fig. 2 indicates the increase of contrast in the image i.e., the intensity levels in the background has been elevated so that the background becomes lighter. This is also evident from the statistical mean and standard deviation of both the images. The mean and standard deviation of the original image are 0.3264 and 0.0586 respectively and for the enhanced image 0.5033 and 0.0727 respectively.

Figure 3 shows the subjective comparison of the results obtained from HE method [6], Lin's method [2] and the proposed method. It is evident from Fig. 3 that the results of the proposed work enhances the image with good visualization.

The results of the HE method [6] shows the enhancement of the foreground portion along with the background that results in a noisy like image. From the result of [2], it is observed that the complete background information is vanished and pedestrians are shown clearly. The subjective visualization of the results shows the segmentation of pedestrians from the given image rather than enhancing the image. In case of further processing of the enhanced image for

Table 2. Statistical evaluation of results shown in Fig. 3

Figure	Mean	Standard deviation	Figure	Mean	Standard deviation
3a	0.3264	0.0586	3b	0.2503	0.0654
3c	0.4992	0.2928	3d	0.5000	0.2934
3e	0.3868	0.3311	3f	0.3979	0.3881
3g	0.5033	0.0727	3h	0.4130	0.0827

feature extraction or recognition, the enhanced version gives poor response due to vanishing of background and the pixels comprising the pedestrians taking the maximum values. The majority of the pixels are low intensity pixels comprising the background and few pixels comprising the foreground has maximum intensity values. Statistical evaluation of the results shown in Fig. 3 is shown in Table 2.

To give a better enhancement result overcoming the problems in the literature, a fuzzy based image enhancement approach is proposed. From the results, it is claimed that the proposed method enhances the given IR image globally and suits well for further processing like edge detection, segmentation of the pedestrian, feature extraction etc.,

4.3 Performance Evaluation of Proposed Work with Quantitative Measures

For the objective evaluation, the metrics discussed in Sect. 3 are used. For every metric, the results obtained from the proposed method are compared with HE's method [6] and Lin's [2] method. The total database contains 284 images divided into 10 classes. The comparative analysis of different metrics are tabulated in Tables 3, 4, and 5. In each table, the value represents the average value obtained over the images in the corresponding class. The final row represents the mean value of all the classes.

The values of the SSIM measure is tabulated in Table 3. It is clear from the values that the SSIM value of every class is close to 1 indicating maximum similarity compared to the other two approaches.

The values of the UIQI measure are tabulated in Table 4. It is evident from the values that the UIQI value of every class are close to 0.9 and superior than the other two approaches.

The values of the SCC measure are tabulated in Table 5 and it is observed that the values obtained are superior than the other two approaches.

The comparison of NCC values shown in Fig. 4 indicates that the value of NCC is close to 1 in every class.

The comparison of PSNR values shown in Fig. 5 shows that the value of PSNR is higher than the other two methods indicating better quality and lower MSE.

The comparison of MAE values shown in Fig. 6 shows that the value of MAE is lower than the other two methods indicating that the proposed method introduces very low error.

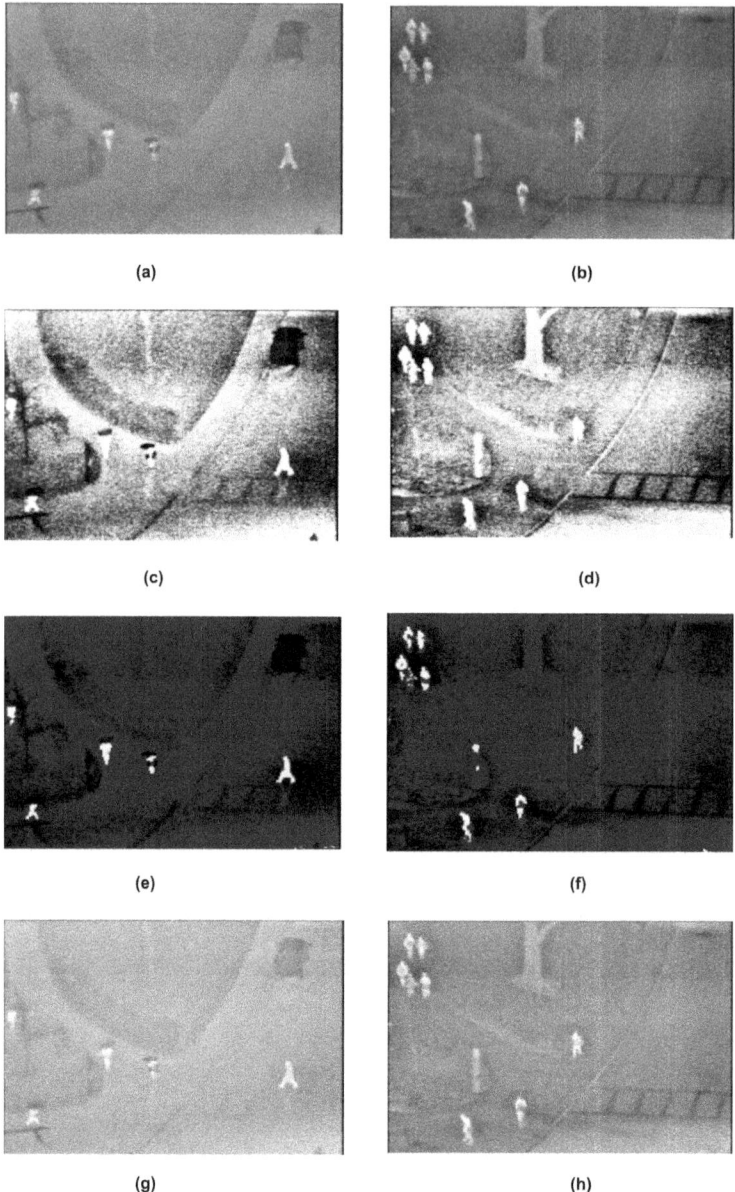

Fig. 3. Subjective comparison of the enhancement results over two sample images (a) Sample image from class 1, (b) sample image from class 6, (c) Histogram Equalization of (a), (d) Histogram Equalization of (b), (e) Result obtained using [2] on (a), (f) Result obtained using [2] on (b), (g) Result obtained on (a) using proposed method, (h) Result obtained on (b) using proposed method

Table 3. Comparative analysis of SSIM values

Class	Methods		
	HE [6]	Lin's method [2]	Proposed method
1	0.9894	0.9411	0.9949
2	0.9917	0.9499	0.9943
3	0.9942	0.9479	0.9956
4	0.9920	0.9494	0.9944
5	0.9927	0.9496	0.9944
6	0.9850	0.9260	0.9960
7	0.9881	0.9365	0.9965
8	0.9884	0.9363	0.9954
9	0.9895	0.9413	0.9951
10	0.9902	0.9417	0.9950
All	0.9901	0.9420	0.9952

Table 4. Comparative analysis of UIQI values

Classes	Methods		
	HE [6]	Lin's method [2]	Proposed method
1	0.2333	0.0011	0.8872
2	0.2956	0.0012	0.9059
3	0.5783	0.0012	0.9115
4	0.3222	0.0012	0.9038
5	0.3723	0.0012	0.9036
6	0.2443	0.0008	0.8439
7	0.2212	0.0011	0.9119
8	0.2588	0.0009	0.8795
9	0.2379	0.0011	0.8936
10	0.3157	0.0012	0.8904
All	0.3080	0.0011	0.8931

4.4 Characteristics of the Input-Output Transfer Function

The performance of the proposed method is further analyzed by the characteristics of the input-output transfer function. It is the plot between the initial fuzzified values and the modified fuzzified values. The plot of the original image and other methods is shown in Fig. 7.

In Fig. 7, the curve in blue indicates the plot for the original image. The curves in pink and brown indicate the plot of intensity values obtained from Histogram Equalization method [6] and Lin's method [2] respectively. The curve

Table 5. Comparative analysis of SCC values

Class	Methods		
	HE [6]	Lin's method [2]	Proposed method
1	0.3279	0.1103	0.4124
2	0.4390	0.1478	0.4388
3	0.4605	0.1551	0.4845
4	0.4424	0.1489	0.4434
5	0.4515	0.1520	0.4479
6	0.1973	0.0664	0.3786
7	0.2799	0.0941	0.4470
8	0.2824	0.0951	0.4064
9	0.3292	0.1108	0.4197
10	0.3405	0.1146	0.4206
All	0.3550	0.1195	0.4299

in green indicates the plot between initial and modified fuzzy values obtained from the proposed method. From Fig. 7 the following observations are made.

1. Pink curve [6] shows a steady increase of all intensity values resulting in high contrast of image as shown in Fig. 3(c) and (d).
2. Brown curve [2] shows that the background is completely washed out and the objects alone are visible as shown in Fig. 3(e) and (f).
3. Green curve showing the plot of intensity values obtained from the proposed method. The plot indicates that the enhancement of the image is done uniformly indicating a similar plot as of the original as shown in Fig. 3(g) and (h).
4. The green curve also indicates that shifting of the intensity values towards right indicating the contrast increase. The same is evident from the shifting of the bin in Fig. 2.

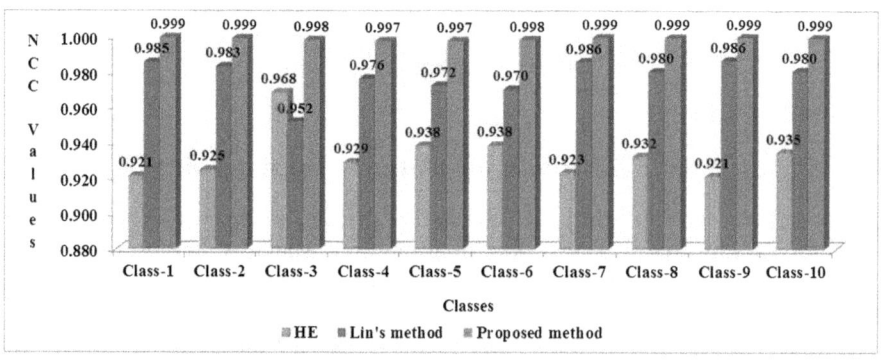

Fig. 4. Comparison of NCC values with HE [6] and Lin's method [2]

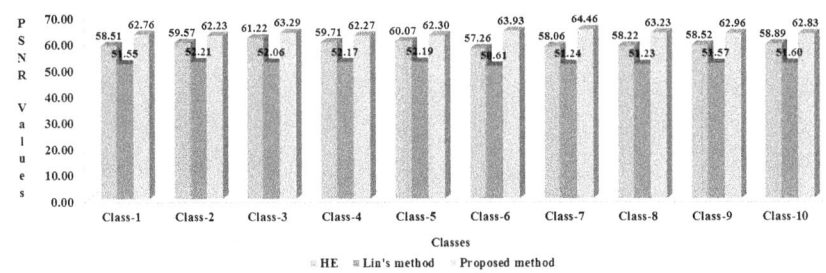

Fig. 5. Comparison of PSNR values with HE [6] and Lin's method [2]

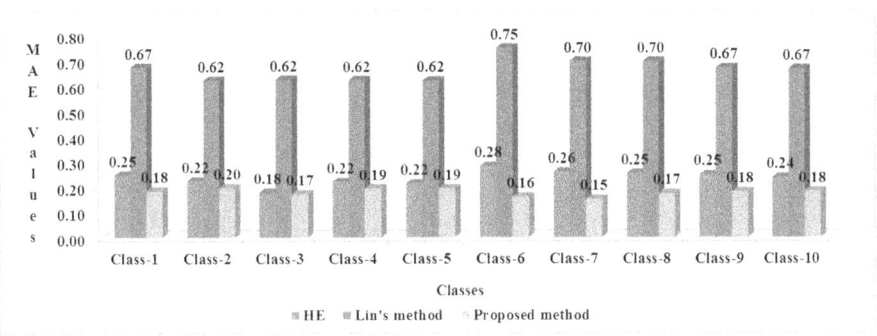

Fig. 6. Comparison of MAE values with HE [6] and Lin's method [2]

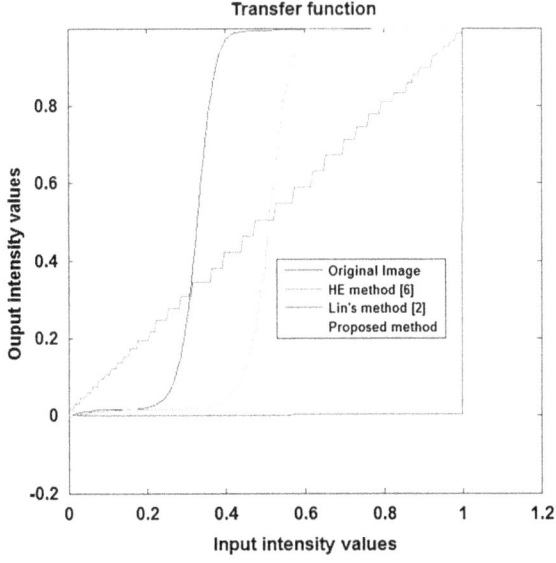

Fig. 7. Input output transfer functions of different enhancement methods.

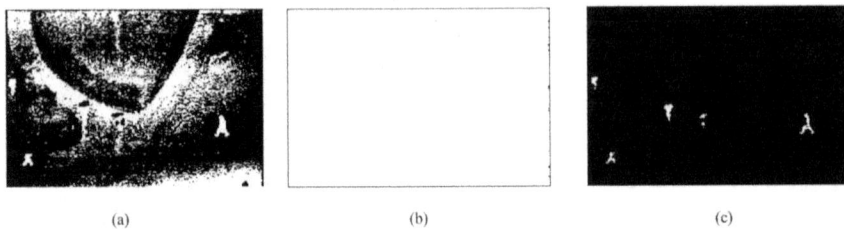

Fig. 8. Result of thresholding on (a) HE [6], (b) Lin's method [2] and (c) Proposed Method representation of binary image.

4.5 Robustness of Proposed Method

To demonstrate the robustness of the proposed method, thresholding and filtering operations are applied on the enhanced image. The results are analyzed here.

Thresholding. Global thresholding is done on the enhanced image using a threshold value of 0.7. Figure 8 shows the thresholded image obtained for HE [6], Lin's method [2] and for the proposed method. From the resultant binary image, the exact number of pedestrians available in the given IR image matches with the ground truth result for the proposed method but failed to detect all the pedestrians in the other two approaches.

Filtering. To show the efficacy of the proposed method, spatial filtering is done on the enhanced image. The average filter, median filter, Gaussian filter, Laplacian filter and Laplacian of Gaussian are applied on the enhanced image. After applying these filters, the results are analyzed using NCC, PSNR and SCC metrics. The quantitative analysis of these metrics are tabulated in Tables 6, 7 and 8 respectively.

The paper is finally summarized as follows. The enhancement of IR images is done successfully in fuzzy domain. The fuzzifiers are calculated adaptively. The exponential fuzzifier is calculated using sigmoid function. The denomination fuzzifier is calculated using the exponential fuzzifier. The plot of input and

Table 6. Performance comparison on filtered image with NCC Measure

Filter	Methods		
	HE [6]	Lin's method [2]	Proposed method
Average	0.9176	0.9882	0.9992
Median	0.9180	0.9866	0.9992
Gaussian	0.9200	0.9865	0.9992
Laplacian	0.1895	−0.0010	0.2172
LoG	0.1874	−0.0010	0.2119

Table 7. Performance comparison on filtered image with PSNR Measure

Filters	Methods		
	HE [6]	Lin's method [2]	Proposed method
Average	58.4541	51.5540	64.1683
Median	58.4430	51.5467	63.8941
Gaussian	58.4942	51.5506	63.5345
Laplacian	51.8771	48.1228	62.0554
LoG	51.9168	48.1018	58.0660

Table 8. Performance comparison on filtered image with SCC Measure

Filters	Methods		
	HE [6]	Lin's method [2]	Proposed method
Average	0.3269	0.1095	0.4597
Median	0.3263	0.1097	0.4504
Gaussian	0.3274	0.1099	0.4384
Laplacian	0.0083	0.0036	0.0850
LoG	0.0194	0.0084	0.0793

output values resemble the s-shaped sigmoid function and hence usage of sigmoid function in calculating the exponential fuzzifier suits well. The robustness of the enhancement is tested using thresholding and spatial filtering. The results of spatial filtering is analyzed quantitatively and the results show the efficacy of the proposed method. The objective evaluation of the whole method gives the results superior to the other compared methods. Subjective comparison also indicate the enhancement of the IR image is perceptually good.

5 Conclusion

A robust and adaptive IR image enhancement approach using fuzzy sets is proposed in this paper. Modification of Fuzzified data is done using contrast intensification and enhancement operator. The novelty of the proposed method is the enhancement of the IR imagery using fuzzy sets, adaptive calculation of exponential and denomination fuzzifiers and testing the robustness of the proposed method. The exponential fuzzifier is calculated using sigmoid function with mean of the image as the parameter. Subjective and objective evaluation of the results is compared with histogram equalization and Lin's method. Subjective evaluation shows the results obtained for the proposed method are superior than the other two approaches. The objective evaluation is done using statistical metrics. In all the metrics, the results of the proposed method are proved to be the best than the other approaches. Further the robustness of the proposed method is tested by applying thresholding and spatial filtering on the enhanced image.

Finally the transfer function shows a wide range of the gray scale values of the enhanced image that caters for further processing like feature extraction and pedestrian detection.

Acknowledgments. This work is supported by the Defense Research and Development Organization (DRDO), New Delhi India for funding the project under the Directorate of Extramural Research & Intellectual Property Rights (ER & IPR) No. ERIP/ER/1103978/M/01/1347 dated July 28, 2011.

References

1. Rajkumar, S., Chandra Mouli, P.V.S.S.R.: Target detection in infrared images using block-based approach. In: Informatics and Communication Technologies for Societal Development, pp. 9–16 (2015)
2. Lin, C.-L.: An approach to adaptive infrared image enhancement for long-range surveillance. Infrared Phys. Technol. **54**(2), 84–91 (2011)
3. Jain, A.K.: Fundamentals of Digital Image Processing. Prentice-Hall Inc., Upper Saddle River (1989)
4. Yu, Z., Bajaj, C.: A fast and adaptive method for image contrast enhancement. In: International Conference on Image Processing (ICIP 2004), vol. 2, pp. 1001–1004 (2004)
5. Lai, R., Yang, Y., Wang, B., Zhou, H.: A quantitative measure based infrared image enhancement algorithm using plateau histogram. Opt. Commun. **283**(21), 4283–4288 (2010)
6. Gonzalez, R.C., Woods, R.E.: Digital image processing (2002)
7. Wang, B., et al.: A real-time contrast enhancement algorithm for infrared images based on plateau histogram. Infrared Phys. Technol. **48**(1), 77–82 (2006)
8. Song, Y., Shao, X., Xu, J.: New enhancement algorithm for infrared image based on double plateaus histogram. Infrared Laser Eng. **2**, 029 (2008)
9. Liang, K., Ma, Y., Xie, Y., Zhou, B., Wang, R.: A new adaptive contrast enhancement algorithm for infrared images based on double plateaus histogram equalization. Infrared Phys. Technol. **55**(4), 309–315 (2012)
10. Deshpande, S.D., et al.: Max-mean and max-median filters for detection of small targets. In: SPIE's International Symposium on Optical Science, Engineering, and Instrumentation. International Society for Optics and Photonics, pp. 74–83 (1999)
11. Highnam, R., Brady, M.: Model-based image enhancement of far infra-red images. In: Proceedings of the Workshop on Physics-Based Modeling in Computer Vision, p. 40 (1995)
12. Tang, M., Ma, S., Xiao, J.: Model-based adaptive enhancement of far infrared image sequences. Pattern Recogn. Lett. **21**(9), 827–835 (2000)
13. Cao, Y., Liu, R., Yan, J.: Small target detection using two-dimensional least mean square (TDLMS) filter based on neighborhood analysis. Int. J. Infrared Millimeter Waves **29**(2), 188–200 (2008)
14. Peregrina-Barreto, H., Herrera-Navarro, A.M., Morales-Hernández, L.A., Terol-Villalobos, I.R.: Morphological rational operator for contrast enhancement. J. Opt. Soc. Am. **28**(3), 455–464 (2011)
15. Bai, X., Fugen, Z.: Hit-or-miss transform based infrared dim small target enhancement. Opt. Laser Technol. **43**(7), 1084–1090 (2011)

16. Shao, X., Fan, H., Lu, G., Xu, J.: An improved infrared dim and small target detection algorithm based on the contrast mechanism of human visual system. Infrared Phys. Technol. **55**(5), 403–408 (2012)
17. Ross, T.J.: Fuzzy Logic with Engineering Applications. Wiley, New York (2009)
18. Pal, S.K., King, R.: Image enhancement using smoothing with fuzzy sets. IEEE Trans. Syst. Man Cybern. **11**(7), 494–500 (1981)
19. Hanmandlu, M., Tandon, S.N., Mir, A.H.: A new fuzzy logic based image enhancement. Biomed. Sci. Instrum. **33**, 590–595 (1996)
20. Hassanien, A.E., Badr, A.: A comparative study on digital mamography enhancement algorithms based on fuzzy theory. Stud. Inform. Control **12**(1), 21–32 (2003)
21. Rangasamy, P., Kuppannan, J., Atanassov, K.T., Gluhchev, G.: Role of fuzzy and intuitionistic fuzzy contrast intensification operators in enhancing images. Notes Intuitionistic Fuzzy Sets **14**(2), 59–66 (2008)
22. Ghodke, V.N., Ganorkar, S.R.: Image enhancement using spatial domain techniques and fuzzy intensification factor. Int. J. Emerg. Technol. Adv. Eng. **3**(10), 430–435 (2013)
23. Mitchell, T.M.: Machine Learning, vol. 45. McGraw Hill, Burr Ridge (1997)
24. Sayood, K.: Introduction to data compression. Newnes (2012)
25. Wang, Z., Bovik, A.C.: A universal image quality index. Signal Process. Lett. **9**(3), 81–84 (2002)
26. Wang, Z., Bovik, A.C., Sheikh, H.R., Simoncelli, E.P.: Image quality assessment: from error visibility to structural similarity. IEEE Trans. Image Process. **13**(4), 600–612 (2004)
27. Lewis, J.P.: Fast normalized cross-correlation. Vis. Interface **10**(1), 120–123 (1995)
28. OTCBVS Benchmark Dataset Collection. http://www.vcipl.okstate.edu/otcbvs/bench/

Dance Composition Using Microsoft Kinect

Reshma Kar[1(✉)], Amit Konar[1], and Aruna Chakraborty[2]

[1] Department of Electronics and Telecommunication Engineering,
Jadavpur University, Kolkata, India
rkar317@gmail.co.in, konar.amit@yahoo.co.in
[2] Department of Computer Science and Engineering, St. Thomas' College
of Engineering and Technology, Kolkata, India
aruna.stcet@gmail.com

Abstract. In this work, we propose a novel approach in which a system autonomously composes dance sequences from previously taught dance moves with the help of the well-known differential evolution algorithm. Initially, we generated a large population of dance sequences. The fitness of each of these sequences was determined by calculating the total inter-move transition abruptness of the adjacent dance moves. The transition abruptness was calculated as the difference of corresponding slopes formed by connected body joint co-ordinates. By visually evaluating the dance sequences created, it was observed that the fittest dance sequence had the least abrupt inter-move transitions. Computer simulation undertaken revealed that the developed dance video frames do not have significant inter-move transition abruptness between two successive frames, indicating the efficacy of the proposed approach. Gestural data specific of dance moves is captured using a Microsoft *Kinect* sensor. The algorithm developed by us was used to fuse the dancing styles of various '*Odissi*' dancers dancing to the same *rasa* (theme) and *tala* (beats) and *loy* (rhythm). In future, it may be used to fuse different forms of dance.

Keywords: Dance composition · Computational creativity · Differential evolution · Microsoft *kinect* · Odissi dance

1 Introduction

Gestures are used as alternative form of expression to enrich or augment vocal and facial expressions. As gestures are a part of natural communication, gestural interfaces may be viewed as the pre-requisites of ambient computing [18]. Dance is a special form of gestural expression portrayed in a rhythmic form to generally communicate the context of a music piece [17]. An important part of dance is establishing a smooth flow of dance moves to create a visually appealing sequence of movements.

Dance is specific of different regions, communities and personal styles. Dance schools world-wide teach different dance moves to students, which they are often required to combine to create new dance sequences. It is an important part of dance creation for teachers and self-learning for students. Various techniques have been proposed to ease dance choreography and most of these works have been tested on the dance form 'Ballet' [1, 2]. However, not much work has been done on composing Indian dance forms. In this work, we focus our attention on an Indian classical dance form known as '*Odissi*' which is a classical dance of the state Orissa [10, 11].

Choreographing dance sequences is definitely an art which different people succeed to different degrees. Thus, it would be an interesting task to see how high-end computational algorithms perform at choreographing dance sequences. Naturally, in a visually appealing and easily executable dance sequence, the steps following each other would execute smooth transitions. In our work, we used the same constraint to judge randomly generated dance sequences and finally select the best among them.

At its heart, computational creativity is the study of building software that exhibits behavior that would be deemed creative in humans [3]. Widmer *et al.,* [4] described a computer which can play a musical piece expressively by shaping the musical parameters like tempo and dynamics. In [5] Gervas provided an excellent review of different computational approaches to storytelling. We can find a brief glimpse of the computational attempts at music composition in [6]. Similarly, computational dance composition techniques find mention in the works of [7, 8]. Some works on ballet are discussed in the following paragraphs however their approach is different from ours as they compose dances from pre-defined choreography structures characteristic of 'ballet'. In contrast, dance composition in Indian classical dance forms are more dependent on the context of the music and follow much less rigid sequencing.

A 3-dimensional animation system was developed based on hierarchic human body techniques and its motion data in [9]. Using the proposed system, One can easily compose and simulate classic ballet dance in real-time on the internet. Their goal was to develop and integrate several modules into a system capable of animating realistic virtual ballet stages in a real-time performance. This includes modeling and representing virtual dancers with high realism, as well as simulating choreography and various stage effects. For handling motion data more easily, they developed a new action description code based on "Pas" which is a set of fundamental movements for classic ballet.

An automatic composition system for ballet choreographies was developed by using 3DCG animation in [1]. Their goal was to develop some useful tools in dance education such as creation-support system for ballet teachers and self-study system for students. The algorithm for automatic composition was integrated to create utilitarian choreographies. As a result of an evaluation test, they verified that the created choreographies had a possibility to be used in the actual lessons. This system is valuable for online virtual dance experimentation and exploration by teachers and choreographers involved in creative practices, improvisation, creative movement, or dance composition. The goals, technical novelty and claims of the paper are briefly given below.

Goals:

- To choreograph dance sequence from previously taught dance sequences.
- To study the applicability of a heuristic algorithm in composing dance.
- To be able to automatically identify visually appealing dance sequences.

Technical Novelty:

- A novel measure of fitness of dance sequences is presented.
- Differential evolution is employed to solve the problem of creating a smooth flowing pattern of dance.
- A novel metric of comparison of different forms of dance is introduced.

Claims:

- Heuristic Algorithms can be used to choreograph dance.
- A visually appealing and easy to execute dance sequence can be recognized using the proposed metric for measuring inter gesture transition abruptness.
- Dances of different forms can be quantitatively compared on a common platform using a metric which evaluates the dances forms based on their commonalities.

2 Differential Evolution Algorithm

Proposed by Storn and Prince [12–14] in 1995, Differential Evolution (DE) Algorithm was found to outperform many of its contemporary heuristic algorithms [15]. Following its discovery, the structural simplicity and efficiency of the algorithm attracted researchers, for use in optimization of rough and multi-modal objective functions. Several extensions of the basic DE algorithm are reported in the literature. The De/rand/1 version of the DE algorithm, containing four main steps are outlined below.

(1) Initialization: DE starts with NP number of D-dimensional parameter vectors, selected in a uniformly random manner from a prescribed search space, given for an engineering optimization problem. The parameter vectors here represent trial solutions of optimization. The i-th parameter vector of the population at the current generation G is formally represented by

$$\vec{Z}_i(G) = [z_{i,1}(G), z_{i,2}(G), z_{i,3}(G), \ldots, z_{i,D}(G)] \tag{1}$$

where each component of $\vec{Z}_i(G)$ lies between corresponding components of $\vec{Z}_{min}$ and $\vec{Z}_{max}$ given by

$$\vec{Z}_{min} = [z_{min-1}, z_{min-2}, z_{min-3}, \ldots, z_{min-D}]$$

and $\vec{Z}_{max} = [z_{max-1}, z_{max-2}, z_{max-3}, \ldots, z_{max-D}]$.

The j-th component of the i-th vector is given by

$$z_{i,j}(0) = z_{j-min} + rand_{i,j}(0,1) \times (z_{j-max} - z_{j-min}), \tag{2}$$

where $rand_{i,j}(0,1)$ is a uniformly distributed random number lying between 0 and 1 and is instantiated independently for each component of the i-th parameter vector.

(2) Mutation: For each individual population target vector $\vec{z_i}(G)$ belonging to population G, a set of three other randomly selected vectors: $\vec{Z_j}(G), \vec{Z_k}(G)$ and $\vec{Z_l}(G)$) are chosen and arithmetically recombined to create a mutant vector.

$$\vec{V_i}(G) = \vec{Z_j}(G) + F(\vec{Z_k}(G) - \vec{Z_l}(G)) \quad (3)$$

The process is repeated for each parameter vector i in $[1, NP]$.

(3) Recombination: Recombination, allows each pair of trial vector $\vec{Z_i}(G)$ to recombine with its corresponding mutant vector $\vec{V_i}(G)$ for i = 1 to NP. Here, recombination is performed position-wise over the length of the parameter vectors. Thus, for trial vectors of length NP, we need to perform NP number of recombination. The principle of recombination for a single position j is given below. Let $rand_{i,j}$ be a uniformly distributed random number in [0, 1] used to select the right element from $V_{i,j}(G)$ and $Z_{i,j}(G)$ into j-th position of the Target vector $u_{i,j}(G)$, where

$$u_{i,j}(G) = \begin{cases} v_{i,j}(G) \text{ if } rand_{i,j} \leq Cr \text{ or } j = j_{rand} \\ z_{i,j}(G) \text{ otherwise} \end{cases} \quad (4)$$

and Cr denotes the crossover rate, which is defined at the beginning of the program once only with a typical value of 0.7.

(4) Selection: In this step, survival of the fittest chromosome is ensured where the offspring replaces the parent vector, if it yields a better value for the objective function.

$$\vec{Z_i}(G+1) = \vec{U_i}(G) \text{ if } f(\vec{U_i}(G)) \leq f(\vec{Z_i}(G))$$
$$= \vec{Z_i}(G) \text{ if } f(\vec{U_i}(G)) > f(\vec{Z_i}(G)) \quad (5)$$

Repeat from step 2 until stopping criterion, defined on convergence on the best fit member of the trial solutions or convergence of the average fitness over iterations or a fixed large number of iterations are met.

3 Metric to Compare Dance Gestures

Our basic principle in placing dance-gestures adjacently in visually appealing dance choreography is based on a simple comparison metric of these gestures. The dance gestures are video clips of variable duration ranging from 6 to 8 seconds. Since the *Kinect* records at the speed of approximately 30 frames per second, the number of frames captured for each dance-gesture is different. Each video clip, comprising a number of frames, is decoded into a sequence of skeletal diagrams, where each skeletal diagram corresponds to an individual frame (illustrated in Fig. 2). These skeletal diagrams are sketches of the body structure indicated by 3D (three dimensional) straight line segments joining 20 fundamental junctions of the dancer's physique (Fig. 1). Each 3D straight line segment is projected on to XY, YZ and ZX planes as illustrated in Fig. 3 a, b, c, and the slopes of the projected 2D straight lines in the three planes with respect to X-, Y- and Z- axes respectively are computed. These slopes are used as metrics to compare two different 3D straight lines representing the orientation of one given body part (say, the right forearm) present in two frames of two videos. While constructing a new dance video from the existing video clips of shorter durations, we need to match the last frame and the first frame of two consecutive videos, which might come in order to ultimately offer a new dance video. Naturally, the matching of 3D straight lines is required between the last frame and the first frame of each pair of videos to test their possible just-apposition in the final video.

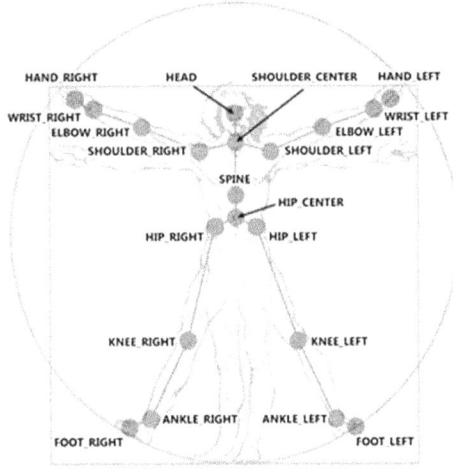

Fig. 1. 20 body joint co-ordinates obtained from Kinect sensor for each frame

Fig. 2. Video clips of dance gestures illustrating frames. It can be seen that Transition Abruptness is calculated by comparing the last and first frames of consecutive dance gestures i and i + 1 respectively.

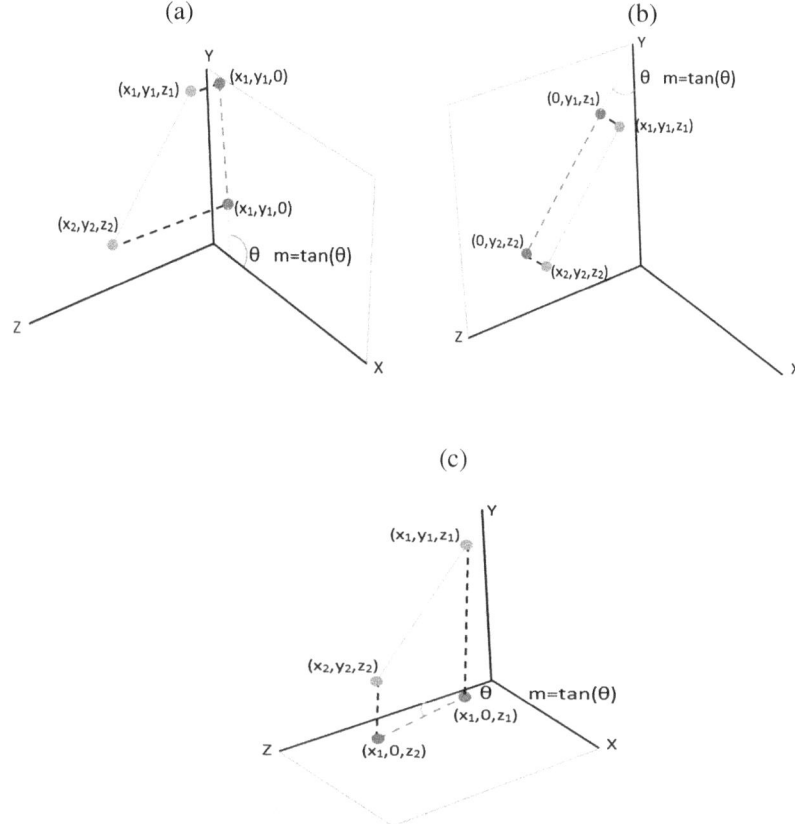

Fig. 3. Calculation of slope of projections of a line on XY, YZ and ZX planes wrt. X, Y and Z axes respectively

A. Definition: We introduced a new term called, Transition Abruptness (TA), to measure the abruptness of inter-gesture transitions in a dance sequence. It is a measure of the total difference between two 3-dimensional body skeletal structures, induced by comparing the angular difference of the projected straight lines of each 3D straight line link of two skeleton structures. TA between two dynamic gestures, G_i and G_{i+1}, each comprising a number of sequential frames, is measured by (6), where $p_{x,i,j,k}$ denotes the slope of the projected straight line k on the X-Y plane with respect to x-axis of the j-th frame of the i-th gesture. The parameters: $q_{y,i,j,k}$ and $r_{z,i,j,k}$) denote slopes of the projected straight line k on the Y-Z plane (Z-X plane) with respect to y-axis (z-axis) of the j-th frame of the i-th gesture.

$$TA(G_i, G_{i+1}) = \sum_{\forall k} \sum_{\forall i, \forall j} (|p_{x,i,1,k} - p_{x,i+1,f,k}| + |q_{y,i,1,k} - q_{y,i+1,f,k}| + |r_{z,i,1,k} - r_{z,i+1,f,k}|) \quad (6)$$

The *total transition abruptness* of the gesture permutation $G_1, G_2, G_3 \ldots G_n$ is calculated in (7) by summing TA of each two consecutive dance gestures

$$\text{Total Transition Abruptness} = \sum_{\forall i} TA\left(G_i, G_{i+1}\right) \qquad (7)$$

4 Selection of Dance Sequences

Evolutionary Algorithms are generally employed to optimize complex non-linear, multi-dimensional objective functions which usually contain multiple local optima. In our experiments, the search surface considered is characteristic of dance-move permutations. The fitness function which ensures the survival of best dance sequences is obtained based on the total abruptness in inter-gesture transitions. In this section, we present a novel scheme of dance composition by selection of dance permutations. The basic structure of parameter vectors used here is of 3K dimension, where K denotes the maximum value of k. The integer 3 appears due to inclusion of three elements: $p_{x, i, j, k}$, $q_{y, i, j, k}$ and $r_{z, i, j, k}$ each K-times in the parameter vector. It is important to note that we have two sets of parameter vectors, the first set for representation of the first frame of each video clip describing a dynamic gesture, and the last set to represent the last frame of the same dynamic gesture. In the evolutionary algorithm we match two dynamic gestures by measuring the total transition abruptness of the last frame and the first frame of any two video clips. The pseudo code of the proposed gesture selection algorithm is outlined next.

Pseudo Code
Input: A set of body joint co-ordinates of *n* dance gestures $G_1, G_2 \ldots G_5$.
Output: A visually appealing permutation of *m* dance gestures.
Begin
   1. Randomly initialize a population of NP solutions (dance sequences) $\vec{Z}_j(g) = \{G_1, G_2 \ldots, G_5\}$. Here j runs from 1 to NP and g signifies generation
   2. **For** Iter=1 to MaxIter
      Begin
         a) Create mutant vector using mutation scheme section 2.
         b) Crossover target vector and mutant vector as outlined in section 2.
         c) Evaluate Fitness by equation 7 i.e.

$$fitness = \sum_{i=1}^{n} Transition\ Abryptness(\vec{G}_i, \vec{G}_{i+1}) \quad \forall G_i \in \vec{Z}$$

         d) **If** trial vector is better (less abrupt) than target
           Then replace trial by target in the next generation
         End if

      End For
   3. Return $\vec{Z}$ after minima value of fitness function converges.
End

Procedure: Transition Abruptness ($\vec{G}_i, \vec{G}_{i+1}$)

Input: $\vec{G}_i, \vec{G}_{i+1}$
Output: Inter-gesture Transition Abruptness TA
Begin
Let K be the number of lines in each skeletal diagram
1. **For** k=1 to K
   a) Extract $l^k_{G_i}, l^k_{G_{i+1}}$ where $l^k_{G_i} \in last\ frame\ of\ (\vec{G}_i)$
   and
   $l^k_{G_{i+1}} \in first\ frame\ of\ (\vec{G}_{i+1})$

   Here each of the above lines are represented by, the projections of their slopes ($p_{x,i,j,k}$, $q_{y,i,j,k}$, $r_{z,i,j,k}$ discussed preceding eq. 6)

   b) Compute the fitness of each consecutive pair of gestures by Eq.6
   $A_l = TA(G_i, G_{i+1})$

End For
2. TA=0

For l=1 to N-1
   a) $TA = TA + A_l$

End For
3. **Return** TA

5 Comparison Metric of Different Dance Forms

The comparison of dance composition algorithms is a difficult task as there is no numerical formula to distinguish the quality of one dance from another. To the best of our knowledge, ours is the first work on *Odissi* dance composition which makes the comparison of our algorithm further difficult. Thus, we also propose a metric for comparison of dance of different forms and use it to compare dance composed by our algorithm with dance composed by other algorithms. Apparently, a good dance composition technique maintains a smooth flow of transitions between gestures and also a high amount of dynamism. The smoothness of inter-gesture transitions can be measured by the calculating *Transition Abruptness* between two consecutive gestures. A smaller *Transition Abruptness* between consecutive gestures indicates a smooth flow of dance. Similarly, if non-adjacent gestures have higher value of *Transition Abruptness* the dance can be said to have more dynamic steps. Thus, we define the *Visual Appeal* of a dance sequence S as follows composed of n gestures G_i, where i ranges from 1 to n.

$$\text{Visual Appeal}(S) = \frac{\sum_{i=1}^{n} \text{Transition Abruptness}(G_i, G_{i+2})}{\sum_{i=1}^{n} \text{Transition Abruptness}(G_i, G_{i+1})} \tag{8}$$

6 Experiments

The Microsoft *Kinect* captures skeletal co-ordinates at an approximate rate of 30 frames per second, with the help of an RGB camera, an infrared projector a monochrome CMOS (complimentary metal-oxide semiconductor) sensor. This configuration allows the *Kinect* to efficiently capture the 3-dimensional skeletal co-ordinates in closed room settings. However, certain precautions are required to be maintained to ensure noise-free collection of data. A white background is maintained to eliminate possible chances of interference of background objects in data collection. To ensure good quality of images, two standing lights are placed facing the dance platform. The dancers are also instructed to avoid wearing clothes which are too loose around the body joints. The subjects should be within an appropriate range of the *Kinect* which is approximately 1.2 to 3.5 meter or 3.9 to 11 ft.

In our experiments, 10 experienced *Odissi* dancers are asked to perform 5 of their preferred dance gestures which are each captured separately with the help of the Microsoft *Kinect*. Thus, we have a total of 50 video clips of dynamic dance gestures. A sequential permutation of 5 of these dance gestures are then selected from a large amount of such randomly created permutations with the help of *differential evolution* algorithm. It is implicit that dancing style of each dancer is dependent on various factors including personal choice and interpretation of dance steps. This lends a unique touch to each of the dancer's gestures though all of them belong to the same dance form. The aim of our experiments is to combine the dance styles of different teachers which has the potential to give rise to interesting patterns and also has future applications in fusing various dance forms. Stills from dance gestures of the different teachers are shown in Fig. 4.

Fig. 4. Gesture stills of different *"Odissi"* dancers

The data captured using *Kinect* represents the bodily movements over time with an approximate distance of 10 cm from ground truth. However, some important considerations must be made before performing analysis of the skeletal co-ordinates obtained.

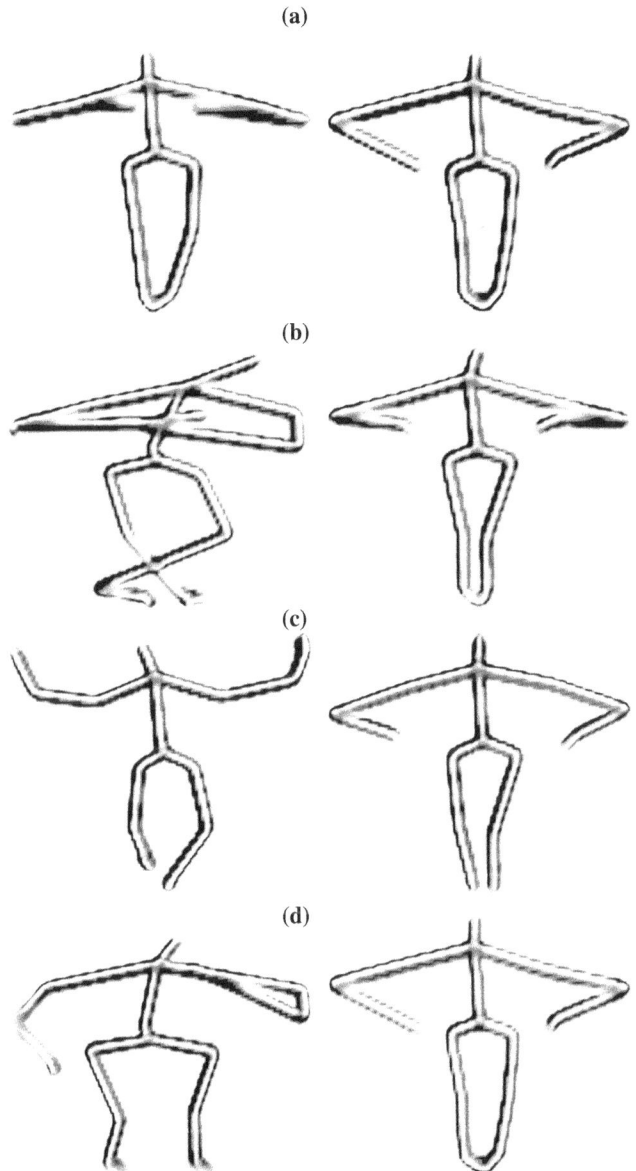

Fig. 5. Inter-Gesture Transition poses

For example two subjects (dancers) may be portraying the same gesture and yet have different X, Y and Z co-ordinates. The main reasons of this are difference in skeletal structure of subjects and variable distance of subjects from *Kinect* camera. To overcome these differences, we have used the slope of the lines in skeletal diagram as the comparison parameter.

In the next phase, differential evolution algorithm is used to evaluate different permutations of the dance sequences and find the best among them. The comparison of dance sequences is based on *total transition abruptness*. The total transition abruptness is simply the sum of all *inter-gesture transition abruptness* $TA = (G_i, G_{j+1})$. The comparison for placing the gestures adjacently is based on the first frame of a gesture and the last frame of the preceding gesture. In Fig. 5, we have illustrated the diagrams such four pairs; in Table 1 we described how the *inter-gesture transition abruptness* (total slope differences of the projections of the indicated skeletal diagrams) are able to detect inter move abruptness of the pairs in Fig. 5. In Fig. 7 we have shown a part of one of the fittest generated dance sequences.

Table 1. Analysis of Inter-gesture Transition Abruptness values obtained

Fig. No.	Transition Abruptness (TA)	Analysis
Figure 5a	292.0031	It can be easily seen that the poses are quite close
Figure 5b	350.9825	TA increases as gradual slope changes occur
Figure 5c	955.3705	Drastic Changes in both upper and lower body increase TA
Figure 5d	900.0376	Comparatively more changes in lower body than upper body cause slight decrease in TA

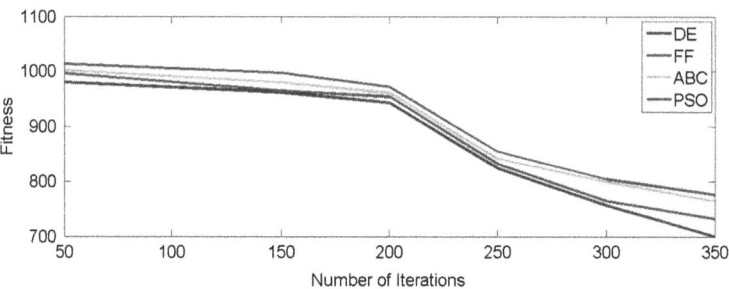

Fig. 6. Value of Fitness Function of different Heuristic Algorithms for Dance Composition, *DE*: *Differential Evolution*, *FF*: *Firefly Algorithm*, *ABC*: *Adaptive Bee Colony optimization*, *PSO*: *Particle Swarm Optimization*.

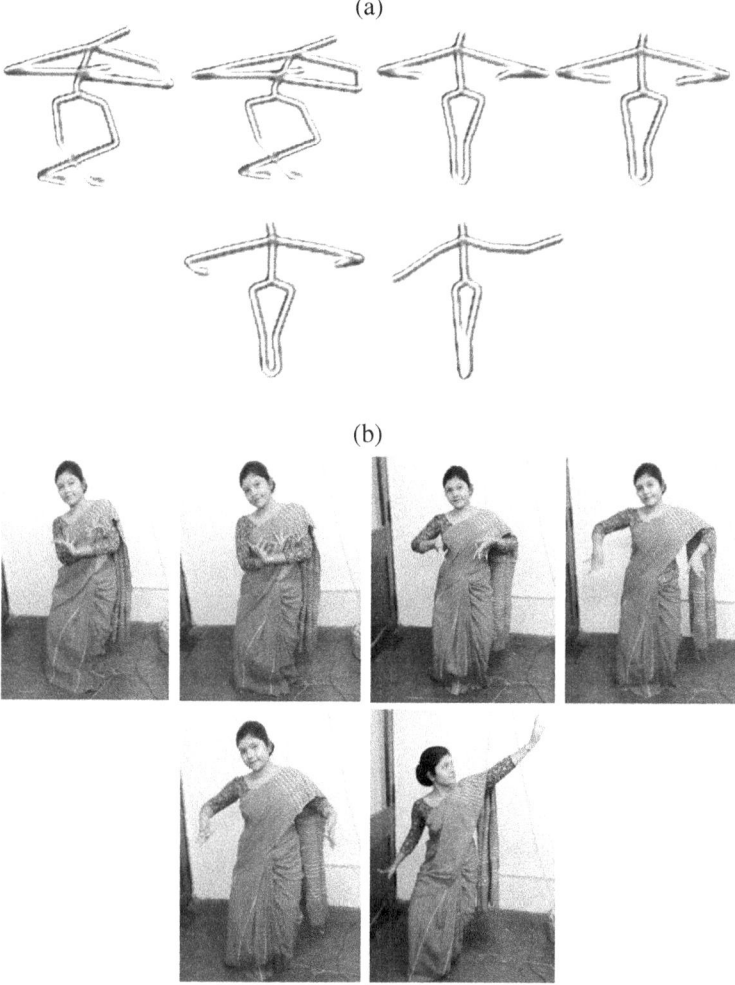

Fig. 7. Subsequence of the final dance sequence generated by differential evolution demonstrated by (a) Skeletal diagrams (b) A dance student's performance

7 Performance Evaluation

Finally, we asked 10 *Odissi* dancers to rate the dance permutation generated by our system on a scale of 1–4 as follows, 1: Bad, 2: Fair, 3: Good, 4: Excellent. The results obtained are given in Fig. 8. The convergence of different optimization algorithms on the dance composition problem is illustrated in Fig. 6, the corresponding data is also given in Table 2. It is seen that *Differential Evolution* algorithm performs better than 3 other algorithms namely *Adaptive Bee Colony algorithm*, *Firefly algorithm* and *Particle Swarm Optimization* for the dance composition problem. Using our proposed metric *visual appeal* outlined in Eq. 8, we compared our dance composition techniques with two other dance composition techniques for different dance forms [1, 16]. Our algorithm performs substantially better than other algorithms on an average as indicated in Table 3.

Table 2. Average fitness value of different heuristic algorithms over different iterations

Iterations	Fitness			
	DE	FF	ABC	PSO
50	980	996	1002	1013
150	962	965	980	997
200	943	954	961	972
250	824	832	842	855
300	756	764	799	804
350	700	732	765	776

Table 3. The comparison of different dance composition algorithms on the basis of *visual appeal*.

Dance composition technique	Average *Visual Appeal* for 3 runs
Ballet Composition [16]	18.67
Contemporary Dance Composition [1]	19.99
Odissi Composition by Differential Evolution	23.44

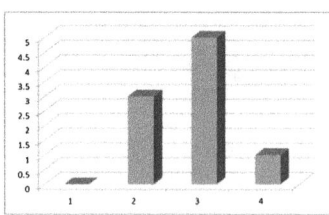

Fig. 8. Performance Evaluation of the Dance composition System as per the opinion of 10 dancers; here 1: Bad 2: Fair 3: Good 4: Excellent

8 Discussion

This paper introduced a meta-heuristic approach to compose dance by optimally selecting inter-gestures movement patterns from multiple dance gestures. The fitness estimate used for dance gesture composition ensures a smooth transition of frames in the dance video. One metric representing visual appeal has been introduced to compare the performance of the proposed Differential Evolution (DE) based meta-heuristic algorithm with existing algorithms of dance composition. The proposed DE-based realization is also compared with other standard realizations including, firefly, PSO and ABC with respect to convergence time, and the results indicate that the DE realization outperforms its partners in the present context.

9 Conclusion

This paper provides a fresh perspective on the technique of dance composition. Dance composers are commonly required to ensure a smooth flow of inter-gesture dance transitions. Our algorithm uses this common know-how and integrates it into the differential evolution algorithm to compose interesting dance patterns. Since the differential evolution algorithm uses a random initial population each time; the chances of dance patterns generated being novel each time is high. The algorithm can be improved by including other constraints in the fitness function which increase the dynamicity of the dance patterns. There is also a wide scope in creating dance composition with context to music-mood as well as lyrics. Apart from this one may also analyse the relative performance of different evolutionary algorithms in dance composition. In a nutshell, our work area relatively unexplored and offers a wide future scope.

References

1. Soga, A., Umino, B., Hirayama, M.: Automatic composition for contemporary dance using 3D motion clips: experiment on dance training and system evaluation. In: International Conference on CyberWorlds (CW 2009), pp. 171–176. IEEE (2009)
2. Dancs, J., Sivalingam, R., Somasundaram, G., Morellas, V., Papanikolopoulos, N.: Recognition of ballet micro-movements for use in choreography. In: IEEE/RSJ International Conference on Intelligent Robots and Systems (IROS), pp. 1162–1167. IEEE (2013)
3. Colton, S., López de Mantaras, R., Stock, O.: Computational creativity: coming of age. AI Mag. **30**(3), 11–14 (2009)
4. Widmer, G., Flossmann, S., Grachten, M.: YQX plays Chopin. AI Mag. **30**(3), 35–48 (2009)
5. Gervás, P.: Computational approaches to storytelling and creativity. AI Mag. **30**(3), 49–62 (2009)
6. Edwards, M.: Algorithmic composition: computational thinking in music. Commun. ACM **54**(7), 58–67 (2011)
7. de Sousa Junior, S.F., Campos, M.F.M.: Shall we dance? A music-driven approach for mobile robots choreography. In: IEEE/RSJ International Conference on Intelligent Robots and Systems (IROS), pp. 1974–1979. IEEE (2011)
8. Jadhav, S., Joshi, M., Pawar, J.: Art to SMart: an evolutionary computational model for BharataNatyam choreography. In: HIS, pp. 384–389 (2012)
9. Soga, A., Endo, M., Yasuda, T.: Motion description and composing system for classic ballet animation on the web. In: 10th IEEE International Workshop on Robot and Human Interactive Communication, pp. 134–139. IEEE (2001)

10. Saha, S., Ghosh, S., Konar, A., Janarthanan, R.: Identification of Odissi dance video using Kinect sensor. In: International Conference on Advances in Computing, Communications and Informatics (ICACCI), pp. 1837–1842. IEEE (2013)
11. Saha, S., Ghosh, S., Konar, A., Nagar, A.K.: Gesture recognition from indian classical dance using Kinect sensor. In: Fifth International Conference on Computational Intelligence, Communication Systems and Networks (CICSyN), pp. 3–8. IEEE (2013)
12. Storn, R., Price, K.: Differential evolution–a simple and efficient heuristic for global optimization over continuous spaces. J. Glob. Optim. **11**(4), 341–359 (1997)
13. Storn, R., Price, K.: Differential Evolution - A Simple and Efficient Adaptive Scheme for Global Optimization Over Continuous Spaces. ICSI, Berkeley (1995)
14. Price, K.V., Storn, R.M., Lampinen, J.A.: Differential Evolution: A Practical Approach to Global Optimization. Springer, Heidelberg (2006)
15. Vesterstrom, J., Thomsen, R.: A comparative study of differential evolution, particle swarm optimization, and evolutionary algorithms on numerical benchmark problems. In: Congress on Evolutionary Computation (CEC), vol. 2, pp. 1980–1987. IEEE (2004)
16. Soga, A., Umino, B. and Longstaff, J.S.: Automatic composition of ballet sequences using a 3D motion archive. In: 1st South-Eastern European Digitization Initiative Conference (2005)
17. Patra, B.G., Das, D., Bandyopadhyay, S.: Unsupervised approach to Hindi music mood classification. In: Prasath, R., Kathirvalavakumar, T. (eds.) MIKE 2013. LNCS, vol. 8284, pp. 62–69. Springer, Heidelberg (2013)
18. Kar, R., Chakraborty, A., Konar, A., Janarthanan, R.: Emotion recognition system by gesture analysis using fuzzy sets. In: Swarm, Evolutionary, and Memetic Computing, pp. 354–363. Springer International Publishing (2013)

A Framework of Moving Object Segmentation in Maritime Surveillance Inside a Dynamic Background

Alok Kumar Singh Kushwaha[✉] and Rajeev Srivastava

Department of Computer Science and Engineering,
Indian Institute of Technology (BHU), Varanasi 221005, UP, India
{alok.rs.cse12,rajeev.cse}@iitbhu.ac.in

Abstract. Maritime surveillance represents a challenging scenario for moving object segmentation due to the complexity of the observed scenes. The waves on the water surface, boat wakes, and weather issues contribute to generate a highly dynamic background. Moving object segmentation using change detection under maritime environment is a challenging problem for the maritime surveillance system. To address these issues, a fast and robust moving object segmentation approach is proposed which consist of seven steps applied on given video frames which include wavelet decomposition of frames using complex wavelet transform; use of change detection on detail coefficients (LH, HL, HH); use of background modeling on approximate co-efficient (LL sub-band); cast shadow suppression; strong edge detection; inverse wavelet transformation for reconstruction; and finally using closing morphology operator. For dynamic background modeling in the water surface, we have used background registration, background difference, and background difference mask in the complex wavelet domain. For shadow detection and suppression problem in water surface, we exploit the high frequency sub-band in the complex wavelet domain. A comparative analysis of the proposed method is presented both qualitatively and quantitatively with other standard methods available in the literature for seven datasets. The various performance measures used for quantitative analysis include relative foreground area measure (RFAM), misclassification penalty (MP), relative position based measure (RPM), normalized cross correlation (NCC), Precision (PR), Recall (RE), shadow detection rate (SDR), shadow discrimination rate, execution time and memory consumption. Experimental results indicate that the proposed method is performing better in comparison to other methods in consideration for all the test cases as well as addresses all the issues effectively.

Keywords: Moving object segmentation · Maritime surveillance · Change detection · Dynamic background · Wavelet transform · Performance measure

1 Introduction

Maritime surveillance is an active area of research because of its various application areas of computer vision and can be used in the fight against a wide range of criminal activities, including pirate attacks, unlicensed fishing trailers and human trafficking. Maritime domain represents one of the most challenging scenarios for moving object detection due to the complexity of the monitored scene: waves on the water surface, boat wakes, and weather issues (such as bright sun, fog, heavy rain) contribute to generate a highly dynamic background. Due to these factors automatic object detection in maritime environment is far too complex for conventional detection methods that are applicable to common indoor, outdoor and traffic scenes. Most often these techniques are either not well capable of detecting the possibly threatening objects or in disregarding the background which results in a large amount of false detections. A basic background extraction technique using a fixed background template as is often used in e.g. traffic monitoring or vehicle detection, will not be suitable in a maritime environment due to the highly dynamic background and the possible camera motion. In this paper, we describe moving object segmentation and shadow suppression method that has been specifically designed for dealing with the dynamic water background.

The main contributions of the proposed method are
(1) A new approach for moving object segmentation under maritime surveillance is proposed (2) Comparative study of the proposed method with other state-of-the-art algorithms on a set of challenging video sequences (3) Analysis of the sensitivity of the most influencing parameters [27–29, 31], and a discussion of their effects. (4) and analysis of the computational complexity and memory consumption of the proposed algorithm.

2 Related Works

There have been a number of attempts to address the problem of moving object segmentation at sea. Some of the main tasks to achieve this goal is to first understand the nature of the sea clutter and its modelling for accurate segmentation of moving objects. To take into account these problems, in the recent years, many moving object segmentation approaches have been proposed [1, 2] and these approaches can be classified in two categories [3] such as non-recursive and recursive techniques.

A non-recursive technique uses a sliding-window approach for background estimation. It stores a buffer of the previous L video frames, and estimates the background image based on the temporal variation of each pixel within the buffer. In this category, Kim *et al.* [4] proposed moving object segmentation method based on codebook where a codebook is formed to represent significant states in the background using quantization and clustering [4]. It solves the some of the above mentioned problems, such as sudden changes in illumination, but does not consider the problems of ghost regions or shadow detection. A more refined application of this algorithm was proposed by Kushwaha *et al.* [5] which is based on construction of basic background model where in the variance and covariance of pixels are computed to construct the model for scene background which is adaptive to the dynamically changing background. Non-recursive techniques need to buffer the frames and its computational complexity is high due to their non-recursive nature.

The major feature of recursive techniques is that they do not maintain a buffer for background estimation. They recursively update either a single or multiple background model(s) based on each input frame. McFarlane and Schofield [6] have proposed an approximate median filter method for segmentation of multiple video objects. This technique has also been used in background modelling for urban traffic monitoring [7]. This method needs many frames to learn the new background region revealed by an object that moves away after being stationary for a long time [3] but it is computationally cost effective. Stauffer *et al.* [8] have proposed a tracking method where in motion segmentation has been done using mixture of Gaussians and on-line approximation to update the model. This model has some disadvantages such as background having fast variations cannot be accurately modeled with just a few Gaussians (usually 3 to 5) causing problems for sensitive detection. Kim and Hwang [9] derived an edge map using change detection method and after removing edge points which belong to the previous frame, the remaining edge map is used to extract the video object plane. This method suffers from the problem of object distortion. To solve this problem, Shih *et al.* [10] used change detection method in three adjacent frames which easily handles the new appearance of the moving object.

In recent years, some wavelet domain analysis techniques have been developed using change detection for surveillance [11–15] which are recursive in nature. Huang *et al.* [11, 12] proposed an algorithm for moving object segmentation to solve the double-edge problem in the spatial domain using a change detection method with different thresholds in four wavelet sub-bands. Baradarani [13, 14] refined the work of Huang *et al.* [11, 12] using dual tree complex filter bank in wavelet domain. These methods [11–14] suffer from the problem of noise disturbances and distortion of moving segmented object due to change in speed of objects. Khare *et al.* [15] refine the work of Baradarani [13, 14] and Huang *et al.* [11, 12] using Daubechies complex wavelet. The method proposed by Khare *et al.* [15] reduces the noise disturbance and speed change, but it suffers from the problem of dynamic background changes and shadow detection and due to this segmenting coherence occurs [16].

All the above discussed methods suffer from the problem of either slow speed of moving object or abrupt lighting variation changes leading to shadow and ghost like appearances. To solve the problem of shadow detection many approaches are proposed in wavelet domain in the literatures. Shadows are mainly of two types: self-shadow and cast shadow [17]. A *"self-shadow"* is the one which occurs on the object itself when hidden from the illumination source. This is usually obscured and has gradual changes in intensity, with no definite boundaries. On the other hand, *"cast-shadow"* is the dark region projected on the ground by occlusion of light due to the object. Guan [18] proposed a shadow detection and removal algorithm, by using HSV color model in dyadic multi-scale wavelet domain. In this approach, wavelet transforms is applied on value and saturation components with automatic threshold in form of standard deviation. Guan [18] used the real valued wavelet transform which suffer from the problem of shift sensitivity and poor edge detection [19]. One solution to overcome these problems is to use complex wavelet transform as they are shift invariant and have better edge detection property [19]. Khare *et al.* [20] proposed shadow detection and removal method which is based on dual tree complex wavelet transform with standard deviation of wavelet coefficients as a threshold but in dynamic background it does not suppress the shadow problem more accurately.

There are many general approaches to background modelling in dynamic environment; only few of them have been tested on water background. A water background is more difficult than other kinds of dynamic background since waves on the water surface do not belong to the foreground even though they involve motion. Also, sun reflections do not have the same behaviour of a reflective surface. Therefore a real-time, complete, and effective solution for maritime surveillance does not yet exist.

Motivated by these facts, we have proposed a new method for segmentation of moving object in water background which solve the above problems using change detection and background modeling applied on Daubechies complex wavelet transform using LL sub-band. For dynamic background modeling, we have used background registration, background difference, and background difference mask in complex wavelet domain. For shadow detection and suppression problem in water surface, we exploit the high frequency sub-band in complex wavelet domain. The main motivation behind performing these tasks in the complex wavelet domain is that the noise resilience nature of complex wavelet domain, as the lower frequency sub-band of the wavelet transform has the capability of a low-pass filter. The other motivation is that the high frequency sub-bands of complex wavelet transform represent the edge information that provides a strong cue to handle shadow.

The proposed method is compared with other methods namely: Khare *et al.* [15], Hsia *et al.* [21], and Bloisi *et al.* [22]. Performance of the proposed method is found better in terms of visual performance and a number of quantitative measures such as relative foreground area measure (RFAM), misclassification penalty (MP), relative position based measure (RPM), normalized cross correlation (NCC), Precision (PR), Recall (RE), shadow detection rate (SDR), shadow discrimination rate, execution time and memory consumption.

Rest of the paper is organized as follows: Sect. 3 explains the proposed method in detail. Experimental results are given in Sect. 4 respectively. Finally, conclusion of the work is given in Sect. 5.

3 Methods and Models

Here we propose a novel moving object segmentation scheme which is able to detect moving objects in a water surface by efficiently minimizing the effects of noise, sun reflections, and wakes of water. In the proposed approach, the above mentioned issues are addressed using background modeling and shadow detection step in complex wavelet domain. In proposed approach, seven major steps are applied on the given video frames which include: wavelet de-composition of frame using complex wavelet transform; use of change detection on detail coefficients (LH, HL, HH); use of dynamic background modelling on approximate co-efficient (LL sub-band); cast shadow suppression; strong edge detection; inverse wavelet transformation for reconstruction; and finally using closing morphology operator. For dynamic background modelling we have used background registration, background difference, and background difference mask in complex wavelet domain. For shadow detection and removal, we exploit the high frequency sub-band in complex wavelet domain. All these steps are iteratively applied until the result does not surpass the set threshold value for object segmentation. The working of the proposed model is shown in the given block diagram in Fig. 1. The brief descriptions of the steps of the proposed model are given as follows:

Step 1: Wavelet Decomposition of Frames. In the proposed approach, a 2-D Daubechies complex wavelet transform [19] is applied on current frame and previous frame to get wavelet coefficients in four sub-bands: LL, LH, HL and HH.

Step 2: Application of Change Detection Method on Wavelet Co-efficient. In step 2, change detection method is applied on detail wavelet coefficients i.e. on sub-bands: LH, HL, and HH. Let $Wf_{n,d}(i,j)$ $(d = \{LH, HL, HH\})$ and $Wf_{n-1,d}(i,j)$ $(d = \{LH, HL, HH\})$ are the wavelet coefficients at location (i,j) of the current frame and previous frame and $V_{th,d}$ is a threshold determined by the significant test [23] then the wavelet domain frame difference $WD_{n,d}(i,j)$ for respective sub-bands are computed as:

for every pixel location (i,j) ϵ the co-ordinate of frame

$$WD_{n,d}(i,j) = \begin{cases} 1 & if \ |Wf_{n,d}(i,j) - Wf_{n-1,d}(i,j)| > V_{th,d} \\ 0 & otherwise \end{cases} \quad (1)$$

Step 3: Application of Background Modeling Using LL Sub-band. Here in step 3, we have applied background modeling on water background surface. For dynamic background modeling, we have used background registration, background difference, and background difference mask in complex wavelet domain using LL sub-band. The background modeling step is divided in to four major steps. The first step calculate the frame difference mask $WD_{n,LL}(i,j)$ of the LL image which is obtained by thresholding the difference between coefficients in two LL sub-bands as follows:

$$WD_{n,LL}(i,j) = \begin{cases} 1 & if \ |Wf_{n,LL}(i,j) - Wf_{n-1,LL}(i,j)| < V_{th,WD} \\ 0 & otherwise \end{cases} \quad (2)$$

where $V_{th,FD}$ is a threshold of $WD_{n,LL}(i,j)$. If $WD_{n,LL}(i,j) = 0$, then the difference between two frames is almost the same.

The second step of background modeling maintains an up-to-date background buffer as well as background registration mask indicating whether the water background information of a pixel is available or not. According to the frame difference mask of the past several frames, water background pixels that are not moving for a long time are considered as reliable background. The reliable water background, $BR_{n,LL}(i,j)$ is defined as

$$BR_{n,LL}(i,j) = \begin{cases} BR_{n-1,LL}(i,j) + 1 & if \ WD_{n,LL}(i,j) = 0 \\ 0 & otherwise \end{cases} \quad (3)$$

The $BR_{n,LL}(i,j)$ value is accumulated until $WD_{n,LL}(i,j)$ holds zero value. At any time that $WD_{n,LL}(i,j)$ is changed from 0 to 1, $BR_{n,LL}(i,j)$ becomes zero.

In third step of background modeling, if the value in $BR_{n,LL}(i,j)$ exceeds a pre-defined value, denoted by L, then the background difference masks $BD_{n,LL}(i,j)$ is calculated. It is obtained by taking the difference between the current frame and the background information stored. This background difference mask is the primary information for object shape generation in water background surface i.e.

$$BD_{n,LL}(i,j) = \begin{cases} 1 & if \ |Bf_{n-1,LL}(i,j) - Wf_{n,LL}(i,j)| > V_{th,BD} \\ 0 & otherwise \end{cases} \quad (4)$$

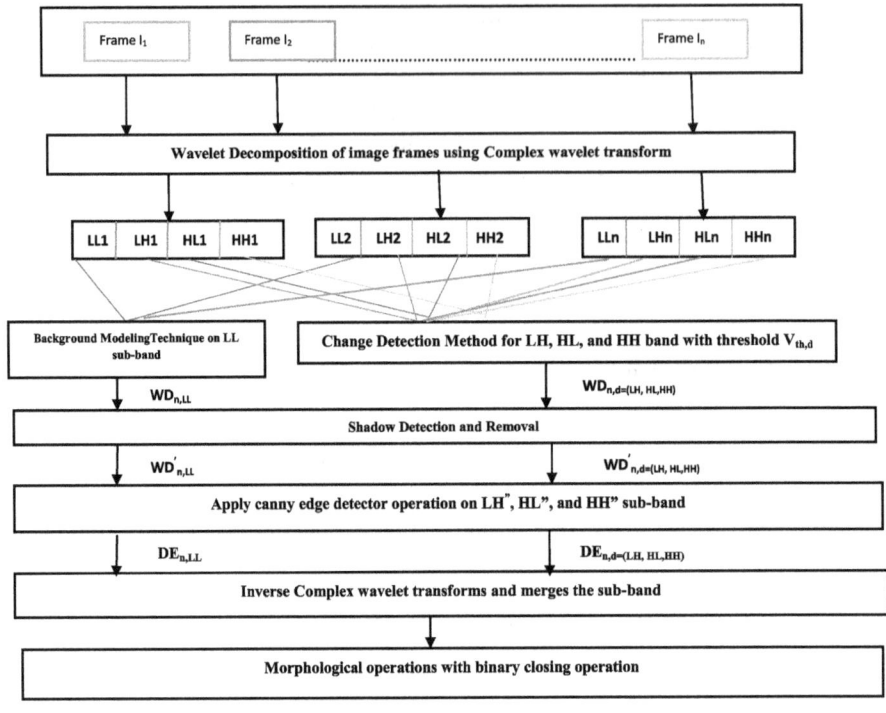

Fig. 1. Block diagram of the proposed method

where $Bf_{n-1,LL}(i,j)$ is the pixel value in the current frame that is copied to the corresponding pixel in the $BR_{n,LL}(i,j)$, and $V_{th,BD}$ is a given threshold. In the case of $BR_{n,LL}(i,j) < L$, it is assumed that the background is not constructed, so frame differences mask $WD_{n,LL}(i,j)$ is used which is calculated in the first step.

In the fourth step of background modeling, a background model is constructed on water surface using the background difference mask, background registration mask and the frame difference mask.

Step 4: Application of Shadow Detection and Removal. Daubechies complex wavelet transform provides significant amount of structural information along the edges and are useful for the shadow detection and suppression tasks. The major properties of shadows obtained after moving object segmentation in water background surface is that they have large discontinuities at edge locations resulting in high frequency components and in the chromacity the shadow regions are relatively smooth and have less variation. This information is useful for detection and removal of shadow. Therefore, in shadow detection and removal step high frequency wavelet coefficients are analyzed. The basic property of complex wavelet transform used here is that wavelet transform provides the local regularity of functions and singularities of an image f(x, y) represent its edges. So edges can be detected effectively by the local maxima of the wavelet transform modulus [24]. The edge map of any sub-band can be computed by using thresholding. For example the edge map of LH sub-band can be computed as follows:

$$SD^L_{\eta^H}(\alpha, \beta) = \begin{cases} 1 & \text{if } WD^L_{\eta^H}F(\alpha, \beta) \geq Th(\alpha, \beta) \\ 0 & \text{Otherwise} \end{cases}$$ (5)

In a similar way, we can compute the edge maps for HL and HH sub-band.

Shadow regions are relatively smooth therefore the edges of the shadow are normally suppressed in high frequency coefficients and are evident only in one of the directional coefficients [24]. So, in the next step horizontal and vertical projection vectors in high frequency sub bands (directional coefficients) are analyzed to extract the actual object region measurements. The shadow detection and removal method consists of the following steps:

(A) Compute the edge test regions (ETR) by applying mask operation in directional coefficients using 'Candidate Test Region' using Eq. 5

$$SD^H_{ER}(\alpha, \beta) = WD^L_{\eta^H}(\alpha, \beta) * F_{obj+sha}(\alpha, \beta)\Big|_{mask}$$ (6)

$$SD^V_{ER}(\alpha, \beta) = WD^L_{\eta^V}(\alpha, \beta) * F_{obj+sha}(\alpha, \beta)\Big|_{mask}$$ (7)

$$SD^D_{ER}(\alpha, \beta) = WD^L_{\eta^D}(\alpha, \beta) * F_{obj+sha}(\alpha, \beta)\Big|_{mask}$$ (8)

where $WD^L_{\eta^H}(\alpha, \beta)$, $WD^L_{\eta^V}(\alpha, \beta)$, and $WD^L_{\eta^D}(\alpha, \beta)$ represent the high frequency coefficients in horizontal, vertical and diagonal direction respectively at L^{th} level. The superscript H, V and D represent the Horizontal, Vertical and Diagonal directional subband respectively.

(B) Compute the vertical and horizontal projection vectors from each direction edge region.

$$v^H = \sum_i^{mH} \{SD^H_{ER}(\alpha_i, \beta_1), \ldots, SD^H_{ER}(\alpha_i, \beta_{nH})\}$$ (9)

$$h^H = \sum_i^{nH} \{SD^H_{ER}(\alpha_1, \beta_j), \ldots, SD^H_{ER}(\alpha_{nH}, \beta_j)\}$$ (10)

$$v^V = \sum_i^{mV} \{SD^H_{ER}(\alpha_i, \beta_1), \ldots, SD^H_{ER}(\alpha_i, \beta_{nV})\}$$ (11)

$$h^v = \sum_i^{mV} \{SD^V_{ER}(\alpha_1, \beta_j), \ldots, SD^V_{ER}(\alpha_{mV}, \beta_j)\}$$ (12)

$$v^D = \sum_i^{nD} \{SD_{ER}^D(\alpha_i, \beta_1), \ldots, SD_{ER}^D(\alpha_i, \beta_{nD})\} \qquad (13)$$

$$h^D = \sum_i^{mD} \{SD_{ER}^D(\alpha_1, \beta_j), \ldots, SD_{ER}^D(\alpha_{mD}, \beta_j)\} \qquad (14)$$

(C) Now using the following equations we can find the best fit measurements of object region (without shadow).

$$W_{obj}^x = \arg\min\{\max(h^H), \max(h^V), \max(h^D)\} \qquad (15)$$

$$W_{obj}^y = \arg\min\{\max(v^H), \max(v^V), \max(v^D)\} \qquad (16)$$

The proposed shadow suppression technique is only applied to foreground pixels rather than the entire image, thus saving significant processing time.

Step 5: Application of Canny Edge Detector to Detect Strong Edges in Wavelet Domain. Canny edge detection method is one of the most useful and popular edge detection methods, because of its low error rate, well localized edge points and single edge detection response [25]. In next step, the canny edge detection operator is applied on $WD_{n,d=(LL,LH,HL,HH)}(i,j)$ to detect the edges of significant difference pixels in all sub-bands as follows:

$$DE_{n,d=(LL,LH,HL,HH)}(i,j) = canny(WD_{n,d=(LL,LH,HL,HH)}(i,j)) \qquad (17)$$

Where $DE_{n,d=(LL,LH,HL,HH)}(i,j)$ is an edge map of $WD_{n,d=(LL,LH,HL,HH)}(i,j)$

Step 6: Application of Inverse Complex Wavelet Transform. After finding edge map $DE_{n,d=(LL,LH,HL,HH)}(i,j)$ in wavelet domain, inverse wavelet transform is applied to get moving object edges in spatial domain i.e. E_n

Step 7: Application of Closing Morphological Operation to Sub-band. As a result of step 6, the obtained segmented object may include a number of disconnected edges due to non-ideal segmentation of moving object edges. Extractions of object using these disconnected edges may lead to inaccurate object segmentation. Therefore, some morphological operation is needed for post-processing of object edge map to generate connected edges. Here, a binary closing morphological operation is used [25] which gives $M(E_n)$ i.e. the set of connected edge. In this step, the segmented output is obtained.

4 Experimental Results

4.1 Dataset Description

In this section, a brief overview of seven datasets used for experimentation purpose is presented in Table 1.

Table 1. Description of datasets used for Experimentation

Video Sequence	Information with respect to Object			Information with respect to Scene			Information with respect to Shadow	
	Object Type	Object Size	Scene Type	Noise Level	Complexity	Shadow Size	Shadow Strength	Shadow Direction
High-view video sequence [26]	Boat/Ship	Small	Outdoor	High	Shooted in much more height	Medium	Weak	Multiple
Occlusions-1 video sequence [26]	Ship	Large	Outdoor	High	Occlusions between object &Camera jittering	Medium	Weak	Multiple
Venice-3 video sequence [26]	Boat	Large	Outdoor	Low	Cast shadow	Large	Strong	Multiple
Venice-7 video sequence [26]	Boat	Large	Outdoor	Low	Wakes	Large	Weak	Multiple
Canoe video sequence [30]	Boat	Small	Outdoor	High	Wakes	Medium	Strong	Multiple
Boats video sequence [30]	Boat	Small	Outdoor	High	Wakes	Medium	Weak	Multiple
Ir-2 video sequence [26]	Ship	Large	Outdoor	Low	Captured by night vision camera in night (i.e. more noisy)	Medium	Weak	Multiple

4.2 Results and Analysis

The proposed method for segmentation of moving object has been applied on a number of video clips dataset [26, 30] discussed as above in Table 1. For the segmentation of the video object by various methods, the numbers of frames taken into consideration at a time include 125, 150 and 175. Here, in this section, the qualitative and quantitative analysis of the proposed method and other methods in consideration are presented.

(A) Experiment-1

Here in this experiment, we have taken High-view video sequence [26] from the MAR data sets. From Fig. 2, one can conclude that the segmentation result obtained by the proposed method has better segments in high view situation. This video is shooted from much more height with camera jittering conditions and it's also suffering from the problem of noise. From the obtained results it can be observed that the other methods [15, 22] suffers from the problems of object distortion, shadow and noise problem but the proposed method is able to suppress these problems (see frame 125–175 (iii–iv)). From Fig. 2, one can conclude that Hsia et al. [21] method depends on the fast motion of object, so it's not segmenting the frame properly (see frame 125–175 (v)). The proposed method handles all these critical condition and segments the result properly (see frame 125–175 (ii)).

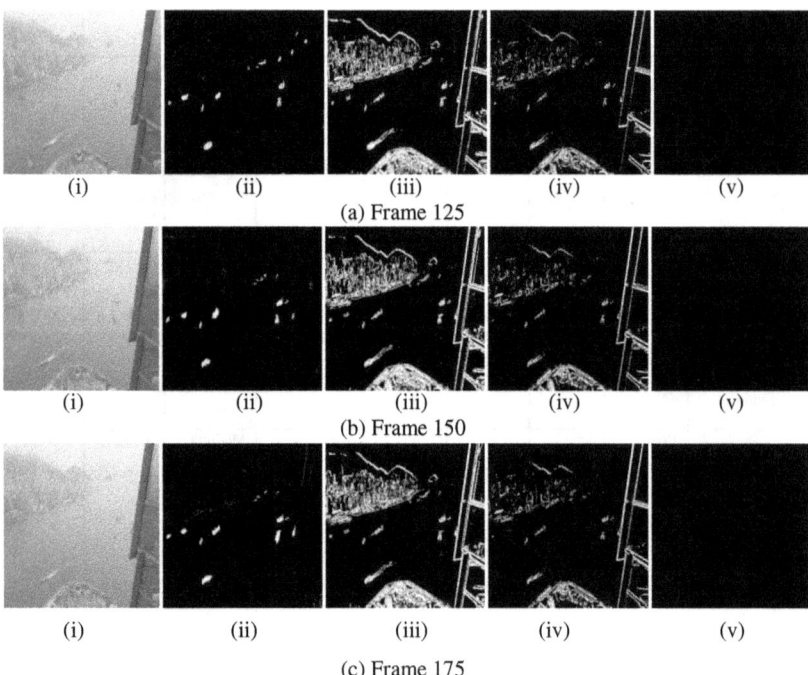

Fig. 2. Segmentation results for high-view video sequence corresponding to (a) Frame 125, (b) frame 150, and (c) frame 175 (i) original frame, and the segmented frame obtained by various methods such as: (ii) the proposed method, (iii) Bloisi et al. [22], (iv) Khare et al. [15], and (v) Hsia et al. [21].

(B) Experiment-2

Here in this experiment, we have taken Occlusions-1 video sequence [26] from the MAR data sets. This video is shooted from full and partial occlusions between ships with camera jittering conditions and it also suffers from the problem of noise. From Fig. 3, one can conclude that the segmentation result obtained by the proposed method has better segments in full and partial occlusions between ships. From the obtained results, it can be observed that other methods [15, 22] are suffering from the problems of object distortion due to occlusions and noise but the proposed method is able to suppress these problems (see frame 125–175 (iii–iv)). From Fig. 3, one can conclude that Hsia *et al.* [21] method depends on the fast motion of object, so it's not capable of segmenting the frame properly (see frame 125–175 (v)). The proposed method handles all these critical conditions and segments the result properly (see frame 125–175 (ii)).

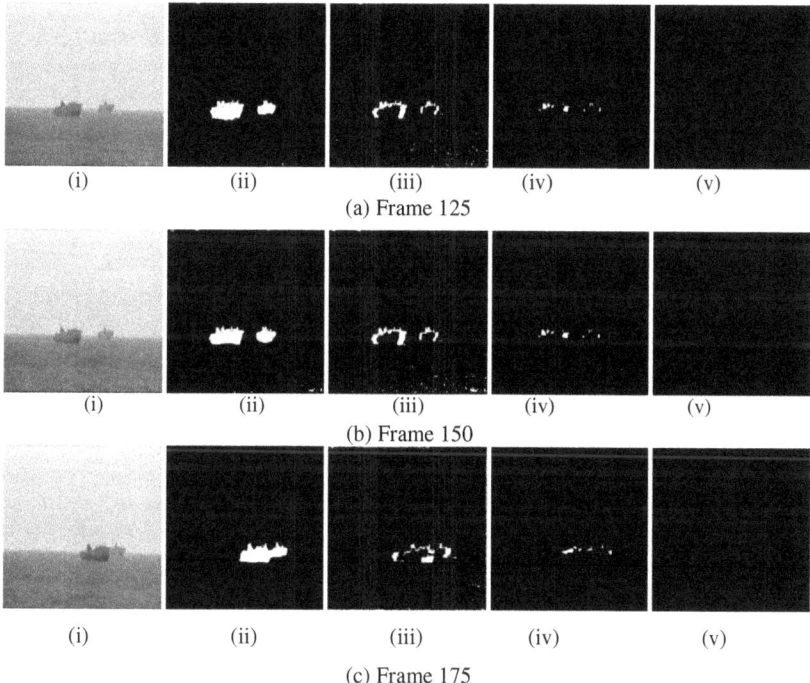

Fig. 3. Segmentation results for Occlusions-1 video sequence corresponding to (a) Frame 125, (b) frame 150, and (c) frame 175 (i) original frame, and the segmented frame obtained by various methods such as: (ii) the proposed method, (iii) Bloisi *et al.* [22], (iv) Khare *et al.* [15], and (v) Hsia *et al.* [21].

(C) Experiment-3

Here in this experiment, we have taken venice-3 video sequence [26] from the MAR data sets. In these video sequence boat shadows are present (see frame 125–175 (i)) and it's also suffering from the problem of noise. From Fig. 4, one can conclude that the segmentation result obtained by the proposed method has better segments in shadow conditions. From the obtained results, it can be observed that the other methods suffer from the problems of cast shadow, object distortion and noise (see frame 125–175 (iii–v)) but the proposed method is able to suppress these problems (see frame 125–175 (ii)).

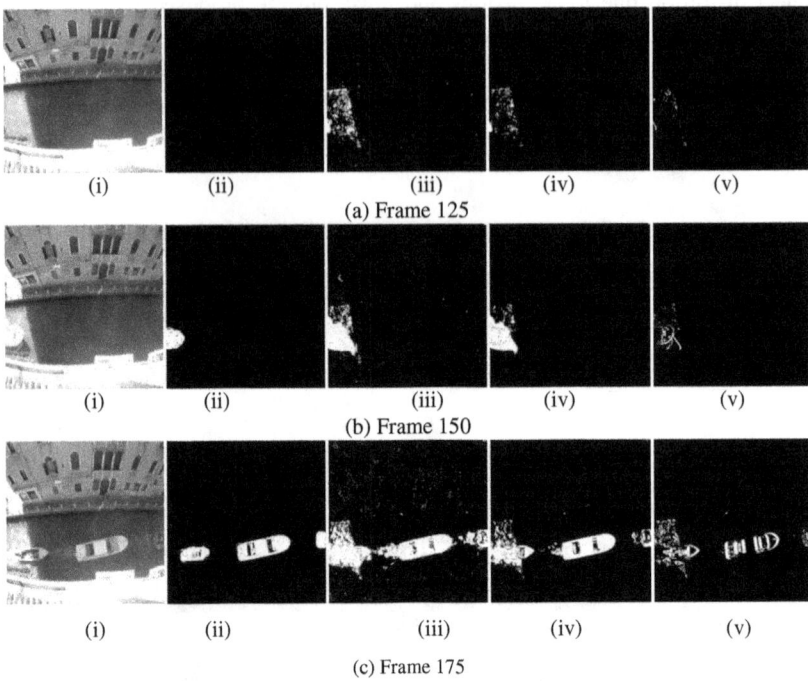

Fig. 4. Segmentation results for venice-3 video sequence corresponding to (a) Frame 125, (b) frame 150, and (c) frame 175 (i) original frame, and the segmented frame obtained by various methods such as: (ii) the proposed method, (iii) Bloisi *et al.* [22], (iv) Khare *et al.* [15], and (v) Hsia *et al.* [21].

(D) Experiment-4

Here in this experiment, we have taken venice-7 video sequence [26] from the MAR data sets. In these video sequence water wakes and multiple direction shadows are present (see frame 125–175 (i)) and it's also suffering from the problem of noise. From the Fig. 5, it is clear that proposed method work properly in water wakes environment (see frame 125–175 (ii)) but other methods [15, 21, 22] suffer from the noise, shadow and dynamic background problems (see frame 125–175 (iii–v))

(E) Experiment-5

Here in this experiment, we have taken canoe video sequence [30] from the change detection data sets. This video sequence suffers from the problem of noise and shadow.

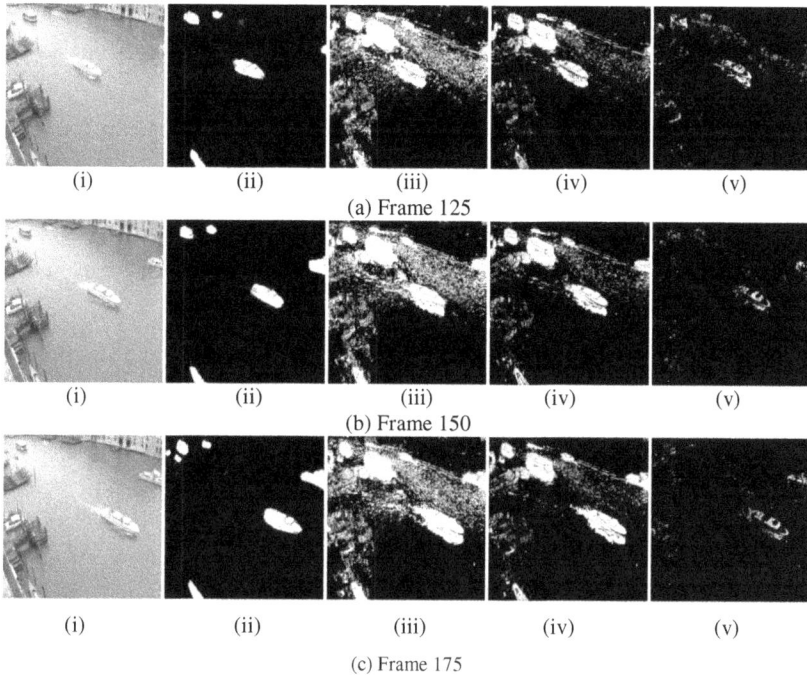

Fig. 5. Segmentation results for venice-7 video sequence corresponding to (a) Frame 125, (b) frame 150, and (c) frame 175 (i) original frame, and the segmented frame obtained by various methods such as: (ii) the proposed method, (iii) Bloisi *et al.* [22], (iv) Khare *et al.* [15], and (v) Hsia *et al.* [21].

From Fig. 6, one can conclude that the segmentation result obtained by the proposed method has better segments in shadow conditions (see frame 850–950 (ii)). From Fig. 6, one can conclude that Hsia *et al.* [21] method depends on the fast motion of object, so it's not segmenting the frame properly (see frame 850–950 (v)).

(F) Experiment-6

Here in this experiment, we have taken boats video sequence [30] from the change detection data sets. In this video sequence water wakes and noise are present. Figure 7, one can conclude that the segmentation result obtained by the proposed method has better segments in water wakes. From the obtained results in Fig. 7, it can be observed that the other methods [15, 22] suffers from the problem of false acceptance of objects but the proposed method is able to suppress these problems (see frame 850–950 (iii-iv)). From Fig. 7, one can conclude that Hsia *et al.* [21] method depends on the fast motion of object, so it's not segmenting the frame properly (see frame 850–950 (v)).

(G) Experiment-7

Here in this experiment, we have taken Ir-2 video sequence [20] from the MAR data sets. This video is captured in night mode environment using night vision camera with camera jittering conditions and it's also suffering from the problem of noise. From the

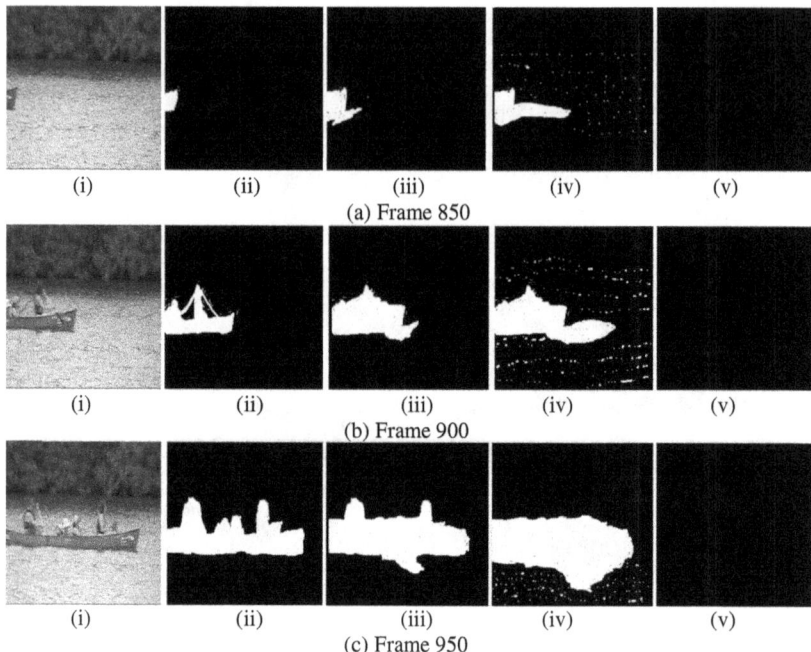

Fig. 6. Segmentation results for canoe video sequence corresponding to (a) Frame 850, (b) frame 900, and (c) frame 950 (i) original frame, and the segmented frame obtained by various methods such as: (ii) the proposed method, (iii) Bloisi et al. [22], (iv) Khare et al. [15], and (v) Hsia et al. [21].

obtained results in Fig. 8, it can be observed that the other methods [15, 22] suffers from the problems of object distortion, shadow and noise problem but the proposed method is able to suppress these problems (see frame 125–175 (iii–iv)). From Fig. 8, one can conclude that Hsia et al. [21] method depends on the fast motion of object, so it's not segmenting the frame properly (see frame 125–175 (v)). The proposed method handles all these critical condition and segments the result properly (see frame 125–175 (ii)). From Fig. 8, it is deduced that the segmentation result obtained by the proposed method has better segments in night mode condition.

In all above experimentations, the proposed method has also been compared with other standard methods [15, 21, 22] in literature in terms of RFAM (Relative foreground area measure) [27], MP (Misclassification Penalty) [27], RPM (Relative position based measure) [27], NCC (Normalized cross correlation) [28], PR (Precision) [31], RE (Recall) [31], SDR (shadow detection rate) [29], SDR (shadow discrimination rate) [29], computation time and memory consumption. All experimentations were performed on a machine with Intel 2.53 GHz core i3 processor with 2 GB RAM using OpenCV 2.8 software. Tables 2, 3 and 4 show the values of RFAM, MP, RPM, NCC, PR, RE [27–29, 31] for the proposed method and other methods [15, 21, 22] for seven video sequences [26, 30]. From Tables 2, 3 and 4, one can observe that the proposed method is associated to high value of RFAM, RPM, NCC, PR, RE and low value of

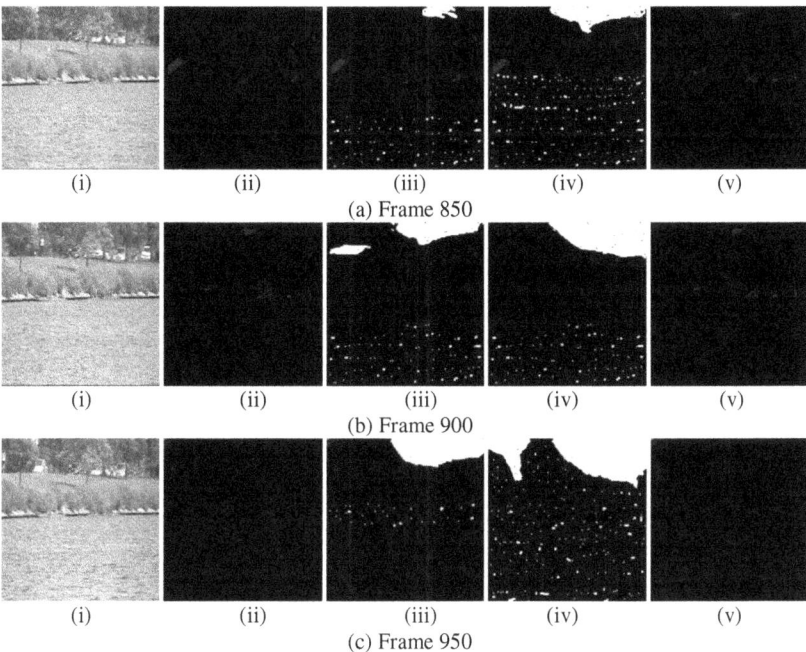

Fig. 7. Segmentation results for boats video sequence corresponding to (a) Frame 850, (b) frame 900, and (c) frame 950 (i) original frame, and the segmented frame obtained by various methods such as: (ii) the proposed method, (iii) Bloisi *et al.* [22], (iv) Khare *et al.* [15], and (v) Hsia *et al.* [21].

MP (see the result in Tables 2, 3 and 4 in bold), in most of the frames in comparison to other methods in consideration [15, 21, 22] for the seven datasets [26, 30] indicating that the proposed method is better in comparison to other methods. From Table 5, it can be inferred that in cases of High-view video sequence [26], Occlusions-1 video sequence [26], Venice-3 video sequence [26], and Venice-7 video sequence [26], canoe video sequence [30], boats video sequence [30], Ir-2 video sequence [26] the proposed method is found to be better than all other methods [15, 21, 22] in terms of shadow detection rate and shadow discrimination rate. In Table 6, average computation time (second/frame) and memory consumption for different methods for Venice-7 video sequence [26] of frame size 480 × 320 with 300 frames are shown. From the Table 6, it can be observed that the proposed method using complex wavelet transform is faster than the method reported in [21, 22]. The proposed method using complex wavelet transform takes approximately same time as the Khare *et al.* [15]. Also from the Table 6, the proposed method consumes only 4.13 megabytes of RAM which is the least in comparison with the other methods discussed [15, 21, 22].

Therefore, after observing the values of ten quantitative measures, it can be concluded that the proposed method using complex wavelet transform give better results as compared to other methods and also takes less processing time and memory in comparison to others.

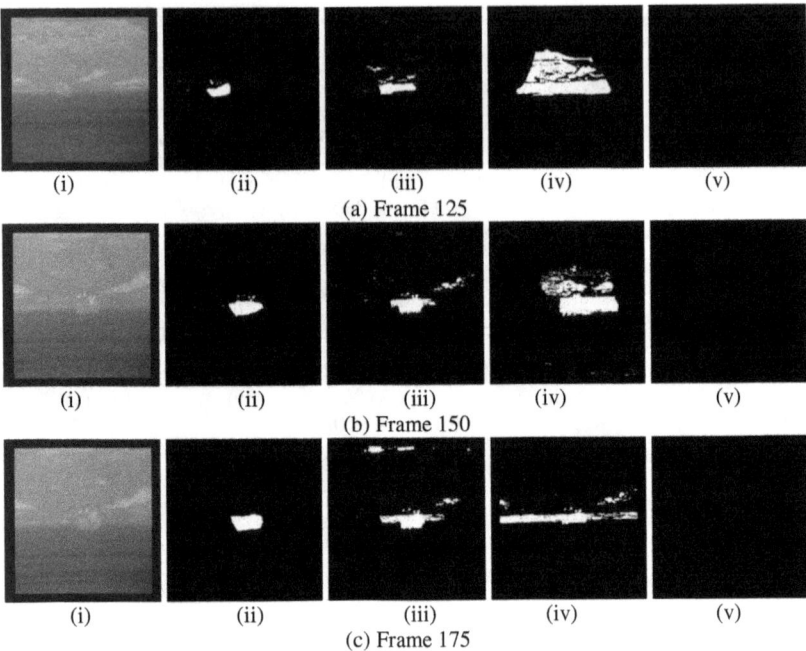

Fig. 8. Segmentation results for Ir-2 video sequence corresponding to (a) Frame 125, (b) frame 150, and (c) frame 175 (i) original frame, and the segmented frame obtained by various methods such as: (ii) the proposed method, (iii) Bloisi et al. [22], (iv) Khare et al. [15], and (v) Hsia et al. [21].

Table 2. Comparison of methods in terms of Relative foreground area measure (RFAM) and Misclassification Penalty (MP) for different video dataset

Frame No.	Bloisi et al. [22]	Hsia et al. [21]	Khare et al. [15]	Proposed Method	Frame No.	Bloisi et al. [22]	Hsia et al. [21]	Khare et al. [15]	Proposed Method
A-High-view video sequence [26]					A-High-view video sequence [26]				
125	0.7914	0.1870	0.6126	**0.9443**	125	0.0057	0.1160	0.0711	**0.0018**
150	0.7665	0.1491	0.6405	**0.9287**	150	0.0062	0.2130	0.0781	**0.0023**
175	0.7719	0.1457	0.6290	**0.9128**	175	0.0037	0.1820	0.0830	**0.0023**
B-Occlusions-1 video sequence [26]					B-Occlusions-1 video sequence [26]				
125	0.8631	0.1514	0.6757	**0.9458**	125	0.0085	0.4128	0.0159	**0.0056**
150	0.8316	0.1087	0.7184	**0.9237**	150	0.0095	0.4521	0.0162	**0.0042**
175	0.8365	0.1920	0.6500	**0.9650**	175	0.0093	0.3978	0.0134	**0.0038**
C-Venice-3 video sequence [26]					C-Venice-3 video sequence [26]				
125	0.7718	0.4433	0.6902	**0.9056**	125	0.0142	0.8975	0.0163	**0.0011**
150	0.7945	0.4287	0.6768	**0.9120**	150	0.0137	0.9136	0.0198	**0.0069**
175	0.7634	0.4645	0.7123	**0.9471**	175	0.0147	0.8285	0.0144	**0.0077**
D-Venice-7 video sequence [26]					D-Venice-7 video sequence [26]				
125	0.6514	0.3396	0.4581	**0.8733**	125	0.0121	0.1698	0.0256	**0.0034**
150	0.6445	0.3089	0.4064	**0.8847**	150	0.0101	0.1970	0.0195	**0.0083**
175	0.6629	0.3762	0.4183	**0.9143**	175	0.0115	0.1296	0.0456	**0.0062**
E-Canoe video sequence [30]					E-Canoe video sequence [30]				
850	0.6329	0.2103	0.5623	**0.8721**	850	0.0092	0.7356	0.0359	**0.0026**
900	0.6192	0.2391	0.5512	**0.8936**	900	0.0096	0.7793	0.0523	**0.0031**
950	0.6683	0.2619	0.5239	**0.8587**	950	0.0089	0.7519	0.0548	**0.0029**
F-Boats video sequence [30]					F-Boats video sequence [30]				
850	0.5672	0.8209	0.3561	**0.8521**	850	0.0112	0.0061	0.0672	**0.0053**
900	0.5518	0.8104	0.3346	**0.8411**	900	0.0216	0.0058	0.0781	**0.0052**
950	0.5329	0.7892	0.3098	**0.8317**	950	0.0119	0.0054	0.0745	**0.0048**
G- Ir-2 video sequence [26]					G- Ir-2 video sequence [26]				
125	0.5573	0.3271	0.4724	**0.7312**	125	0.0141	0.1823	0.0436	**0.0085**
150	0.5465	0.2931	0.4384	**0.7012**	150	0.0155	0.1762	0.0445	**0.0093**
175	0.5710	0.2857	0.4476	**0.7394**	175	0.0164	0.1783	0.04866	**0.0089**

A Framework of Moving Object Segmentation   51

Table 3. Comparison of methods in terms of Relative position based measure (RPM) and Normalized cross correlation (NCC) for different video datasets

Frame No.	Bloisi et al. [22]	Hsia et al.[21]	Khare et al.[15]	Proposed Method	Frame No.	Bloisi et al. [22]	Hsia et al.[21]	Khare et al.[15]	Proposed Method
A-High-view video sequence [26]					A-High-view video sequence [26]				
125	0.7537	0.1840	0.6268	**0.9056**	125	0.6598	0.0739	0.5505	**0.9325**
150	0.7489	0.1616	0.6602	**0.9253**	150	0.6371	0.0991	0.5785	**0.9618**
175	0.7328	0.1053	0.6842	**0.9381**	175	0.6692	0.0980	0.5799	**0.9513**
B-Occlusions-1 video sequence [26]					B-Occlusions-1 video sequence [26]				
125	0.7525	0.1800	0.6125	**0.9135**	125	0.6980	0.0215	0.5799	**0.9271**
150	0.7900	0.1490	0.6576	**0.9249**	150	0.6621	0.0411	0.6070	**0.9576**
175	0.7115	0.1495	0.6107	**0.9568**	175	0.6534	0.0446	0.6030	**0.9168**
C-Venice-3 video sequence [26]					C-Venice-3 video sequence [26]				
125	0.7773	0.3910	0.7137	**0.9346**	125	0.6631	0.1543	0.6263	**0.9040**
150	0.7549	0.3804	0.7289	**0.9127**	150	0.6174	0.1374	0.6094	**0.9162**
175	0.7521	0.3471	0.7096	**0.9439**	175	0.6590	0.1364	0.6130	**0.9418**
D-Venice-7 video sequence [26]					D-Venice-7 video sequence [26]				
125	0.7894	0.2149	0.7232	**0.9472**	125	0.7496	0.2128	0.6027	**0.9621**
150	0.7659	0.2145	0.7137	**0.9257**	150	0.7029	0.2093	0.6217	**0.9518**
175	0.7475	0.2451	0.7457	**0.9328**	175	0.7837	0.2944	0.6133	**0.9463**
E-Canoe video sequence [30]					E-Canoe video sequence [30]				
850	0.6721	0.1181	0.5310	**0.8819**	850	0.6619	0.1782	0.5618	**0.9013**
900	0.7129	0.1988	0.5461	**0.8653**	900	0.6983	0.1673	0.5865	**0.9167**
950	0.6452	0.1734	0.5213	**0.8893**	950	0.6435	0.1173	0.5241	**0.9356**
F-Boats video sequence [30]					F-Boats video sequence [30]				
850	0.6161	0.8119	0.5134	**0.8328**	850	0.6252	0.7918	0.5872	**0.8318**
900	0.6452	0.8245	0.5328	**0.8542**	900	0.6534	0.8034	0.5648	**0.8625**
950	0.6237	0.8013	0.5563	**0.8458**	950	0.6051	0.8253	0.5923	**0.8493**
G- Ir-2 video sequence [26]					G- Ir-2 video sequence [26]				
125	0.7349	0.1911	0.6534	**0.8964**	125	0.7342	0.1911	0.5634	**0.8239**
150	0.7211	0.1548	0.6219	**0.9217**	150	0.7629	0.1728	0.5178	**0.8472**
175	0.7318	0.1419	0.6673	**0.9183**	175	0.7268	0.1639	0.5839	**0.8650**

Table 4. Comparison of methods in terms of Precision (PR) and Recall (RE) for different video datasets

Frame No.	Bloisi et al. [22]	Hsia et al.[21]	Khare et al.[15]	Proposed Method	Frame No.	Bloisi et al. [22]	Hsia et al.[21]	Khare et al.[15]	Proposed Method
A-High-view video sequence [26]					A-High-view video sequence [26]				
125	0.9288	0.5015	0.7810	**0.9654**	125	0.7826	0.3522	0.6978	**0.9060**
150	0.9069	0.5155	0.7645	**0.9663**	150	0.7011	0.3463	0.6141	**0.9056**
175	0.8912	0.5445	0.7645	**0.9307**	175	0.7460	0.3609	0.6520	**0.9218**
B-Occlusions-1 video sequence [26]					B-Occlusions-1 video sequence [26]				
125	0.7941	0.5245	0.7490	**0.8718**	125	0.7822	0.4441	0.6588	**0.9040**
150	0.7577	0.4859	0.6911	**0.8084**	150	0.7107	0.4399	0.5109	**0.9071**
175	0.7213	0.5629	0.7433	**0.8787**	175	0.7452	0.4230	0.5818	**0.9365**
C-Venice-3 video sequence [26]					C-Venice-3 video sequence [26]				
125	0.7726	0.5755	0.7106	**0.9519**	125	0.7349	0.3268	0.6991	**0.9303**
150	0.7839	0.5718	0.7490	**0.9520**	150	0.7844	0.3408	0.6482	**0.9432**
175	0.7563	0.5239	0.7356	**0.9356**	175	0.7639	0.3019	0.6848	**0.9010**
D-Venice-7 video sequence [26]					D-Venice-7 video sequence [26]				
125	0.7176	0.4041	0.6462	**0.9717**	125	0.6909	0.2997	0.6655	**0.9059**
150	0.7503	0.4315	0.6583	**0.9485**	150	0.7286	0.2257	0.6718	**0.9133**
175	0.7019	0.4566	0.6259	**0.9348**	175	0.6670	0.2456	0.6328	**0.9239**
E-Canoe video sequence [30]					E-Canoe video sequence [30]				
850	0.7261	0.4354	0.6363	**0.8745**	850	0.7318	0.3960	0.6624	**0.9304**
900	0.7534	0.4747	0.6494	**0.8581**	900	0.7925	0.3493	0.6953	**0.9778**
950	0.7782	0.4610	0.6672	**0.8818**	950	0.7532	0.3768	0.6410	**0.9462**
F-Boats video sequence [30]					F-Boats video sequence [30]				
850	0.7273	0.7546	0.6322	**0.8273**	850	0.7751	0.8444	0.6929	**0.9743**
900	0.7858	0.7490	0.6470	**0.8213**	900	0.7704	0.8645	0.6029	**0.9779**
950	0.7630	0.7271	0.6620	**0.8458**	950	0.7451	0.8274	0.6640	**0.9561**
G- Ir-2 video sequence [26]					G- Ir-2 video sequence [26]				
125	0.8791	0.6443	0.7598	**0.9693**	125	0.7794	0.2217	0.6914	**0.9766**
150	0.8614	0.6640	0.8127	**0.9349**	150	0.7803	0.2869	0.6750	**0.9574**
175	0.8496	0.6340	0.7903	**0.9128**	175	0.7619	0.2455	0.6604	**0.9217**

Table 5. Shadow detection rate χ and shadow discrimination rate ζ of seven video sequence frames (Nos. 125, 150, 175)

Bloisi et al. [22]	Hsia et al.[21]	Khare et al.[15]	Proposed Method	Bloisi et al. [22]	Hsia et al.[21]	Khare et al.[15]	Proposed Method
A-High-view video sequence [26]				A-High-view video sequence [26]			
78.25	25.67	75.46	**92.35**	76.81	36.56	77.16	**93.25**
B-Occlusions-1 video sequence [26]				B-Occlusions-1 video sequence [26]			
75.13	26.65	76.52	**93.14**	75.97	35.73	75.69	**95.47**
C-Venice-3 video sequence [26]				C-Venice-3 video sequence [26]			
81.39	58.54	77.72	**95.43**	79.28	37.47	77.27	**92.67**
D-Venice-7 video sequence [26]				D-Venice-7 video sequence [26]			
70.56	64.83	74.57	**94.27**	78.86	36.32	75.29	**94.81**
E-Canoe video sequence [30]				E-Canoe video sequence [30]			
71.27	56.11	69.72	**92.19**	75.24	29.16	71.11	**9231**
F-Boats video sequence [30]				F-Boats video sequence [30]			
76.11	70.33	72.17	**90.15**	73.94	70.11	72.68	**91.55**
G- Ir-2 video sequence [26]				G- Ir-2 video sequence [26]			
73.52	21.18	71.19	**91.88**	79.11	23.28	73.16	**92.42**

Table 6. Computational time and consumption memory for Venice-7 video sequence [26]

Methods	Computational Time (in second/frame)	Memory Consumption (MB)
Bloisi et al. [22]	3.945	22.75
Hsia et al. [21]	1.867	11.75
Khare et al. [15]	1.341	7.19
The Proposed Method	1.154	4.13

5 Conclusions

In this paper, an approach for moving object segmentation under maritime surveillance conditions with a fast computational speed and low memory requirement was proposed. The proposed method was well capable of dealing with gradual and sudden illumination changes, camera jitter, shadows, and reflections that can provoke false detections in maritime surveillance. The proposed method consisted of seven steps applied on given video frames which included: wavelet de-composition of frame using complex wavelet transform; use of change detection on detail coefficients (LH, HL, HH); use of background modeling on approximate co-efficient (LL sub-band); cast shadow suppression; strong edge detection; inverse wavelet transformation for reconstruction; and finally using closing morphology operator. For background modeling, we have used background registration, background difference, and background difference mask in complex wavelet domain. For shadow detection and removal, we exploited the high frequency sub-band in complex wavelet domain. The extensive experimental results on seven challenging data sets demonstrated that the proposed method performed better in comparison to other state -of-the-art moving object segmentation methods in terms of visual performance and a number of quantitative performance metrics [27–29, 31] in various complex video sequences.

References

1. El-Sayed, S.K., Ahmed, S.: Moving object detection in spatial domain using background removal techniques - state-of-on computer science. Recent Pat. Comput. Sci. **1**, 32–54 (2008)
2. Cristani, M., Farenzena, M., Bloisi, D., Murino, V.: Background subtraction for automated multisensor surveillance: a comprehensive review. EURASIP J. Adv. Sig. Process. **2010**, 1–24 (2010)
3. Cheung, S-C., Kamath, C.: Robust techniques for background subtraction in urban traffic video. In: Proceedings of the SPIE 5308 Conference of Visual Communications and Image Processing, vol. 5308, pp. 881–892 (2004)
4. Kim, K., Chalidabhongse, T.H., Harwood, D., Davis, L.: Real time foreground background segmentation using codebook model. Real Time Imaging **11**, 172–185 (2005)
5. Kushwaha, A.K.S., Sharma, C.M., Khare, M., Prakash, O., Khare, A.: Adaptive real-time motion segmentation technique based on statistical background model. Imaging Sci. J. **62**, 285–302 (2014)
6. McFarlane, N., Schofield, C.: Segmentation and tracking of piglets in images. Mach. Vis. Appl. **8**, 187–193 (1995)
7. Remagnino, P., Baumberg, A., Grove, T., Hogg, D., Tan, T., Worrall, A., Baker, K.: An integrated traffic and pedestrian model-based vision system. In: Proceedings of the Eighth British Machine Vision Conference, pp. 380–389 (1997)
8. Stauffer, C., Grimson, W.: Adaptive background mixture models for real-time tracking. In: IEEE Computer Society Conference on Computer Vision and Pattern Recognition (CVPR 1999), vol. 2, pp. 246–252 (1999)
9. Kim, C., Hwang, J.-N.: Fast and automatic video object segmentation and tracking for content-based applications. IEEE Trans. Circ. Syst. Video Technol. **12**, 122–129 (2002)
10. Shih, M.-Y., Chang, Y.-J., Fu, B.-C., Huang, C.-C.: Motion-based back-ground modeling for moving object detection on moving platforms. In: Proceedings of the International Conference on Computer Communications and Networks, pp. 1178–1182 (2007)
11. Huang, J.C., Hsieh, W.S.: Wavelet based moving object segmentation. Electron. Lett. **39**, 1380–1382 (2003)
12. Huang, J.C., Su, T.S., Wang, L.J., Hsieh, W.S.: Double change detection method for wavelet based moving object segmentation. Electron. Lett. **40**, 798–799 (2004)
13. Baradarani, A., Wu, Q.M.J.: Wavelet based moving object segmentation: from scalar wavelets to dual-tree complex filter banks. In: Herout, A. (ed.) Pattern Recognition Recent Advances. InTech Open Access, Rijeka (2010)
14. Baradarani, A.: Moving object segmentation using 9/7-10/8 dual tree complex filter bank. In: Proceeding of IEEE 19th International Conference on Pattern Recognition (ICPR), pp. 1–4 (2008)
15. Khare, M., Srivastava, R.K., Khare, A.: Single change detection-based moving object segmentation by using Daubechies complex wavelet transform. IET Image Proc. **8**, 334–344 (2014)
16. Liu, H., Chen, X., Chen, Y., Xie, C.: Double change detection method for moving-object segmentation based on clustering. In: IEEE ISCAS 2006 Circuits and Systems, pp. 5027–5030 (2006)
17. Prati, A., Mikic, I., Trivedi, M.M., Cucchiara, R.: Detecting moving shadows: algorithms and evaluation. IEEE Trans. Pattern Anal. Mach. Intell. **25**, 918–923 (2003)
18. Guan, Y.P.: Spatio-temporal motion-based foreground segmentation and shadow suppression. IET Comput. Vis. **4**, 50–60 (2010)

19. Daubechies, I.: Ten Lectures on Wavelets. SIAM, Philadelphia (1992)
20. Khare, M., Srivastava, R.K., Khare, A.: Dual tree complex wavelet transform based shadow detection and removal from moving objects. In: Proceeding of 26th SPIE Electronic Imaging, vol. 9029, pp. 1–7 (2014)
21. Hsia, C.-H., Guo, J.-M.: Efficient modified direction al lifting-based discrete wavelet transform for moving object detection. J. Sig. Process. **96**, 138–152 (2014)
22. Bloisi, D.D., Pennisi, A., Iocchi, L.: Background modeling in the maritime domain. Mach. Vis. Appl. **25**, 1257–1269 (2014)
23. Aacj, T., Kaup, A., Mester, R.: Statistical model-based change detection in moving video. J. Sig. Process. **31**, 165–180 (1993)
24. Romberg, J.K., Choi, H., Baraniuk, R.G.: Multiscale edge grammars for complex wavelet transforms. In: Proceedings of the IEEE International Conference on Image Processing, pp. 614–617 (2001)
25. Sridhar, S.: Digital image processing, 3rd edn. Oxford Publication, Oxford (2008)
26. Bloisi, D., Iocchi, L., Pennisi, A., Previtali, F.: http://www.dis.uniroma1.it/~labrococo/MAR/dataset.htm
27. Gao-bo, Y., Zhao-yang, Z.: Objective performance evaluation of video segmentation algorithms with Ground-Truth. J. Shanghai University. **8**, 70–74 (2004)
28. Eskicioglu, A.M., Fisher, P.S.: Image quality measures and their performance. IEEE Trans. Commun. **43**, 2959–2965 (1995)
29. Prati, A., Mikic, I., Trivedi, M.M., Cucchiara, R.: Detecting moving shadows: algorithms and evaluation. IEEE Trans. Pattern Anal. Mach. Intell. **25**, 918–923 (2003)
30. Wang, Y., Jodoin, P.-M., Porikli, F., Konrad, J., Benezeth, Y., Ishwar, P.: http://changedetection.net/
31. Subudhi, B.N., Ghosh, S., Ghosh, A.: Change detection for moving object segmentation with robust background construction under wronskian framework. Mach. Vis. Appl. **24**, 795–809 (2013)

Novel Technique in Block Truncation Coding Based Feature Extraction for Content Based Image Identification

Sudeep Thepade[1], Rik Das[2(✉)], and Saurav Ghosh[3]

[1] Department of Computer Engineering, Pimpri Chinchwad College of Engineering,
Pune, India
sudeepthepade@gmail.com
[2] Department of Information Technology, Xavier Institute of Social Service,
Ranchi, Jharkhand, India
rikdas78@gmail.com
[3] A.K. Choudhury School of Information Technology, University of Calcutta,
Kolkata, West Bengal, India
sauravghoshcu@gmail.com

Abstract. Feature vector extraction has been the key component to define the success rate for content based image recognition. Block truncation coding is a simple technique which has facilitated various methods for effective feature vector extraction for content based image recognition. A new technique named Sorted Block Truncation Coding (SBTC) has been introduced in this work. Three different public datasets namely Wang Dataset, Oliva and Torralba (OT-Scene) Dataset and Caltech Dataset consisting of 6,221 images on the whole was considered for evaluation purpose. The technique has stimulated superior performance in image recognition when compared to classification and retrieval results with other existing techniques of feature extraction. The technique was also evaluated in lossy compression domain for the test images. Various parameters like precision, recall, misclassification rate and F1 score has been considered to evaluate the performances. Statistical evaluations have been carried out for all the comparisons by introducing paired t test to establish the significance of the findings. Classification and retrieval with proposed technique has shown a minimum of 14.4 % rise in precision results compared to the existing state-of-the art techniques.

Keywords: Image classification · Sorted BTC · Binarization · Retrieval · Query classification

1 Introduction

Content based image identification has its budding demand due to various applications in vital areas like weather forecasting, medical science, defence activities and many more. Image recognition has been an algorithmic process to identify a given input data into one among the various given categories [1]. The visual contents have been used to classify images into their categories of interests in case of content based image recognition [2]. Thus, feature extraction has played a vital role in the success factor of image identification. In this paper, a new Block Truncation Coding (BTC) based feature extraction technique named Sorted Block Truncation Coding (SBTC) has been proposed and was compared with existing state-of-the art techniques of feature extraction to evaluate the efficiency of the respective techniques in terms of facilitator for content based recognition process. The experimentation was carried out in RGB color space. Red, Green and Blue have been considered to be the base colors which have formed the RGB color space [29].

- The objective of the paper is to propose a novel technique of feature extraction for improved content based image identification.
- The novel technique of feature extraction has effectively reduced the feature vector size.
- It has made the size of feature vector independent of the dimension of images.
- It has considerably reduced the time for feature vector extraction.
- The results of classification with the proposed technique of feature extraction have shown significant improvement over existing techniques.

A content based retrieval methodology has been proposed which has outclassed the established techniques.

2 Related Work

Threshold selection has been considered as a widely used technique for feature vector extraction using binarization of images. Threshold selection has been affected by a number of factors including ambient illumination, variance of gray levels within the object and the background, inadequate contrast, etc. [7–9]. A variety of techniques has been implemented to extract feature vectors based on mean threshold selection. The techniques have involved binarization with mean threshold selection and ternary threshold selection to extract the features from generic images and fused images [14, 15, 17–19]. Mean threshold selection was not effective to determine the spread of data as it has not considered standard deviation of the gray values. Selection of local threshold has implemented standard deviation and variance to calculate the threshold [3–5, 20, 24, 25]. Efficient feature extraction has been performed with application of genetic algorithm for color and texture based features by 3D color histogram and Gabor filters [11]. Proposed technique of feature extraction in [6] has divided the image into non overlapping blocks and calculated local descriptors of color and texture from the Color moments and moments on Gabor filter responses of these blocks. Point features of visual significance were chosen from images and were used as signatures for image recognition [10]. Combination of color layout descriptor and Gabor texture descriptor was considered as image features in [12]. Extraction of features with color, texture and spatial structure descriptors was carried out in [21]. The authors in [22] have explored wavelet packets and Eigen values of Gabor filters for extraction of feature vectors from images. The authors in [23] have proposed the intra-class and inter-class feature extraction from images. Color Difference Histogram and Angular Radial Transform were fused to form feature vectors for retrieval [26]. Color histogram and texture features based on a co-occurrence matrix were exploited to form the feature vectors for efficient retrieval [13]. The characteristics of the images were explored with color histogram and spatial orientation tree for feature extraction [16]. The existing techniques of feature extraction have often generated hefty feature vector size. Hence, the space required for storing the feature vectors was huge and time for image classification or retrieval has increased radically. The computational overhead for extraction of feature vectors with global or local threshold selection techniques has been enormous. In case of global threshold selection exhaustive search for optimal threshold has been carried out with repeated iterations. The local threshold selection techniques have considered the selection of multiple thresholds with reference to each pixel in the image which is complex and time consuming. The mean threshold selection techniques have a lengthy process of considering the comparison of each pixel value with the mean value for generating feature vectors. The fusion based techniques has been observed to be slow because of the late fusion of classifier decisions. The authors have identified the above mentioned demerits of large feature vector size, increased training time and late decision making prevailing with the existing techniques. Hence, a new BTC based technique named Sorted BTC (SBTC) has been introduced in this work and was compared with existing techniques of feature extraction for performance evaluation in content based image classification and retrieval. The technique has extracted feature vectors of size 24 irrespective of the size of the images. The proposed method has not considered any threshold selection process. Therefore, the comparison of each pixel value with threshold was not required which in turn has reduced the feature extraction time. The novel technique has outclassed the existing techniques in classification and retrieval performances and has retained consistency in compressed domain.

3   Block Truncation Coding (BTC)

Block Truncation Coding (BTC) has been implemented for image compression since early days of image processing in the year 1979 [28]. It has been extended for the color images after successful performance of BTC with grayscale images. Non overlapping blocks were coded one at a time for an image, after being segmented in the dimension of $n \times n$. Mean and standard deviation was applied to find the new values of the reconstructed blocks which remained same as the original blocks [27]. Each color component Red (R), Green (G) and Blue (B) was considered as a block to implement the concept of block truncation coding based feature extraction technique in the proposed approach discussed in this work as in Fig. 1.

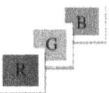

Fig. 1. Red, Green and Blue component as blocks (Color figure online)

4 Image Compression Scheme

A Discrete Cosine Transform (DCT) based lossy Image compression approach has been performed to evaluate the classification performances of the proposed algorithm in the compressed domain. The compression algorithm involved loss of image detail for higher compression ratio [30, 31]. Efficiency of energy compaction in DCT has been higher than that of FFT. The general equation for a two dimensional DCT has been given as in Eqs. 1 and 2.

$$C(u, v) = W(u)W(v) \sum_{x=0}^{N-1} \sum_{y=0}^{N-1} f(x,y) \cdot \cos\left(\frac{\Pi(2x+1)u}{2N}\right) \cos\left(\frac{\Pi(2y+1)v}{2N}\right) \quad (1)$$

for u, v = 0, 1, 2,............, N
and the inverse transform is given as

$$f(x, y) = \sum_{x=0}^{N-1} \sum_{y=0}^{N-1} W(u)W(v)C(u,v) \cos\left(\frac{\Pi(2x+1)u}{2N}\right) \cos\left(\frac{\Pi(2y+1)v}{2N}\right) \quad (2)$$

for x, y = 0, 1, 2,...., N−1.
The following diagram in Fig. 2 shows the steps used for image compression.

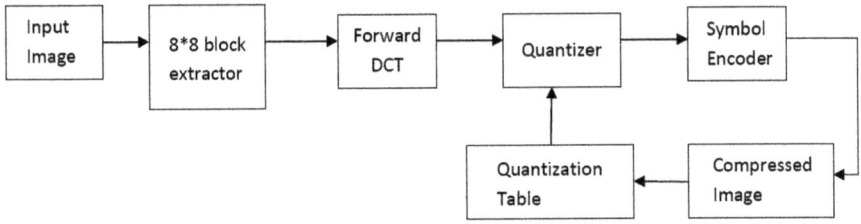

Encoder Section

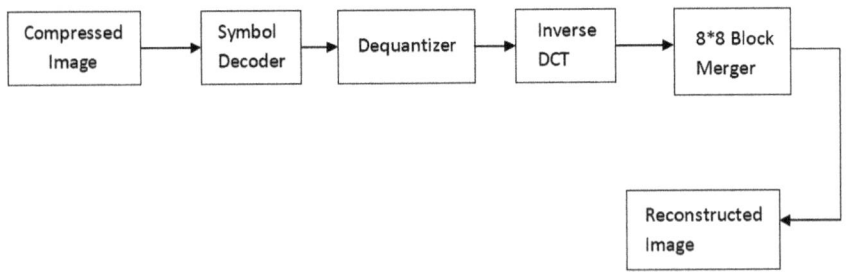

Decoder Section

Fig. 2. Process of image compression and reconstruction

Fig. 3. Images with different compression ratios derived from original image

The compression ratios used for image compression has been given in Fig. 3.

5   Proposed Technique (Sorted Block Truncation Coding (SBTC))

Image data gets contaminated with the presence of noise which has adverse influence on image processing algorithms. Various noise removal algorithms have been developed to reduce the effect of noise from data. Binning has been considered as a popular method to smooth sorted data values present in a dataset [32]. Execution process of binning method for noise removal has been based on taking the average of sorted values in a dataset by consulting the neighbours and then to perform local smoothing. Therefore, each value in the respective bins was being replaced by the corresponding average value of the bin. The same process was followed for all the bins to carry out the smoothing process. If the smoothed values were considered as feature vectors then for an image of dimension S*S, the number of feature vectors would have been S^2. Thus, the dependence of the size of feature vectors on the dimension of the image should have generated hefty feature vector size. The huge size of feature vector in turn have added computational complexity and increased training time. Proposed approach of Sorted BTC has implemented modified binning methodology on sorted gray values of images to extract feature vectors from each of the color component Red (R), Green (G) and Blue (B). The size of feature vectors generated with this method was equivalent to the number of bins instead of the number of gray values. For example, if all the gray values were sorted and divided into $N = 8$ bins or partitions, then the number of feature vectors generated was also 8 which was equal to the number of bins or partitions. This has radically reduced the size of feature vector and has significantly increased the computational efficiency for feature vector extraction. The process has divided the intensity values into N blocks where

($N >= 2$). Feature extraction has been carried out following the Block Truncation Coding (BTC) technique, where each of the color components Red (R), Green (G) and Blue (B) were considered as a block. Each block was divided into bins of sorted intensity values. The average of sorted intensity values in each bin was considered to form the feature vector of that block. The feature vectors of the blocks thus generated have been combined to create the feature vector of the image. The process represented the intensity values of an image within a single dimensional array. The single dimensional array was then sorted in ascending order. The sorted array was divided into N blocks to calculate the average of intensities in each block to generate the feature vectors as shown in Algorithm 1. The procedure *SBTC()* has been repeated for feature vector generation from *N* blocked (while $N >= 2$) images and compared with the results obtained for misclassification rate and F1 Score with feature vectors of a *(N–1)* blocked images (while *(N > 2)*. The misclassification rate (MR) has given the measure of wrongly classified instances and the F1 Score has been computed as the harmonic mean of precision and recall. Higher value of F1 Score is an indication of better classification results. The misclassification rate (MR) and F1 Score were observed for increasing number of blocks and were compared. Further subdivisions of images into blocks were restricted when the performance of classification degrades.

Algorithm 1
Begin

1. Input an image I with three different color components Red (R), Green (G) and Blue (B) respectively of size m*n each.
2. m*n intensity values can be represented with single dimensional array SDR.
3. SDR is having elements with indices 1 : m*n for each color component R, G and B.
4. The gray values of each extracted component for the given image are sorted in ascending order as 'SORTED SDR'.
5. The intensity values of the respective color components are divided into N ($N >= 2$) partitions for feature extraction.

/*The feature vector of each color component for the given color space in the given image is calculated from N partitions by using the procedure SBTC ()*/
SBTC(*i*, *m*n*)
{
    Read (i[j], j= 1....m*n)
    for x = 0 to N-1
        for $j = \left(\frac{x*m*n}{N}\right)+1$ to $\frac{(x+1)*(m*n)}{N}$

$$FeatureVectorN_{colorcomponent} = \left(\frac{N}{m*n}\right) * \sum_{i=\left(\frac{x*m*n}{N}\right)+1}^{(x+1)*(m*n)/N} sortedSDR[I]$$

    /*where color component = R, G and B for RGB Color Space */
    end
end

6. Repeat procedure *SBTC()* for *N* partitions (while *N* >= 2) and compare classification performances with *(N−1)* (while *(N > 2)*) partitions.
7. Stop when classification performance of current *N* partitions is inferior compared to *N−1* partitions.

End

The maximum number of feature vectors extracted in RGB color space is equivalent to the number of partitions *N*.

6 Classifiers Used for Classification

Two different classifiers were used for the comparison of performance of classification processes, namely, K-Nearest Neighbor (KNN) classifier [33, 34] and Neural Network (NN) Classifier [35]. KNN classifier was used to assign the output of classification process with a class membership which was common among its k nearest neighbors. It has followed the mean square error method for comparing the query image to the database image as in Eq. 3.

$$MSE = \frac{1}{MN} \sum_{y=1}^{M} \sum_{x=1}^{N} [I(x,y) - I'(x,y)]^2 \qquad (3)$$

KNN has been considered as an instance based classifier which has the lowest possible error rate as it has a maximum error rate of not more than twice the Baye's error rate. Hence, it was chosen for initial evaluation of classification results. The NN classifier has combination of simple processing units capable of doing complex pattern matching tasks. The high noise tolerance level and self adaptive properties of NN classifier has made it flexible for real world applications. The process of classification has been a supervised process where the back propagation technique of multi layer perceptron artificial neural network has a major role. Back propagation was used to train the network to optimize the performance of classification. The process has compared the output

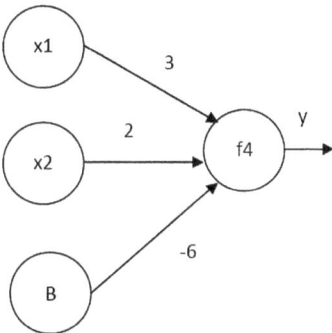

Fig. 4. Neural Network classifier

values with the correct answers to calculate a predefined error function. The errors were then fed back to the network for adjustment of weights of each connection to reduce the value of the error functions. The process was repeated for large number of training cycles for reducing the error of the overall calculation. Back propagation method has been used with a known or desired output for each input value in order to compute the predefined error function. Hence it was considered as a suitable choice for classification purpose. Figure 4 has shown a perceptron with two inputs and a bias input having three different weights of 3, 2 and −6 respectively. The activation function f4 was applied to the value $S = 3 \times 1 + 3 \times 2 - 6$. A unipolar step activation function gives the values of f4 as shown in Eq. 4.

$$f_4 = \begin{cases} 1 & if \ldots S > 0 \\ 0 & otherwise \end{cases} \quad (4)$$

On the other hand, the consistency of the feature extraction process was also examined with the help of two different classifier environments.

7 Architecture for Proposed Retrieval Technique

A novel technique has been proposed for retrieval purpose as shown in Fig. 5. The query image was first classified into the nearest image category.

The classification process was carried out by measuring the distance between the query image and the database images. The classification was done to the category which has the minimum distance from the query image. Henceforth, the retrieval process was carried out. Due to the classification of the query image before retrieval of similar images, the searching process during the retrieval phase was restricted only within the classified category or the class of interest. This has significantly improved the classification process with considerably high retrieval results compared to state-of-the art methods.

8 Datasets Used

The proposed technique was evaluated on three different datasets namely Wang dataset (10 Categories with 1000 images) [19], Caltech dataset (20 Categories with 2533 images) and Oliva and Torralba (OT-Scene) Dataset (8 categories, 2688 images) [26]. The descriptions of the datasets have been given in the following subsections.

8.1 Wang's Dataset

It is an extensively utilized public dataset offered by Wang et al. It has 1000 images of 10 different categories. Dimension for each image is 256 × 384 or 384 × 256 and each category consists of 100 images. The various categories in this dataset are Tribals, Sea Beaches, Gothic Structures, Buses, Dinosaur, Elephants, Flowers, Horses, Mountains and Food. A sample collage for Wang's dataset has been given in Fig. 6.

Novel Technique in Block Truncation Coding

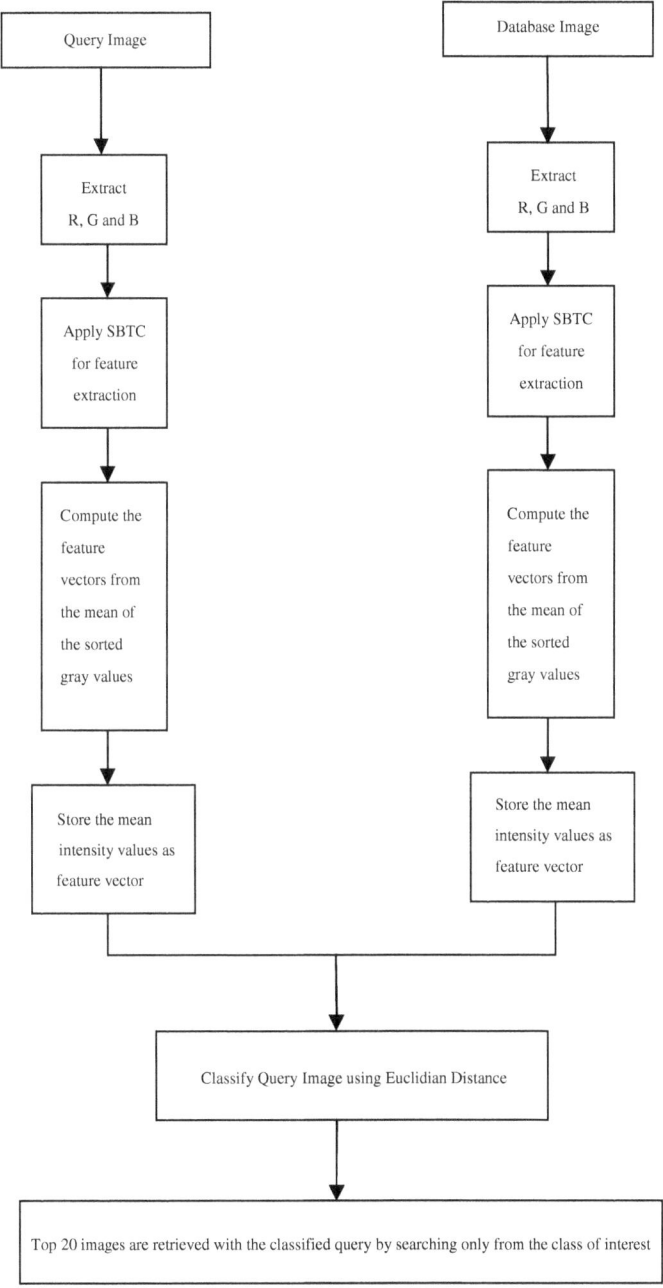

Fig. 5. Block diagram for proposed feature extraction technique

Fig. 6. Sample collage for Wang dataset

8.2 Oliva and Torralba (OT-Scene) Dataset

This dataset is provided by MIT and consists of 2688 images which are divided into eight different categories. Multiple categories in the dataset have included Coast and Beach (with 360 images), Open Country (with 328 images), Forest (with 260 images), Mountain (with 308 images), Highway (with 324 images), Street (with 410 images), City Centre (with 292 images) and Tall Building (with 306 images). A sample collage for OT Scene dataset is given in Fig. 7.

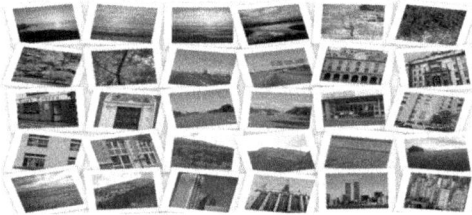

Fig. 7. Sample collage for OT-Scene dataset

8.3 Caltech Dataset

The dataset has considered 2533 images divided into 20 different categories. Each of the categories has different number of images with a dimension of 300 × 200. The categories are airplane, bonsai, panther, dalmatian, dolphin, faces, flamingo, deer, piano, skates, metronome, minar, motorbike, panda, football, stopsign, sunflower, trees, monuments and watches. A sample collage for the Caltech dataset has been given in Fig. 8.

Fig. 8. Sample collage for Caltech dataset

9 Evaluation Techniques

Cross validation scheme has been applied to assess the classification performances for different feature vector extraction techniques. The scheme was k-fold cross validation [29]. The value of k was an integer value and was considered as 10. In this process the entire dataset was divided into 10 subsets. 1 subset was considered as the testing set and the rest 9 subsets were considered to be training set. The method was repeated for 10 trials and the performance of the classifier was evaluated by combining the 10 results thus obtained after evaluating the 10 folds. The value 10 was chosen randomly as the number of subdivisions and has been generally preferred in other literatures [29] also for carrying out the task of cross validation. The repeated random sub sampling property of the technique has used all the images in the datasets for both training and validation purposes. Performance estimation for content based image classification with different feature extraction techniques has been performed using different evaluation parameters. Primarily two different parameters were considered, Misclassification Rate (MR) and F1score to assess the performance of Sorted BTC (SBTC) as in Eqs. 5 and 7. Misclassification rate (MR) has been defined as the error rate of the classifier that indicates the proportion of instances that have been wrongly classified and has been given as in Eq. 5.

$$MR = \frac{FP + FN}{TP + TN + FP + FN} \tag{5}$$

F1 Score has been defined as the harmonic mean of precision and recall. Calculation of harmonic mean HM for n real numbers has been carried out as in Eq. 6.

$$HM = \frac{n}{\frac{1}{a_1} + \frac{1}{a_2} + \ldots \frac{1}{a_n}} = \frac{n}{\sum_{k=1}^{n} \frac{1}{a_k}} = \frac{n \cdot \prod_{l=1}^{n} a_l}{\sum_{k=1}^{n} \frac{\prod_{l=1}^{n} a_l}{a_k}} \tag{6}$$

Therefore, the value of n has been considered as 2, for calculation of F1 Score by combining the two values of precision and recall respectively in Eq. 7.

$$F1score = \frac{2 * \text{Precision} * \text{Recall}}{\text{Precision} + \text{Recall}} \tag{7}$$

Henceforth, the existing BTC based techniques were compared to TSBTC method of feature extraction in terms of precision, recall along with misclassification rate and F1 score for content based image recognition as in Eqs. 8 and 9.

$$TPRate/Recall = \frac{TP}{TP + FN} \tag{8}$$

$$\Pr ecision = \frac{TP}{TP+FP} \tag{9}$$

Several other metrics namely, absolute error, mean squared error, squared error, means absolute error etc. could have been used for performance measurement. Nevertheless, those metrics have been useful for error predictions in regression model where the predicted variables are numerical instead of being categorical. The subtraction between predicted and actual values may turn out to be negative. Hence the absolute errors have been considered to avoid the case. But, in case of classification the output is categorical and the considered metrics have been the benchmarked measures for classification performance evaluation.

10 Experimental Results

The experiments were conducted with Matlab 7.11.0(R2010b) on Intel core i5 processor with 4 GB RAM. Initially, the classification was carried out using KNN classifier with Wang Dataset. Now the results obtained from N = 3 were compared to that of N = 2. Improvement in F1 Score was observed and the MR value was lower for N = 3 compared to N = 2. Hence further subdivisions were carried out to extract feature vectors and the results were compared to that of the immediate previous subdivision. It was detected that till N = 8 the results were improving, while the results degraded for N = 9 as seen in Fig. 9. F1 Score was 0.668 and MR was 0.068 respectively for N = 9 whereas the F1 Score was 0.706 and MR was 0.064 for N = 8. So, an increase in misclassification rate (MR) and a decrease in F1 Score was monitored for N = 9 when compared to N = 8. According to Algorithm 1 for feature extraction, further subdivisions were restricted as degradation in classification performance was noticed and N = 8 was considered to be optimal for feature extraction with Sorted BTC technique.

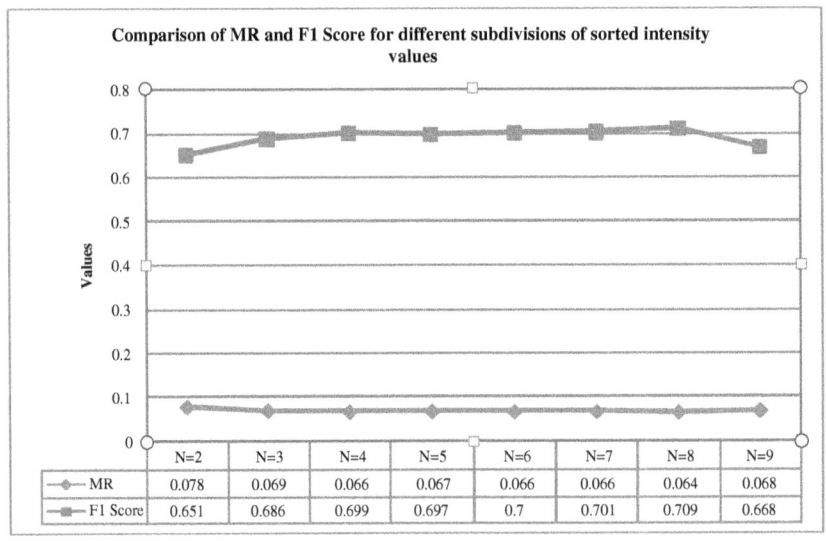

Fig. 9. Comparison of MR and F1 Score for different values of *N*

The category wise misclassification rate (MR) and F1 Score has been shown in Table 1 for two different classifier namely KNN classifier and Neural Network classifier. The classification has been done with 10 fold cross validation.

Table 1. MR and F1 Score for Wang dataset with KNN and NN classifier

Categories	NN (N = 8)		KNN (N = 8)	
	MR	F1 Score	MR	F1 Score
Tribals	0.07	0.69	0.088	0.655
Sea Beach	0.07	0.66	0.082	0.644
Gothic Structure	0.11	0.47	0.132	0.447
Bus	0.06	0.68	0.08	0.604
Dinosaur	0.01	0.98	0.002	0.99
Elephant	0.06	0.71	0.053	0.758
Roses	0.02	0.9	0.018	0.918
Horses	0.02	0.9	0.014	0.935
Mountains	0.08	0.6	0.108	0.433
Average	0.05	0.73	0.06	0.71

The proposed algorithm for feature extraction was also tested for precision and recall values with two more well known public datasets namely Caltech dataset (20 Categories with 2533) images and Oliva and Torralba (OT-Scene) Dataset (8 categories, 2688 images). The precision and recall results for classification have been given in Table 2 along with Wang Dataset.

Table 2. Precision and recall value with KNN and Neural Network classifier for 3 datasets

Classifier	Wang		Caltech		OT Scene	
	Precision	Recall	Precision	Recall	Precision	Recall
KNN	0.72	0.70	0.537	0.578	0.571	0.55
NN	0.882	0.869	0.682	0.688	0.644	0.625

It was observed that the proposed technique has better precision and recall values for classification with Neural Network Classifier. It was found that classification with Neural Network classifier has higher F1 Score and less misclassification rate (MR) compared to KNN Classifier. The classification performance of the proposed algorithm was consequently compared to the classification results obtained from state-of-the art techniques of feature extraction. Wang dataset was considered for evaluation for both of the proposed and existing techniques and Neural Network classifier was used to evaluate the performance of all the feature extraction techniques. The comparison has been given in Fig. 10. It was observed that the proposed technique has better precision and recall compared to the remaining techniques. Statistical comparison of the precision results obtained from classification with the proposed technique and the existing techniques were carried out as shown in Table 3. A paired *t*-test (2 tailed) was conducted to find out the *p*-values of the existing techniques with respect to the proposed technique [36]. The *t*-test was carried out to compare the actual difference between two means corresponding to the variation in the data of the proposed technique and the existing techniques.

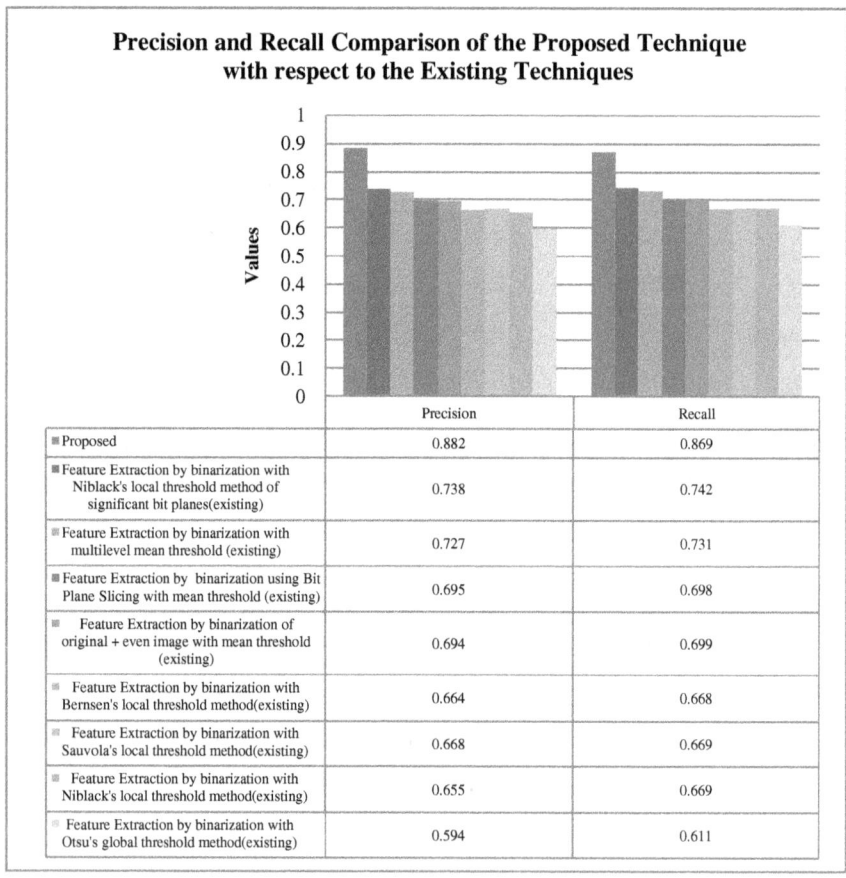

Fig. 10. Graph for comparison of precision and recall for classification with the proposed technique with respect to the existing technique

The test was performed to evaluate whether the differences in precision values were generated from a population with zero mean:

$$H0: \mu d = 0 \text{ vs. } H1: \mu d < 0$$

Table 3 has given the calculated values of t as t-calc and the p-values. Calculation of t-calc was performed by taking the difference between two sample means considered for each comparison in Fig. 10. The p-value has measured the strength of evidence against the null hypothesis. The p-values generated after the comparison has revealed highly significant difference in precision results compared to the existing techniques. Therefore, the null hypotheses of equal precision rates for the existing algorithm compared to the proposed algorithm were rejected. Thus, it was well established that the proposed technique has remarkably contributed for boosting up the classification results compared to the state of the art techniques.

Table 3. t-test for evaluating significance of the proposed technique

Comparison	t-calc	p-value	Significance of difference in value
Feature Extraction by binarization with Niblack's local threshold method of significant bit planes (existing)	2.8793	0.0205	Significant
Feature Extraction by binarization with multilevel mean threshold (existing)	4.2028	0.003	Significant
Feature Extraction by binarization using Bit Plane Slicing with mean threshold (existing)	4.9903	0.0011	Significant
Feature Extraction by binarization of original + even image with mean threshold (existing)	4.8484	0.0013	Significant
Feature Extraction by binarization with Bernsen's local threshold method (existing)	4.9173	0.0012	Significant
Feature Extraction by binarization with Sauvola's local threshold method (existing)	4.1226	0.0033	Significant
Feature Extraction by binarization with Niblack's local threshold method (existing)	4.8125	0.0013	Significant
Feature Extraction by binarization with Otsu's global threshold method (existing)	5.7077	0.0005	Significant

Sorted BTC (SBTC) technique of feature extraction was tested for different compression ratios applied to the test images as shown in Table 4. The analysis divulges the fact that lossy compression has not adversely affected content based classification, as the precision and recall values for different compression ratios was not statistically significant as observed in Table 5.

Table 4. Comparison of precision and recall in compressed domain

Images	Precision	Recall
Original image	0.740	0.737
Image compression ratio (49:64)	0.745	0.741
Image compression ratio (36:64)	0.744	0.741
Image compression ratio (25:64)	0.738	0.737
Image compression ratio (16:64)	0.737	0.736
Image compression ratio (9:64)	0.735	0.733
Image compression ratio (4:64)	0.733	0.732
Image compression ratio (1:64)	0.728	0.727

Table 5. *t*-test to evaluate consistency of the proposed technique in Compressed Domain

Comparison	t-calc	p-value	Significance of difference in value
Compression ratio (49:64)	0.9676	0.3585	Insignificant
Compression ratio (36:64)	0.2179	0.8324	Insignificant
Compression ratio (25:64)	0.3157	0.7595	Insignificant
Compression ratio (16:64)	0.5365	0.6046	Insignificant
Compression ratio (9:64)	1.2098	0.2572	Insignificant
Compression ratio (4:64)	2.0681	0.0686	Insignificant
Compression ratio (1:64)	2.2347	0.0523	Insignificant

The *t*-test displayed in Table 5 was calculated with respect to the precision and recall values of the uncompressed image. The test was performed to examine whether the differences in precision values were generated from a population with zero mean:

$$H0: \mu d = 0 \text{ vs. } H1: \mu d < 0$$

The *p*-values for 2 tailed paired t test have not indicated any significant difference for the precision and recall values for different compression ratios. Hence the null hypothesis was accepted in this case. Thus, it was inferred that Sorted BTC has consistent performance for feature extraction in compressed domain.

The retrieval performance was evaluated on Wang dataset with the proposed retrieval architecture. Five random images were selected from each category and a total of 50 images were selected as query images from 10 different categories. The query images were fired one at a time and were initially classified to the nearest class measured by Euclidean distance. Further, the classified query was forwarded to retrieve images by searching only within the class of interest instead of searching the entire dataset. In both the cases of classified and unclassified query for retrieval, the retrieved images were ranked initially using Euclidian Distance measure. Ranking process was followed by retrieval of top 20 images. Initially a comparison of retrieval has been shown for searching images with classified query and for searching images with unclassified query as in Table 6. Henceforth, a comparison of the proposed technique of retrieval with reference to state- of- the art techniques has been illustrated in Table 8.

Table 6. Comparison of retrieval for query with classification and without classification

Categories	Results with query classification (proposed retrieval technique)	Results without query classification (existing retrieval technique)
Tribals	80	42
Sea Beach	80	55
Gothic Structure	80	37
Bus	80	51
Dinosaur	100	100
Elephant	80	44
Roses	80	61
Horses	100	97
Mountains	40	27
Tribals	60	52
Average precision	78	56.6

The statistical comparison of proposed retrieval technique was done initially with existing retrieval technique with unclassified query in Table 7.

Table 7. *t*-test to evaluate the significance of the proposed retrieval technique

Comparison	*t*-calc	*p*-value	Significance of difference in value
Results without query classification	2.2723	0.0356	Significant

The test has verified whether the differences in precision values for the proposed retrieval technique and existing retrieval technique were generated from a population with zero mean:

$$H0 : \mu d = 0 \text{ vs. } H1 : \mu d < 0$$

The *p*-value has shown significant difference in precision values for the compared techniques in Table 7 and the null hypothesis was rejected which has indicated the superiority of the proposed technique of retrieval with classified queries. Further the proposed technique of retrieval was compared to the state-of-the art techniques based on precision values as in Table 8. Both the proposed and the existing techniques were tested with Wang Dataset under the same retrieval environment which has followed the ranking process based on top 20 retrieved images. The precision results for retrieval with the proposed technique of feature extraction have outperformed the existing techniques in Table 8.

Table 8. Comparison of precision for retrieval with the proposed technique of feature extraction with state-of-the art techniques

	Proposed	Technique [33]	Technique [21]	Technique [32]	Technique [19]	Technique [34]	Technique [24]
Tribals	80	54.1	32.3	54	48	58.75	41.8
Sea Beach	80	48.3	61.2	51	34	41.19	44.6
Gothic Structure	80	40.2	39.2	38	36	42.35	49.2
Bus	80	89.5	39.5	46	61	71.69	30.5
Dinosaur	100	97.7	99.6	100	95	74.53	55.4
Elephant	80	39.1	55.7	63	48	65.08	69.9
Roses	80	85.9	89.3	90	61	83.24	61.1
Horses	100	81.4	65.2	93	74	69.3	57.2
Mountains	40	32	56.8	48	42	44.86	43.7
Food	60	41	44.1	39	50	44.54	43.5
Average precision	78	60.9	58.29	62.20	54.9	59.55	49.69

A *t*-test was performed to confirm whether the differences in precision values for the proposed retrieval technique and state-of-the art retrieval techniques were generated from a population with zero mean:

$$H0 : \mu d = 0 \text{ vs. } H1 : \mu d < 0$$

Table 9. *t*-test to evaluate significance of proposed technique w.r.t state-of-the art techniques

Comparison	t-calc	p-value	Significance of difference in value
Technique [33]	3.0003	0.0149	Significant
Technique [21]	2.7961	0.0208	Significant
Technique [32]	2.7913	0.021	Significant
Technique [19]	4.5786	0.0013	Significant
Technique [34]	3.7933	0.0043	Significant
Technique [24]	5.2046	0.0006	Significant

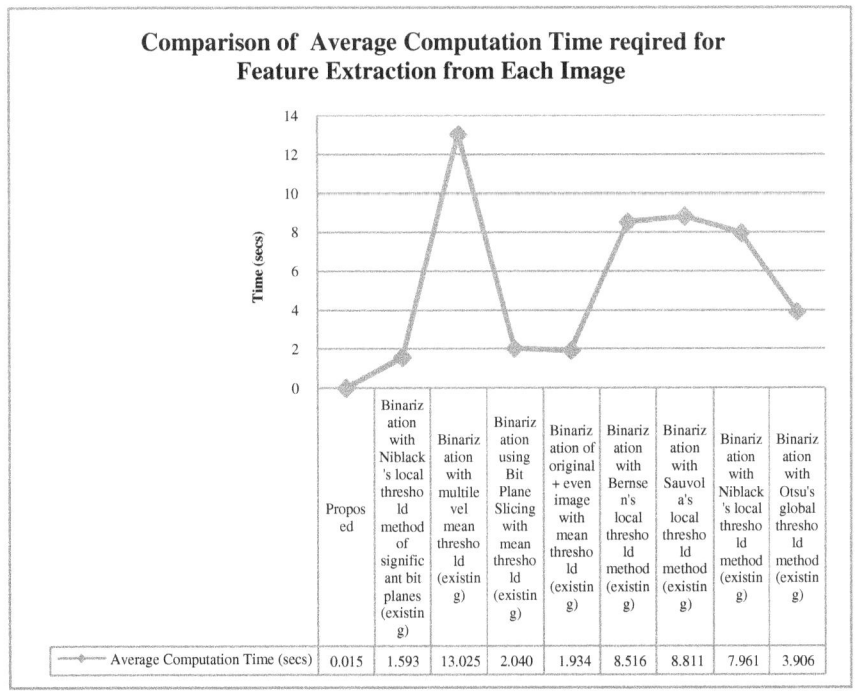

Fig. 11. Comparison of average computation time for feature extraction from each image.

The p-values for the test were found to be significant in Table 9. Hence the null hypothesis was rejected. Thus it was established that the proposed method of retrieval with proposed technique of feature extraction has outclassed the popular techniques of feature extraction and retrieval. Finally, the proposed technique was compared to the existing technique with respect to the average time taken for feature extraction form each image. The comparison has been illustrated in Fig. 11.

It was observed in Fig. 11 that the proposed method has consumed minimum time compared to the state-of-the art techniques.

The statistical comparisons have established improved image identification with the proposed methodology of feature extraction. A small feature vector of size 24 was considered for classification and retrieval purpose. The size of feature vector was 24 and it was independent of different dimensions of the images such as 256×384, 200×300 etc. Figure 10 has revealed highest precision and recall value for classification with proposed method of feature extraction compared to existing techniques. Figure 11 has clearly established that the proposed method has consumed minimum time for feature extraction. Table 8 has shown the highest precision results for retrieval with the proposed technique.

11 Conclusion

The paper carried out in depth comparison of different feature extraction techniques. The authors have also proposed a novel retrieval technique with classified queries. A new technique named Sorted BTC (SBTC) method of feature extraction was introduced in this paper. The technique was compared with other existing techniques in four different parameters viz., misclassification rate (MR), precision, recall, and F1 score. The proposed technique has outperformed all the existing techniques in case of both classification and retrieval. It has shown highly significant statistical difference to establish its superiority. The proposed feature extraction technique has also shown consistent performance in compressed domain without having any significant degradation in classification performance. SBTC has proved to be a consistent and efficient technique and has contributed towards noteworthy improvement in content based image recognition process.

References

1. Keyvanpour, M.R., Charkari, N.M.: A content based model for image categorization. In: 20th International Workshop on Database and Expert Systems Application, pp. 1–4 (2009)
2. Mohanty, N., John, A.L.S., Manmatha, R., Rath, T.M.: Shape-based image classification and retrieval. Handb. Stat. **31**, 249–267 (2013)
3. Niblack, W.: An Introduction to Digital Image Processing. Prentice Hall, Eaglewood Cliffs (1986)
4. Bernsen, J.: Dynamic thresholding of gray level images. In: ICPR 1986: Proceedings of the International Conference on Pattern Recognition, pp. 1251–1255 (1986)
5. Sauvola, J., Pietikainen, M.: Adaptive document image binarization. Pattern Recogn. **33**(2), 225–236 (2000)

6. Hiremath, P.S., Pujari, J.: Content based image retrieval using color, texture and shape features. In: 15th International Conference on Advanced Computing and Communications, vol. 9(2), pp. 780–784 (2007)
7. Gatos, B., Pratikakis, I., Perantonis, S.J.: Efficient binarization of historical and degraded document images. In: The Eighth IAPR Workshop on Document Analysis Systems, pp. 447–454 (2008)
8. Valizadeh, M., Armanfard, N., Komeili, M., Kabir E.: A novel hybrid algorithm for binarization of badly illuminated document images. In: 14th International CSI Computer Conference (CSICC), pp. 121–126 (2009)
9. Chang, Y.-F., Pai, Y.-T., Ruan, S.-J.: An efficient thresholding algorithm for degraded document images based on intelligent block detection. In: IEEE International Conference on Systems, Man and Cybernetics, SMC, pp. 667–672
10. Banerjee, M., Kundu, M.K., Maji, P.: Content-based image retrieval using visually significant point features. Fuzzy Sets Syst. **160**(23), 3323–3341 (2009)
11. El Alami, M.E.: A novel image retrieval model based on the most relevant features. Knowl.-Based Syst. **24**, 23–32 (2011)
12. Jalab, H.A.: Image retrieval system based on color layout descriptor and Gabor filters. In: IEEE Conference on Open System (ICOS), pp. 32–36 (2011)
13. Yue, J., Li, Z., Liu, L., Fu, Z.: Content-based image retrieval using color and texture fused features. Math. Comput. Model. **54**(3–4), 1121–1127 (2011)
14. Kekre, H.B., Thepade, S., Das, R.K.K., Ghosh, S.: Image Classification using block truncation coding with assorted color spaces. Int. J. Comput. Appl. **44**(6), 9–14 (2012). ISSN: 0975-8887
15. Kekre, H.B., Thepade, S., Das, R.K.K., Ghosh, S.: Performance boost of block truncation coding based image classification using bit plane slicing. Int. J. Comput. Appl. **47**(15), 45–48 (2012). ISSN: 0975-8887
16. Subrahmanyam, M., Maheshwari, R.P., Balasubramanian, R.: Expert system design using wavelet and color vocabulary trees for image retrieval. Expert Syst. Appl. **39**(5), 5104–5114 (2012)
17. Kekre, H.B., Thepade, S., Das, R.K.K., Ghosh, S.: Multilevel block truncation coding with diverse colour spaces for image classification. In: IEEE-International Conference on Advances in Technology and Engineering (ICATE), pp. 1–7 (2013)
18. Thepade, S., Das, R.K.K., Ghosh, S.: Image classification using advanced block truncation coding with ternary image maps. In: Unnikrishnan, S., Surve, S., Bhoir, D. (eds.) ICAC3 2013. CCIS, vol. 361, pp. 500–509. Springer, Heidelberg (2013). doi: 10.1007/978-3-642-36321-4_48
19. Thepade, S., Das, R.K.K., Ghosh, S.: Performance comparison of feature vector extraction techniques in RGB color space using block truncation coding or content based image classification with discrete classifiers. In: India Conference (INDICON), pp. 1–6. IEEE (2013). doi:10.1109/INDCON.2013.6726053
20. Shaikh, S.H., Maiti, A.K., Chaki, N.: A new image binarization method using iterative partitioning. Mach. Vis. Appl. **24**(2), 337–350 (2013)
21. Shen, G.L., Wu, X.J.: Content based image retrieval by combining color texture and CENTRIST. In: IEEE International Workshop on Signal Processing, vol. 1, pp. 1–4 (2013)
22. Irtaza, A., Jaffar, M.A., Aleisa, E., Choi, T.S.: Embedding neural networks for semantic association in content based image retrieval. Multimedia Tool Appl. **72**, 1911–1931 (2013)
23. Rahimi, M., Moghaddam, M.E.: A content based image retrieval system based on Color ton Distributed descriptors. Sig. Image Video Process. **9**, 691–704 (2013)

24. Thepade, S., Das, R.K.K., Ghosh, S.: A novel feature extraction technique using binarization of bit planes for content based image classification. J. Eng. **2014**, Article ID 439218, 13 (2014). doi:10.1155/2014/439218, Hindawi Publishing Corporation
25. Chaki, N., Shaikh, S.H., Saeed, K. (eds.): Exploring Image Binarization Techniques. SCI, vol. 560. Springer, Heidelberg (2014)
26. Walia, E., Pal, A.: Fusion framework for effective color image retrieval. J. Vis. Commun. Image R. **25**, 1335–1348 (2014)
27. Wang, J.W.J., Min, K., Jeung, Y.-C., Chong, J.-W.: Improved BTC using luminance bitmap for color image compression. In: 2nd International Congress on Image and Signal Processing, pp. 1–5. IEEE (2009). doi:10.1109/CISP.2009.5304208
28. Chou, Y.-C., Chang, H.-H.: A high payload data hiding scheme for color image based on BTC compression technique. In: IEEE Fourth International Conference on Genetic and Evolutionary Computing ICGEC, pp. 626–629 (2010)
29. Sridhar, S.: Digital Image Processing. Oxford University Press, Oxford (2011)
30. Wallace, G.K.: The JPEG still picture compression standard. IEEE Trans. Consum. Electron. **38**(1), 18–34 (1992)
31. Yang, A.Y., Wright, J., Ma, Y., Sastry, S.S.: Unsupervised segmentation of natural images via lossy data compression. Comput. Vis. Image Underst. **110**(2), 212–225 (2008)
32. Han, J., Kamber, M.: Data mining: concepts and techniques. The Morgan Kaufmann Series in Data Management Systems, pp. 89–90 (2001)
33. Cunningham, P., Delany, S.J.: k-Nearest neighbour classifiers. Multiple Classifier Syst. **34**, 1–17 (2007)
34. Kotsiantis, S.B.: Supervised machine learning: a review of classification techniques. Informatica **31**, 249–268 (2007)
35. Dunham, M.H.: Data Mining Introductory and Advanced Topics, p. 127. Pearson Education, Upper Saddle River (2009)
36. Yıldız, O.T., Aslan, Ö., Alpaydın, E.: Multivariate statistical tests for comparing classification algorithms. In: Coello, C.A. (ed.) LION 2011. LNCS, vol. 6683, pp. 1–15. Springer, Heidelberg (2011)

Objective Evaluation Method of Usability Using Parameters of User's Fingertip Movement

Nobuyuki Nishiuchi[✉] and Yutaka Takahashi

Graduate School of System Design, Tokyo Metropolitan University,
6-6 Asahigaoka, Hino, Tokyo 191-0065, Japan
nnishiuc@tmu.ac.jp, ytakahashi.alo@gmail.com

Abstract. The subjective evaluation method of usability is costly and time-consuming, and is sometimes more unreliable data than objective evaluation method because of the subjective view. On the other hand, the objective evaluation method is traditionally useful and reliable, but expensive. Further, this method is often not feasible, as acquiring the operation logs of many electrical products can be difficult. To overcome current limitations, we propose an objective evaluation method of usability that is applicable to various types of interfaces, such as those of actual electrical products or reproduced interfaces on a touch screen. Our proposed method involves extracting recorded fingertip movements of users during operation via image processing and then evaluating usability based on measurable parameters. Experimental results demonstrate that the proposed method was able to identify problems with usability even when the traditional objective evaluation method could not.

Keywords: Usability · Image processing · Interface · Objective evaluation

1 Introduction

In recent years, it has been noticeable that a lot of new system and application software have been developed and the diffusion of them has been rapidly expanding in various generation users. For the users, ease of use and operation of an interface without a manual are considered extremely important. In the consumer-electronics industry, it has been very difficult to make a difference regarding the functionality of products between the owned products and competitors. Then most electronic companies are now focusing on the advancement of the usability of user interfaces. From these backgrounds, it is considered that the importance of the advancement of usability is increasingly growing, and an effective usability evaluation method is expected for the achievement of it.

Current methods for evaluating usability [1–3] are divided into subjective and objective evaluation methods. The subjective evaluation method is costly, time-consuming, demands professional skill, and is sometimes more unreliable data than objective evaluation [4] because of the subjective view. On the other hand, the objective evaluation method is traditionally considered useful and reliable. According to Nielsen [1], data about people's actual behavior should have precedence over people's claims of what they think they do. However, this method is expensive on resources, and is often not feasible due to difficulties acquiring the operation logs of many electrical products. As such, it is expected to develop a new objective usability evaluation.

To overcome these limitations, we propose a novel objective usability evaluation method involving the extraction of recorded fingertip movements of users during operation via image processing, and evaluation of the usability of the interface based on the measurements of several parameters. In particular, operation time, and the distance and patterns of the locus of fingertip movement, including stationary time and frequency of directional changes were measured. The operation time and distance traveled by the moving locus were evaluated using the ratio of each parameter between novice and expert users (NE ratio [5, 6]).

This article is based on the preliminary results reported in a conference paper published in the 15th International Conference on Human-Computer Interaction (HCI 2013) [7]. We extended the work by investigating the objective evaluation of usability using eye tracking or brain waves and so on. Based on this investigation, we actually integrated a parameter of fingertip movement which was mentioned in the conference paper but not proposed in the specific algorithm and was not actually used in the conference paper as well. Therefore, the present study reports a new aspect of the method presented in the previous conference paper. Further, extensive experimentation has been conducted to validate the effectiveness of this method more deeply. Notably, a new set of experiments has been conducted on more complex tasks to evaluate the performance of the proposed method. The extensive experimental results demonstrate the effectiveness of the proposed method.

The present study is organized as follows: in Sect. 2, a literature review is summarized; in Sect. 3, the methodology of our proposed usability evaluation is described in detail; in Sect. 4, the results of our evaluative experiment are discussed; and in Sect. 5, our conclusions are summarized.

- The objective of the paper is to propose a novel objective evaluation method of usability.
- The technical novelty of the proposed methodology is the objective usability evaluation involving video recordings of user operation, extraction of fingertip movements via image processing, and evaluation of usability based on measurements of several parameters.
- Our claim is: our objective evaluation method is applicable to various types of interfaces and exhibits strong performance. The proposed method can be used to objectively evaluate various types of interfaces, such as actual electrical products or a reproduced interface on a touch screen. In addition, the proposed method can identify the same usability problems which can be identified with the traditional method, and can identify the usability problems even when the traditional objective evaluation method cannot.

2 Literature Review

Usability is defined by the International Standards Organization as "The extent to which a product can be used by specified users to achieve specified goals with effectiveness, efficiency, and satisfaction in a specified context of use" [8]. Under this definition, there are three critical terms of usability: effectiveness, efficiency and satisfaction. Current method for usability evaluation is divided into subjective and objective usability evaluation methods of assessing these three terms.

The subjective evaluation is a type of method to analyze usability based on opinions from a subjective point of view. The subjective usability evaluation encompasses several approaches, such as conducting interviews, questionnaires [1–3], think-aloud protocols [9], and applying usability guidelines and usability heuristics [1]. These methods are used for the evaluation of all three critical measures of the usability described above, with particular focus on satisfaction. El-Halees [10] proposed the automatic technique of evaluating subjective usability using opinion mining, an approach which is quite interesting in terms of subjective evaluation but not actually implemented, as its mean accuracy is low.

On the other hand, the objective evaluation is a type of method to analyze the usability based on objective measurements. Methods of objective evaluation include video capture [1], the keystroke-level model [11], eye-tracking [12–17] and measuring brain waves [18, 19] during user operation, and recording user operation logs [1–3]. A number of studies have been conducted using eye movement. Sugimura [13] quantified habituation using eye movement related to the usability evaluation, and while it did not directly reflect the objective usability evaluation, it remained an interesting approach to the usability evaluation. Wong [14] evaluated the usability of website focused on the e-commerce. A lot of studies as such [14–16] were conducted, but the evaluation was limited in a situation of utilization. These previous findings suggest that consideration of general objective usability evaluation may be insufficient. As a novel approach, brain waves were also used in the objective usability evaluation. Kimura [17] and Inoue [18] proposed the objective evaluation of usefulness via the electroencephalogram (EEG) measurement. Although their proposed method was only in the early stages of development when it was introduced and the number of subjects was insufficient, this research has also garnered attention.

Now we summarized studies from the view point of the target of evaluation. The evaluation of the hardware was for mobile phones, tablets and e-book readers [19–22]. And the evaluation of the software was for an application of smart phones or tablets, and for a websites of travel or commercial [23–28]. The most research was not evaluated by the objective evaluation but by the subjective evaluation, such as questionnaires or using usability heuristics. So, there exists growing demand for a new objective usability evaluation method.

3 Methodology for Usability Evaluation

3.1 Extraction of Fingertip Movement and Action

Users operated the target interface wearing a rubber sock with a green-colored fingertip on the index finger of the right hand to aid in image extraction and processing. As shown in Fig. 1, the users' index fingertip movements were recorded from above using a video camera (HDR-CX370 V, Sony, Japan) during operation.

First, the captured image was projective transformed (Fig. 2, center), to get the locus of fingertip movement on an operational planar. A square-shaped monitor was used in Fig. 2 because the result of the projective transform could be easily confirmed as an example. Then, green-colored fingertip area was extracted from the projective transformed image (Fig. 2, right). The locus of fingertip movement was obtained by connecting the gravity points of the extracted green areas of captured images, as indicated by yellow lines in Fig. 3.

To detect button depression, an electric bulb that is activated whenever a button on the target interface is pressed was attached on the fingertip of the rubber sock (Fig. 3). Thus, in addition to tracking fingertip movement, our system can be used to detect when buttons are pressed during the operation of an interface, a capability that is particularly useful for commercial products that do not record operational logs.

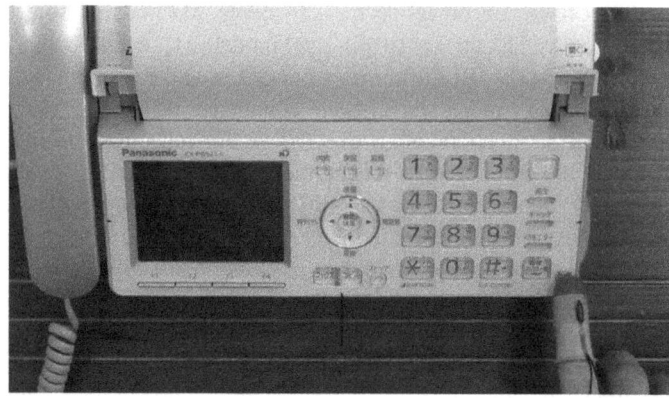

Fig. 1. Experimental setup (left) and captured image (right).

Fig. 2. Captured image (left), projective transformed image (center) and binarized image for extracting fingertip area (right) (Color figure online).

3.2 Parameters for Usability Evaluation

Operation time, distance traveled by the user's fingertip, stationary time, and frequency of directional changes were used as parameters to evaluate usability. Parameters were extracted from recorded videos using image processing algorithms.

Fig. 3. Image processing for extracting fingertip movement (yellow lines) and stationary time (circle size) (Color figure online).

Operation Time. We proposed a new parameter for usability evaluation, termed the iNE ratio (improved Novice Expert ratio), which is derived from the previously described NE ratio [5]. To estimate the iNE ratio, the ideal operation time Tm was modeled using Fitts' law (Sect. 3.3) and is considered to represent the indispensable time for fingertip movement and button operation. In addition, the ratio is a measure of the operation time of an expert user Te. This includes the parameter Tm and the delay time Td, which is the response delay of the interface and can be calculated from Eq. (1), as follows:

$$\mathrm{iNE} = (Tn - Td) / (Te - Td) = (Tn - Td) / Tm$$

$$Td = Te - Tm \qquad (1)$$

where Tn denotes the operation time of novice user, Te the operation time of expert user, Tm the ideal operation time, and Td the delay time.

Distance. In addition to iNE, a second new evaluation parameter, the $\mathrm{NE_d}$ ratio (Novice Expert ratio of distance), was also used. $\mathrm{NE_d}$ is the ratio between Ln, which is the total distance traveled by the movement locus (fingertip) during interface operation by a novice user, and the ideal operation distance Le, which is the sum of the shortest distance between the buttons depressed during operation of an expert user. Specific explanation of Le is described in Sect. 3.3.

$$\mathrm{NE_d} = Ln / Le \qquad (2)$$

Stationary Time. From the recorded fingertip movements, the stationary time of the hand was determined. When the following Eq. (3) was fulfilled, the user's hand was judged to be stationary.

$$\sum_{i=1}^{T} L_i \leq L \times T \tag{3}$$

where L_i represents the distance between the positions of the finger in the current and preceding (i) video frame, and T indicates the number of previous frames in which the user's hand is considered to be stationary for at least $T \times (1/30)$ s. L represents the mean distance that a user's fingertip moves between each frame for $T \times (1/30)$ s. Constants T and L were determined by a preliminary experiment. Figure 3 shows an image of the locus of finger movement (yellow lines) and stationary time, which is represented by circles that are proportional in size to the duration of non-movement.

Frequency of Directional Changes. When the distance before and after the change of the moving direction exceeded a threshold value, the user's hand was judged to be in a state of directional change. The case of horizontal directional change is explained. As shown in Fig. 4, white circle shows a reference point, points A, B, B' C, C' and black circles show the extracted position of the fingertip, and arrows show the direction of fingertip movement.

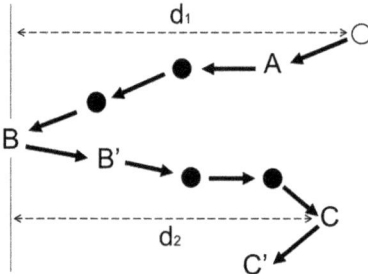

Fig. 4. Explanation of directional changes (horizontal direction)

First, each point is detected. First moved point (left direction in this example) except the act of pressing the button or the stationary becomes A, and the point before point A becomes the reference point. The candidate point of directional change becomes B if B-B' (right direction) is opposite direction of A-B (left direction). Using the same algorithm, another candidate point of directional change becomes C if C-C' (left direction) is the opposite direction of B-C (right direction).

The points of directional change are next determined. As the conditions of directional change, distance d_1 and d_2 shown in Fig. 4 were used. When both values exceed the threshold decided in preliminary experiment, point B is considered as a point of directional change. This determination algorithm prevents any erroneous assignment of decision due to vibration of the fingertip.

The vertical direction change uses the same algorithm, and each directional change of up-down and left-right is obtained.

3.3 Model of Ideal Operation

Fitts' law [29, 30] was used for modeling ideal operation time. MT (ms), the average time taken to acquire the target, was estimated using Eq. (4). In this model, Fitts' law was applied to estimate the operation time from the time required to depress two buttons based on the distance between the buttons and the button size. The sum of these operation times from a series of button-pressing operations represented the ideal operation time Tm, as follows:

$$MT = a + b\log_2\left(0.5 + \frac{D}{W}\right) \quad (4)$$

where W denotes the width of the target, D the distance from the starting point to the center of the target, and a and b the empirical constants determined through linear regression analysis. A preliminary experiment was conducted to estimate the two empirical constants (a, b) for eight directions (Table 1).

Table 1. Two constants (a, b) of Fitts' law for eight directions

	a	b
Average	54.27	357.06
Up	52.42	346.97
Right-Up	45.88	360.28
Right	49.85	368.36
Right-Down	70.57	360.44
Down	60.26	366.49
Left-Down	50.40	355.56
Left	48.43	360.72
Left-Up	57.68	335.31

The ideal operation distance was obtained by the image processing connecting the position where the expert user presses the button of the interface using the minimum number of steps required to complete the task (Fig. 5).

$N_c \times T_c$ (ms) calculates the time of continuous pressing the same button. N_c is the number of times the same button was pressed, as obtained from the number of flickers of the electric bulb (Fig. 3) by image processing. On the other hand, T_c is the time spent pressing the same button continuously and set as 357.06 ms in our evaluative experiment, based on the average empirical constants b of Fitts' law (Table 1). When the value of T_c markedly differs from the actual time of an evaluative experiment, the expert user's time can be used instead of T_c.

Using these parameters, the ideal operation time and the ideal distance are calculated before the evaluative experiment.

Fig. 5. Image processing for ideal operation distance.

4 Evaluative Experiment

4.1 Experiment Description

We conducted an evaluative experiment involving 5 users (right-handed male Japanese university and graduate students, aged 22–24 years). They operated two different manufacturer's facsimile in a standing position. All users had experience using a general facsimile, but it was the first time operating the facsimiles used in this experiment. Before starting the experiment, verbal instruction was provided to users to operate the interface in a normal way.

As shown in Fig. 6, the interfaces of the facsimiles are composed of buttons and a display (Facsimile P; KX-PW621DL, Panasonic, Japan), or buttons and a touch screen (Facsimile S; UX-900CL, Sharp, Japan). Using two facsimiles, users performed the two tasks below without manuals. The order of the tasks was conducted randomly for each user.

Task1: Transmission of a fax using the redialing function of the facsimile interface

Ideal operation steps of Facsimile P:

(1) Press redial button
(2) Select call recipient

Ideal operation steps of Facsimile S:

(1) Press phone call button
(2) Press redial button
(3) Select call recipient

Task2: Transmission of a fax using the phonebook function of the facsimile interface

Ideal operation steps of Facsimile P:

(1) Open phonebook function
(2) Decide method of searching
(3) Shift prompt to find call recipient
(4) Select call recipient
(5) Send a fax

Ideal operation steps of Facsimile S:

(1) Open phonebook function
(2) Find call recipient
(3) Select call recipient
(4) Send a fax

Fig. 6. Interfaces of Facsimile P (left) and Facsimile S (right).

4.2 Results of Task 1 and Discussion

The average values for the usability evaluation parameters of iNE, NE_d, and stationary time for the Facsimiles P and S interfaces of Task 1 are shown in Tables 2 and 3, respectively.

For the operation step "Select call recipient" on Facsimile P interface (Table 2), both iNE and NE_d values were large, and an average stationary time of 1.5 s was observed. As iNE and NE_d exhibited the same tendency, this operation step on the P interface appeared to have a problem regarding usability. The length of the observed stationary time also shows that the user's fingertip had stopped during the "Select call recipient" operation step. This finding was confirmed during post-task interviews with users, who reported that this operation step was difficult to perform on the P interface.

Table 2. Evaluation parameters of Task1 (Facsimile P)

Operation steps	iNE	NE_d	Stationary time (s)
(1) Press redial button	1.94	1.10	0.0
(2) Select call recipient	7.93	9.26	1.5

Table 3. Evaluation parameters of Task1 (Facsimile S)

Operation steps	iNE	NE_d	Stationary time (s)
(1) Press phone call button	12.89	2.42	2.9
(2) Press redial button	5.75	2.57	0.4
(3) Select call recipient	3.93	7.14	0.6

For the Facsimile S interface (Table 3), a long stationary time (2.9 s) and high iNE were detected for the operation step "Press phone call button", likely because there was no re-dial button in the initial display of this interface, resulting in user confusion and operational errors. For the operation step of "Select call recipient", iNE was not notably large. However, NE_d was large because it was necessary that users remove a hand from the operation panel to check the operation. This result indicates that this operation step requires further optimization. This result also showed that if the usability problem couldn't be found by the traditional Novice Expert ratio [5] or iNE, the usability problem could be identified only by NE_d.

Based on the experiment, the frequency of directional changes became large as well as iNE and NE_d, which has caused confusion to most users about the next procedure. This was also supported by comments in post-task interview. The occurrences of directional changes were generally different depending on the user; however, there is a tendency that this parameter is linked to find the exact usability problem. It was difficult to relate it directly to the usability evaluation method at the current stage, but we can consider the usability problems using the frequency of direction changes combined with other parameters.

4.3 Results of Task 2 and Discussion

The average values for the usability evaluation parameters of iNE, NE_d, and stationary time for the Facsimiles P and S interfaces of Task 2 are shown in Tables 4 and 5, respectively. In the operation step "Shift prompt to find call recipient" on the Facsimile P interface (Table 4), hyphen shows that it was impossible to calculate NE_d because the same button as in the previous operation was pressed.

While the operation step "Decide method of searching" on the Facsimile P interface, both iNE and NE_d were large, and an average stationary time of 3.7 s was observed. From these results, it was considered that this operation step had a problem with usability and the operation step of the Facsimile P interface should be improved. On the other hand, in the post-task interview, the majority of users experienced confusion in this operation step, which was consistent with our results. For the operation step "Send a fax" on the Facsimile P interface, the average stationary time was the longest in the Task 2. Most users tried to press the several different buttons in this step and no guidance for the next step was provided due to the usability problem.

For the Facsimile S interface (Table 5), there was no critical usability problem. Unnecessary movement and stationary was slightly observed after the operation step "Find call recipient," as there was a time lag between pressing the button and screen

Table 4. Evaluation parameters of Task 2 (Facsimile P)

Operation steps	iNE	NE_d	Stationary time (s)
(1) Open phonebook function	2.73	1.23	0.4
(2) Decide method of searching	15.09	14.06	3.7
(3) Shift prompt to find call recipient	3.44	4.09	0.0
	1.70	–	0.4
(4) Select call recipient	7.43	6.80	1.0
(5) Send a fax	18.37	9.37	4.2

Table 5. Evaluation parameters of Task 2 (Facsimile S)

Operation steps	iNE	NE_d	Stationary time (s)
(1) Open phonebook function	2.51	1.15	0.0
(2) Find call recipient	3.99	3.49	1.2
(3) Select call recipient	3.72	1.42	0.9
(4) Send a fax	3.92	2.83	0.1

changing; however, the frequency of directional changes was observed with the same tendency as in Task 1. Depending on the users, when the frequency of directional changes became large, iNE and NE_d also became large, and most users were confused about the next operation. This was also clarified by the post-task interview. The frequency of directional changes for the Facsimile P (2–6 times) was higher than that for Facsimile S (maximum of 2 times). Taken together, the results of our evaluative experiment showed that Facsimile S has a more intuitive interface for beginners than Facsimile P.

Throughout the experiment, we demonstrated the main two advantages of the proposed method: applicable to various types of interfaces and high performance. The facsimile as a representative of the actual electrical products could be evaluated from an objective view. Using the proposed objective evaluation, which involves extracting the video-recorded fingertip movements by the image processing, and then objectively evaluating the usability of an interface based on measurable parameters, a number of specific usability problems were identified even if the traditional objective evaluation method had missed.

5 Conclusions

We propose a new method for objective usability evaluation that involves video recording the user's operation, extracting their fingertip movements via image processing, and then evaluating usability based on operation time, distance, stationary time, and frequency of directional changes. From the results of an evaluative experiment involving two interfaces, a number of problems with usability were identified with our method, and the effectiveness of the proposed method was confirmed. Our proposed usability evaluation method appears to be potentially suited for quantitative analysis and has applicability that is comparable to classical methods.

Acknowledgement. This work was supported by JSPS KAKENHI Grant Number 25330238.

References

1. Nielsen, J.: Usability Engineering. Academic Press, Boston (1993)
2. Faulkner, X.: Usability Engineering. Palgrave, New York (2000)
3. Barnum, C.M.: Usability Testing Essentials. Morgan Kaufmann, Burlington (2011)
4. Herman, L.: Towards effective usability evaluation in Asia: cross-cultural differences. In: Proceedings of the 6th Australian Conference on Computer-Human Interaction, pp.135–136 (1996)
5. Urokohara, H., Furuta, K., Tanaka, K., Kurosu, M.: A usability evaluation method that compares task performance between expert and novice. In: Proceedings of Human Interface Symposium, pp. 537–542 (1999)
6. MacDorman, K.F., Whalen, T.J., Ho, C., Patel, H.: An improved usability measure based on novice and expert performance. Int. J. Hum. Comput. Interact. **27**(3), 280–302 (2011)
7. Nishiuchi, N., Takahashi, Y., Hashizume, A.: Development of a usability evaluation method based on finger movement. In: Stephanidis, C. (ed.) HCII 2013, Part I. CCIS, vol. 373, pp. 144–148. Springer, Heidelberg (2013)
8. ISO 9241-11:1998 Ergonomic Requirements for Office Work with Visual Display Terminals (VDTs) - Part 11: Guidance on usability
9. Ericsson, K.A., Simon, H.A.: Protocol Analysis: Verbal Reports as Data. MIT Press, Cambridge (1993)
10. El-Halees, A.: Software usability evaluation using opinion mining. J. Softw. **9**(2), 343–349 (2014)
11. Card, S.K., Moran, T.P., Newell, A.: The keystroke level model for user performance time with interactive systems. Commun. ACM **23**(7), 396–410 (1980)
12. Sugimura, H., Uwano, H.: Quantitative evaluation of habituation to user interface using eye movement. Informational Processing Society of Japan SIG Technical report (2012)
13. Wong, W., Bartels, M., Chrobot, N.: Practical eye tracking of the ecommerce website user experience. In: Stephanidis, C., Antona, M. (eds.) UAHCI 2014, Part IV. LNCS, vol. 8516, pp. 109–118. Springer, Heidelberg (2014)
14. Bojko, A.: Using eye tracking to compare Web page design: a case study. J. Usability Stud. **1**(3), 112–120 (2006)
15. Schall, A.: Eye tracking insights into effective navigation design. In: Marcus, A. (ed.) DUXU 2014, Part I. LNCS, vol. 8517, pp. 363–370. Springer, Heidelberg (2014)
16. Walton, L., Bergstrom, J.C., Hawkins, D.C., Pierce, C.: Eye tracking on a paper survey: implications for design. In: Stephanidis, C., Antona, M. (eds.) UAHCI 2014, Part II. LNCS, vol. 8514, pp. 175–182. Springer, Heidelberg (2014)
17. Kimura, M., Uwano, H., Ohira, M., Matsumoto, K.: An experimental study toward constructing an electroencephalogram measurement method for usability evaluation. In: Proceedings of Human Interface Symposium, pp.735–742 (2008)

18. Inoue, H., Shimizu, S., Nara, H., Tsuruga, T., Miwakeichi, F., Hirai, N., Kikuchi, S., Watanabe, E., Kato, S.: Attempts to quantitative analyze for the change of human brain activity with physical and psychological load. In: Marcus, A. (ed.) DUXU 2014, Part I. LNCS, vol. 8517, pp. 240–249. Springer, Heidelberg (2014)
19. Ji, Y., Park, J., Lee, C., Yun, M.: A usability checklist for the usability evaluation of mobile phone user interface. J. Usability Stud. **20**(3), 207–231 (2006)
20. Wetzlinger, W., Auinger, A., Dörflinger, M.: Comparing effectiveness, efficiency, ease of use, usability and user experience when using tablets and laptops. In: Marcus, A. (ed.) DUXU 2014, Part I. LNCS, vol. 8517, pp. 402–412. Springer, Heidelberg (2014)
21. Ozok, A.A., Benson, D., Chakraborty, J., Norcio, A.F.: A comparative study between tablet and laptop PCs: user satisfaction and preferences. Int. J. Hum. Comput. Interact. **24**, 329–352 (2008)
22. Siegenthaler, E., Wurtz, P., Groner, R.: Improving the usability of e-book readers. J. Usability Stud. **6**(1), 25–38 (2010)
23. Kronbauer, Artur H., Santos, Celso A.S., Vieira, Vaninha: Smartphone applications usability evaluation: a hybrid model and its implementation. In: Winckler, M., Forbrig, P., Bernhaupt, R. (eds.) HCSE 2012. LNCS, vol. 7623, pp. 146–163. Springer, Heidelberg (2012)
24. Ahmad, N., Boota, M., Masoom, A.: Smart phone application evaluation with usability testing approach. J. Softw. Eng. Appl. **7**, 1045–1054 (2014)
25. Quaresma, M., Gonçalves, R.: Usability analysis of smartphone applications for drivers. In: Marcus, A. (ed.) DUXU 2014, Part I. LNCS, vol. 8517, pp. 352–362. Springer, Heidelberg (2014)
26. Vilar Neto, E., Campos, F.F.C.: Evaluating the usability on multimodal interfaces: a case study on tablets applications. In: Marcus, A. (ed.) DUXU 2014, Part I. LNCS, vol. 8517, pp. 484–495. Springer, Heidelberg (2014)
27. Carstens, D.S., Patterson, P.: Usability study of travel website. J. Usability Stud. **1**(1), 47–61 (2005)
28. Benbunan-Fich, R.: Using protocol analysis to evaluate the usability of a commercial web site. Inf. Manage. **39**, 151–163 (2001)
29. MacKenzie, I.S., Buxton, W.: Extending Fitts' law to two-dimensional tasks. In: Proceedings of the SIGCHI Conference on Human Factors in Computing Systems, pp. 219–226 (1992)
30. Iwase, H., Murata, A.: Extending the model of Fitts' law to a three-dimensional pointing movement caused by human extremities. Trans. Inst. Electron. Inf. Communi. Eng. **J85-A**(11), 1336–1346 (2002)

Medical Image Fusion Using Daubechies Complex Wavelet and Near Set

Pubali Chatterjee[1], Somoballi Ghoshal[1(✉)], Biswajit Biswas[1], Amlan Chakrabarti[2], and Kashi Nath Dey[1]

[1] Department of Computer Science and Engineering,
University of Calcutta, Calcutta, India
{somoballipubali,biswajit.cu.08,kndey55}@gmail.com
[2] AKCSIT, University of Calcutta, Calcutta, India
acakcs@caluniv.ac.in

Abstract. Medical image fusion is the process of registering and combining multiple images from single or multiple imaging modalities. It helps to improve the imaging quality and reduces the redundancy, which improves the clinical applicability of medical images for diagnosis. The idea is to improve the content of an image by fusing images of multiple modalities viz. positron emission tomography (PET), computerized tomography (CT), single-photon emission computerized tomography (SPECT), magnetic resonance imaging (MRI) etc. Registration is an important step before fusion. In general, the problem of image registration can be identified as the determination of geometric transformations between the respective source image and target image.

In this paper, we have used Daubechies wavelet and near fuzzy set for registration of multi-modal images and a new pixel-level multi-modal technique for medical image fusion based on complex wavelet and near set approach. Our proposed technique produces excellent fused images and minimizes fusion associated problems giving a high quality image, restoring almost every information of the source images. In this work, we have considered various image modalities like PET, CT, SPECT and MRI. The experimental evaluation for various benchmark images shows that the proposed fusion framework can generate excellent fused images as compared to the other state-of-the-art methods.

Keywords: Image registration · Image fusion · Daubechies complex wavelet transform · Near set · Magnetic resonance image · Positron emission tomography · Computerized tomography · Single-photon emission computerized tomography

1 Introduction

One of the major motivations of image fusion is to enhance the underexposed low resolution image by fusing it with simultaneously captured high resolution image [1]. Potentially multi-sensor image fusion (MIF) is the technique by which the source images acquired by two or more sensors characteristically different from each other but of the same object/scene, produce a single composite image [2]. Image fusion can effectively increase the amount of information of the scene by mixing the images captured by different sensors [3].

Image registration is the determination of a geometrical transformation that aligns points in one view of an object with corresponding points in another view of the same [4]. It is required in image analysis applications where we need to generate a correspondence among various objects in multiple images. There exists a challenge to register two color-images in different modality with high accuracy. In case of color image registration we need to handle a large amount of comprising of pixel values in R, G and B planes. Hence, color image registration is challenging and we need to employ intelligent techniques to perform the registration. There are very few promising works in color image registration [5,6] and whatever exists is mainly in the field of surveillance. In this paper, our proposed methodology uses Daubechies wavelet theory and near fuzzy set concepts to find the similarity between the pixel intensities of the two color images - source and target, and generates the registered image. Our methodology works fine in registering images for biomedical applications involving PET, MRI and SPECT images.

Image fusion can be performed utilizing information of various kinds such as pixel level, feature level and decision level [1,7]. Pixel level image fusion produces a fused image in which each pixel is determined by a set of pixels from various sources. Feature-level algorithms normally fuse the source images using their different feature such as regions, edges or corner points [8,9]. At times, it may lead to loss of information. Decision level fusion scheme combines set of rules defined over image descriptions straightforwardly, for instance, relational graphs [1,10]. Moreover, the decision-level fusion methods are complicated. The advantage of pixel level fusion is that the fused image contains additional original information [11,12]. In addition, compared to feature or decision level fusion, the pixel level fusion is easy to implement and efficient with respect to time. This paper is concerned with the pixel-level image fusion problem. An excellent overview and a general introduction to multi-sensor data fusion can be found in [8,9]. Further scientific papers on multi-sensor image fusion have been published highlighting improved fusion quality and finding more application areas [13–15]. Reasonably a few survey papers have been published recently [16–18], providing overviews of the history, developments and the current state of the art of image fusion in the image-based application fields [3] and scopes of improvement in this field.

In recent years, many pixel-level image fusion methods have been proposed. Among the majority of those techniques, multi-scale transform methods have been widely used in image fusion field very successfully. In general, multi-scale decomposition consist of different methods such as Laplacian pyramid, Morphological pyramid, Discrete wavelet transform (DWT)[9,13,19], Gradient pyramid, Stationary wavelet transform (SWT)[13], and Dual-tree complex wavelet transform (DTCWT) [20,21] etc. The fundamental idea is to perform certain multi-scale decomposition on each of the source images and then to combine all these decompositions to achieve one merged representation based on a fusion rule [10]. Finally, applying the inverse transformation to the combined representation, the fused image is constructed. Multi-scale decomposition is translation-variant technique so their performances quickly deteriorate when a little object movement occurs or the source images cannot be rightly registered. Its advantage is that it is very efficient for proper information analysis and integration but its disadvantage is its complexity [7]. In recent times many multi-scale geometric analysis schemes [13–15,19,22] has been proposed. To get detailed understanding of the various multi-scale transforms and their comparison, one can study [3,7,8,23]. This led us to use Daubechies complex wavelet transform (DCWT) in our work.

Medical imaging systems are categorized into two categories, which are structural or functional systems [24]. Based on sensor property the magnetic resonance image (MRI) and computed tomography (CT) provides high-resolution images with structural and anatomical information. On the other hand positron emission tomography (PET) and single-photoemission computed tomography (SPECT) images provide functional information with low spatial resolution [25]. A detailed understanding of the various medical imaging modalities can be obtained from [20,22]. The excellence of image fusion technique is solely dependent on the local salient features of source images. Mathematically, several alternative techniques have been proposed to represent and handle the local information of source images [26].

The source image and the target image are not identical. They are of the same object taken from different viewpoints or through different sensors. Hence we would not get valid result for fusion without registering the images. This led us to propose the new methodology. This paper presents a novel Daubechies complex wavelet transform based fusion scheme to avoid the weak points of the image fusion technique [20]. We have integrated Daubechies complex wavelet and near set theory to design and implement the algorithm. For best approximation and similarity estimation between frequencies of high spectral and high resolution images, the proposed algorithm have used closest points measure with near set method and entropy. Near set is effectively applied to substitute similar frequency bands from source images that are inherited into the fused image [24]. The results show that the proposed algorithm significantly improves the fusion quality in terms of entropy, mutual information, edge strength and average gradient compared to other popular image fusion methods. The key contributions of our work are as follows:

- Implementation of a new image registration technique for multi-modal color images using Daubechies complex wavelet and near fuzzy set.
- Proposal for a novel color image fusion framework involving Daubechies complex wavelet and near set.
- Performance estimation of our proposed techniques for benchmark images using various quantitative evaluation metrics.

2 Background

In this section we brief the preliminary concepts of Daubechies wavelet, Shift invariance, Near set, Fuzzy set and Near fuzzy set, which are used in our proposed methodology of image fusion.

2.1 Daubechies Complex Wavelet Transform

In multi-resolution theory, the scaling function $\phi(x)$ [11] is defined as:

$$\phi(x) = 2 \sum_k a_k \phi(2x - k) \tag{1}$$

where a_k is finitely nonzero coefficient that can be real or complex number and $\sum a_k = 1$. For one dimension Daubechies wavelet, $\psi_{j,k}(x)$ is defined using the above scaling function and multi-resolution analysis of $\mathbf{L}^2(\mathbf{R})$[27]. For the construction of complex Daubechies wavelet transform [22], the mother wavelet $\psi(x)$ is defined as:

$$\psi(x) = 2 \sum_k (-1)^k a_{1-k} \bar{\phi}(2x - k) \tag{2}$$

where $\psi(x)$ and $\phi(x)$ are wavelet function and scaling function respectively, that support same compact interval $[-N, N+1]$. Let us assume for any function $f(x)$, which can be represented by the combination of scaling function $\phi(x)$ and wavelet function $\psi(x)$ can be given by

$$f(x) = \sum_k c_k^{j_0} \phi_{j_0,k}(x) + \sum_{j=j_0}^{j_{max}-1} d_k^j \psi_{j,k}(x) \tag{3}$$

here j_0 is given level of resolution, $c_k^{j_0}$ and d_k^j are approximation and detailed coefficients respectively. The complex scaling function and wavelet will be written as:

$$\phi(x) = h(x) + ig(x) \text{ and } \phi(x) = w(x) + iv(x) \tag{4}$$

where h, g, w and v are real function.

Shift invariant and openness of phase information are the two essential properties of the Daubechies complex wavelet transform, which directly manipulate the performance of image fusion.

It has been shown in [28] that Daubechies complex wavelet can be symmetric. The symmetric property of the filter makes it easy to handle the boundary problems for finite length signals. In [29], a method is proposed to achieve symmetric property as well as approximate linear phase on a complex Daubechies wavelet. The linear phase response of the filter rules out the nonlinear phase distortion and preserves the shape of the signal.

2.2 Shift Invariance

Shift invariance property also has an effect on the informational content at multilevel. In Discrete wavelet transform (DWT), the nature of wavelet coefficients at different sub-bands changes erratically. But, in the case of complex wavelet transform it remains preserved and nature of magnitude of complex wavelet coefficients at multiple level remains the same [11]. However, applying any operation at multi-scale wavelet coefficients would work in uniform way for complex wavelet coefficients, not like real wavelet transform. Therefore, thresholding of complex wavelet coefficient is more effective than thresholding of real wavelet coefficient [22]. Thus, the Daubechies complex wavelet transform (DCWT) is a compact shift invariant wavelet transform. For small shift of the signal, the wavelet coefficients fluctuate around singularities [27]. However, Daubechies complex wavelet transform (DCWT) acts for better shift invariable property. Figure 1 demonstrates a curved edge structure reconstructed using real and complex Daubechies wavelets transform at single scale decomposition level. From Fig. 1, it is obvious that the square edge structure shifts through over the image space and the image reconstruction using real valued Discrete wavelet transform (DWT) coefficient varies irregularly, where as complex wavelet transform reconstructs all local shifts and orientations of image perfectly in the same mode. Now to avoid miss-registration, we can use shift invariant wavelet transform for image fusion, otherwise fusion process may result in mismatched or non aligned image artifacts.

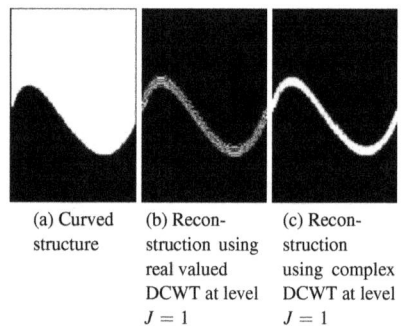

(a) Curved structure   (b) Reconstruction using real valued DCWT at level $J=1$ (c) Reconstruction using complex DCWT at level $J=1$

Fig. 1. Shift sensitivity formation of curved structure

2.3 Phase Information

The phases contain most of the consistent structure of the image whereas the magnitude mostly encodes the strength of local information. We viewed that the imaginary component of complex scaling coefficients takes significant edge information [27]. Thus the imaginary wavelet coefficients of Daubechies complex wavelet transform (DCWT) provide phase information of image. For most of the part the structural information of the image is controlled by the phase, not by the magnitude of wavelet coefficients [11]. This is obvious that phase information of image is a desirable feature of a wavelet transform, which includes most of the structural information from source images to the fused image [22]. From Fig. 2, it is clear that phase information accumulate structural content of the images. For that reason, we have used Daubechies complex wavelet transform (DCWT) to create excellent fused image.

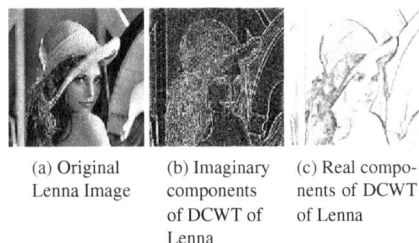

(a) Original Lenna Image   (b) Imaginary components of DCWT of Lenna   (c) Real components of DCWT of Lenna

Fig. 2. Phase information of Lena image

2.4 Near Set

A set X is said to be near relative to a set Y if a probe function ϕ defined over the objects in sets X, Y is assigned to each object by the same probe function ϕ [24], and there is a least one pair of objects $x, y \in X \times Y$ such that $\|\phi(x)-\phi(y)\|_2 \leq \theta$. The description of x is similar to the description of y within some θ, where θ is the threshold parameter defined over feature space based on resemblance. So, a probe function $\phi(\cdot)$ evaluates the effectiveness of a feature value extracted from each feature space.

Thus, if we assume O represents the set of all objects then description of an object $x \in O$ is given by [24]:

$$\phi_B(x) = (\phi_1(x), \phi_2(x), \cdots, \phi_i(x), \cdots, \phi_l(x)) \tag{5}$$

where l is the length of the description, and each $\phi_i :\to \mathbf{R}$ in B, is a probe function that represents a feature used in the description of the object x.

2.5 Fuzzy Set

Sets whose elements have degrees of membership are called Fuzzy sets [30]. Fuzzy set theory allows gradual assessment of the membership of elements in a set; this is described with the help of a membership function in the real unit interval [0, 1].

A fuzzy set A is identified by a membership function $\mu_A(x)$, which assigns each element $x \in X$ a real-valued in the range [0, 1]: $A = \{(x, \mu_A(x))\}$ where $\mu_A(x) : \mathbf{X} \to [0, 1]$. The membership function $\mu_A(x)$ signifies the extent by which the element x has the attribute A.

2.6 Near Fuzzy Set

Now we briefly discuss on the near fuzzy set model used in our algorithm for image registration. The membership of each pixel is calculated using histogram based fuzzyfication method [24] and the two sets are checked to be near or not, based on the near set logic by defining the near set index as the fuzzy histogram intersection threshold value [31]. Let there be two images of the same object, a source image S and a target image T. We decompose the images into three planes R,G and B. After this decomposition we further decompose the R plane's image components using Daubechies complex wavelet. We extract the high and the low components from each of the source and target images (S_R^h, S_R^l) and (T_R^h, T_R^l) respectively in R plane. Then, fuzzification of each pixel of S_R^h, S_R^l, T_R^h and T_R^l is carried out using the following [30]:

$$\mu_f = 1 - \frac{\max(F) - F[i][j]}{\max(F) - \min(F)} \quad (6)$$

where μ_f is the fuzzy value that is to be calculated and F is the matrix whose elements are to be normalized. Hence equation (6) is separately carried out for S_R^h, S_R^l, T_R^h and T_R^l to get the normalized matrices. Fuzzy histogram [31] is drawn for S_R^h, S_R^l, T_R^h and T_R^l based on the membership and the histograms are merged to get an intersection point which gives us the threshold value α for calculating the nearness. If $S[i][j] - T[i][j] \leq \alpha$ then the pixels are said to be near where $S[i][j]$ and $T[i][j]$ are the intensity values of the source and the target images respectively. The same process is applied for the G and the B plane's components.

2.7 Geometric Transformation

In image registration, geometrical transformation is a tool that uses estimation of spatial distortion of target image. In this work we used rigid base transformation with translation and rotation. Assuming that (X, Y) are the coordinates of the source image and (P, R) are the pixel position and line of target image, which should be registered. The geometrical transformation may be represented as [32]:

$$\begin{bmatrix} X \\ Y \end{bmatrix} = \begin{bmatrix} \cos\theta & -\sin\theta \\ \sin\theta & \cos\theta \end{bmatrix} \begin{bmatrix} s_x & 0 \\ 0 & s_y \end{bmatrix} \begin{bmatrix} P \\ R \end{bmatrix} + \begin{bmatrix} \delta_x \\ \delta_y \end{bmatrix} \quad (7)$$

However the origin is considered to be the upper left corner of the source image, θ is the angular orientation difference and (δ_x, δ_y) are the amount of shift between the two images. In this paper, we have carried out robust evaluation of θ. First we find out the pixel values with minimum matches and then we find out the frequency of the matching neighbors. If the frequency of matching neighbors is the highest then we chose that location in the image to calculate θ for rotating and registering the image. (δ_x, δ_y) are evaluated in a similar manner.

3 Proposed Methodology

In this section we elaborate the various steps of our proposed methodologies for image registration and fusion and its schematic representation is shown in Fig. 3.

3.1 Image Registration

At first, noise is removed from two images: source S and target T, using low pass filtration [4]. Then, in order to achieve color image registration, we perform decomposition of both the images in three components R, G and B and then

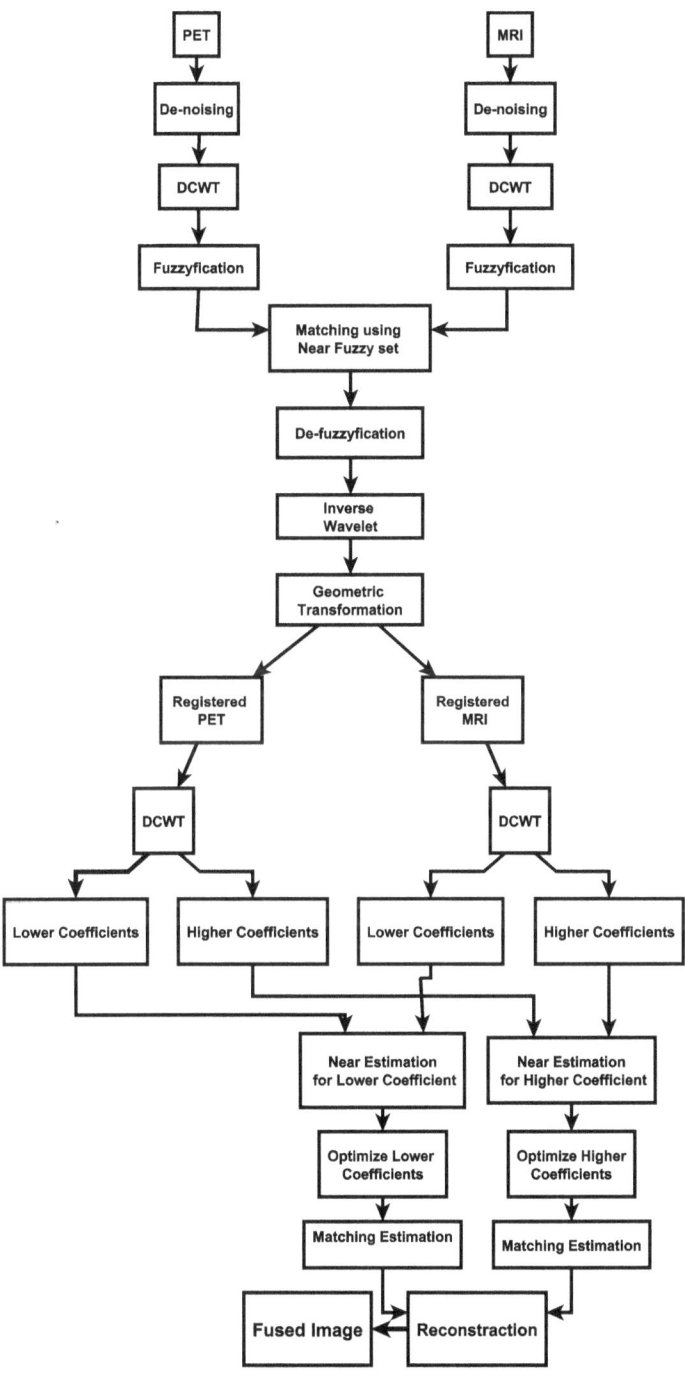

Fig. 3. Various steps of the proposed methodology

wavelet transform as specified in Sect. 2.1. Through wavelet transform we obtain the high and low components of both the images in each plane. Then we proceed to find the membership of each pixel value i.e. to normalize the pixel values using standard fuzzyfication method as stated in Eq. 5, 6. Fuzzy membership histogram [31] of both the images is drawn and concatenated to get the intersection point, which is our threshold value α. Near set function $\phi(x)$ is defined as [24]:

$$\phi(x) = x|\text{intensity of } S_R(x) - \text{intensity of } T_R(x)| \leq \alpha \qquad (8)$$

Each pixel intensity of S_R is matched with every pixel intensity of T_R. If a match is found then the flag is increased by 1 and the matching co-ordinate of the source corresponding to the matched target is stored in a list. In order to achieve high quality of the registered image we have considered 99 % matching between the source and the target images. It may be inferred that if match found is over 99 % then the two images are of the same object. We get the image T' by necessary geometrical transformation, defuzzyfication and inverse wavelet transform technique. The defuzzification equation is defined as follows :

$$T'[i][j] = \max(T_R) - (\max(T_R) - \min(T_R)) \times (1 - \mu_T) \qquad (9)$$

where $\max(T_R)$ and $\min(T_R)$ are maximum, minimum intensity value of T_R respectively, and μ_T is the fuzzy membership value of the pixel [30]. We carry out the same process for the G and B plane components and then combine the outputs to get a registered image matrix. This new image matrix is compared with the source image matrix by evaluating the root mean square error of the two. The schematic diagram of our proposed algorithm is presented in Fig. 3 followed by detailed explanation.

The pseudo-code of the design is illustrated in the Algorithm : Daubechies Complex wavelet and Near Fuzzy Set for Image Registration (DNFR).

3.2 Image Fusion

In the fusion step we consider the images to be fused as the source images and the fused image is generated through the fusion of these images. At first we decomposed the source images into low pass and high pass wavelet coefficients respectively using Daubechies complex wavelet transform (DCWT). After decomposition of source images we have normalized the wavelet coefficients of Daubechies complex wavelet transform (DCWT) for estimating nearness between MRI and PET. The steps of the proposed fusion method illustrated in Fig. 3.

Let W_A^l and W_B^l are approximation coefficients of Daubechies complex wavelet transform (DCWT) of PET and MRI images respectively. For similarity measure between complex wavelet coefficient of W_A^l and W_B^l, we have defined two probe functions $\phi_A(x)$ and $\phi_B(x)$ respectively. The probe function $\phi_A(x)$ for wavelet coefficient of W_A^l is defined as follows [24]:

$$\phi_A(x) = \left\| \frac{1}{\mu_A} + \frac{1}{\sigma_A} + \left(1 - \frac{a \times \mu_A}{\sigma_A - 1}\right) \right\| \qquad (10)$$

Algorithm 1. Proposed Algorithm (DNFR)

Input: Source image S and target image T.
Output: Registered image (T').
begin
Step 1: Remove noise from S and T using low pass filtering.
Step 2: Decompose S and T into thee components R, G and B.
Step 3: Using wavelet transform extract the low and high components from R-Plane's component of both the source and target images, (S_R^l, S_R^h) and (T_R^l, T_R^h)
Step 4: Normalize the membership of each pixel in S_R^l and T_R^l by using fuzzyfication technique as in equation (5) and (6).
Step 5: Draw fuzzy histograms to calculate α as described in Sect. 2.6.
Step 6:
while each pixel of S_R^l is not traversed **do**
  Match each pixel $S_R^l[i][j]$ with $T_R^l[k][l]$ as in equation (8)

  if match found **then**
    flag = flag+1.
    Store pixel position for match in the source corresponding to the target's pixel
  end if
  Move to next pixel of target image $T_R^l[k][l+1]$.
end while
Step 7: Repeat Step 4 and 5 for S_R^h and T_R^h
Step 8:
if match found is over 99 % **then**
  geometric-transformation (T_R)
  de-fuzzyfication (T_R)
  inverse-wavelet-transform (T_R)
end if
Step 9: Repeat Step 3 - Step 6 for the G and the B-Plane's component.
Step 10: Combine the R, G and B components to derive the new image matrix.
Step 11: Compare the source image and the newly formed image by evaluating their root mean square values as in equation (24) to show that the images are registered.

where μ_A and σ_A are mean and standard deviation of complex wavelet coefficient W_A^l, $a = \dfrac{\sigma_A}{\mu_A}$ is the ratio of mean and standard deviation of coefficient W_A^l. Similarly the probe function $\phi_B(x)$ for wavelet coefficient of W_B^l is defined as follows [24]:

$$\phi_B(x) = \left\| \frac{1}{\mu_B} + \frac{1}{\sigma_B} + \left(1 - \frac{b \times \mu_B}{\sigma_B - 1}\right) \right\| \qquad (11)$$

where μ_B, σ_B are mean and standard deviation of complex wavelet coefficient W_B^l and $b = \dfrac{\sigma_B}{\mu_B}$ is the ratio of mean and standard deviation of coefficient W_B^l. According to Near set method, we have $\|\phi_A(x) - \phi_B(x)\| \leq \theta$ here θ is the threshold value under approximation level of feature. For estimation of threshold θ, we have used a matching criteria between wavelet coefficient, W_A^l and W_B^l.

$$\theta = 1 - \frac{2C_{corr}^{AB}}{log(H_A + H_B)} \qquad (12)$$

where H_A and H_B are entropy of coefficients matrix A and B and C_{corr}^{AB} [23] is correlation coefficient of matrix A and B respectively. The entropy H_A for A and The entropy H_B for B is estimated by using equation [16] as follows:

$$H_A = -\sum_{i=1}^{n} p_A(i) log_2 \{p_A(i)\} \qquad (13)$$

$$H_B = -\sum_{i=1}^{n} p_B(i) log_2 \{p_B(i)\} \qquad (14)$$

where n is the number of samples in coefficient matrix A and B and $p_A(i), p_B(i)$ are the normalized frequency in occurrence of each sample in these coefficients matrix A and B. The normalized frequency of $p_A(i), p_B(i)$ is calculated by the following equation :

$$p_A(i) = \frac{A_{max} - A}{A_{max} - A_{min}} \qquad (15)$$

$$p_B(i) = \frac{B_{max} - B}{B_{max} - B_{min}} \qquad (16)$$

where A_{max}, A_{min} are maximum, minimum value of complex wavelet coefficient of matrix A and B_{max}, B_{min} are maximum, minimum value of complex wavelet coefficient of matrix B respectively.

Along with threshold θ, we define two discrepancy matrix W_A and W_B for complex wavelet coefficient of matrix A and B. As the two images are of different modalities with varied characteristics, the discrepancy matrix W_A for complex wavelet coefficient of matrix A is calculated by Euclidean norm which is given by:

$$W_A = \sqrt{A^2 + B^2} \qquad (17)$$

and, the discrepancy matrix W_B for complex wavelet coefficient of matrix B is calculated by maximum norm which is given by:

$$W_B = \max(A, B) \qquad (18)$$

Two discrepancy matrices W_A and W_B are aggregated by following weighted average equation:

$$F = \alpha \times W_A + \beta \times W_B \qquad (19)$$

where α and β are two adaptive weighted parameters. Let us assume α_A and β_B are maximal parametric values of coefficient matrix A and B, which are computed by following equation

$$\alpha_A = \omega log \left(\frac{1 + \theta + 2\tau}{1 + \tau} \right) \qquad (20)$$

$$\beta_B = 1 - \alpha_A \qquad (21)$$

where θ (12) and ω, τ are two arbitrary parameters that are calculated by the following equation:

$$\omega = \frac{\sigma_A}{\sigma_A + \sigma_B} \quad (22)$$

$$\tau = \frac{\mu_A}{\mu_A + \mu_B} \quad (23)$$

where σ_A, σ_B and μ_A, μ_B are standard deviation and mean value of coefficient matrix A, B respectively.

The above mentioned fusion process is also applied for fusion of SPECT and MRI, and CT and MRI images. The result of the fusion procedure and the related performance analysis is presented in the next section. The pseudo-code of the design is illustrated in Algorithm DCWNF.

4 Result and Analysis

In this section, we brief the simulation results of DCWNF along with five different popular fusion algorithms namely, Principal component analysis (PCA), Intensity-hue-saturation (IHS), Discrete wavelet transform (DWT), Contourlet transform (CLT) and Shift inveriant shearlet transform (SIST)[33]. All individual methods have been applied to source image data sets specially positron emission tomography (PET) and magnetic resonance image (MRI)[22,34]. In recent years a number of image fusion quality assessment metrics have been proposed by the researchers [16–18] for evaluating the performance of fusion. We have compared the performance of our proposed fusion algorithm in terms of entropy (EN), spatial frequency (SF), mutual information (MI) and edge strength metric respectively. We have validated our registration method DNFR using the root mean sqaure error method (RMSE) [6]. For performance evaluation of DCWNF we have estimated entropy (EN), spatial frequency (SF), mutual information (MI) and edge strength successively for each image data set. We give a brief introduction of these metrics in the following text.

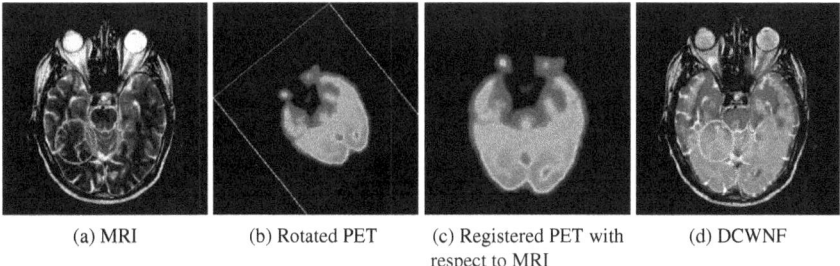

(a) MRI   (b) Rotated PET   (c) Registered PET with respect to MRI   (d) DCWNF

Fig. 4. The fusion result of the proposed method (DCWNF) on data set 1

Algorithm 2. Proposed Algorithm (DCWNF)

Input: Registred images X and Y of different Modality.
Output: Fused image (F').
Step 1: Read source image X and Y;
Step 2: Decompose source images X and Y using DCWT (3).
Step 3: Compute discrepancy matrix W_A and W_B using equations (17) and (18) respectively.
Step 4: Compute threshold θ using equation (12).
Step 5:
if $\|\phi_A(x) - \phi_B(x)\| \leq \theta$ then
  calculate α_A and β_B using equations (20) and (21).
else
  assign $\alpha_A = 0$ and $\beta_B = 1$
end if
Step 6:
calculate H_A and H_B using equations (13) and (14)
if $H_A > H_B$ then
  assign $\alpha = \alpha_A$ and $\beta = \beta_B$
else
  assign $\alpha = \beta_B$ and $\beta = \alpha_A$
end if
Step 7: Compute aggregate Daubechies complex wavelet coefficients using equation (19)
Step 8: Reconstruct fused image by using inversion of DCWT
Step 9: Display (F').

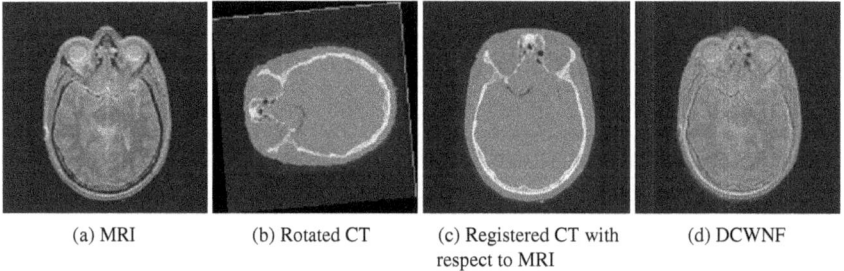

(a) MRI   (b) Rotated CT   (c) Registered CT with respect to MRI   (d) DCWNF

Fig. 5. The fusion result of the proposed method (DCWNF) on data set 2

Root Mean Square Error (RMSE): The performance of the registration algorithm is based on the measure of root mean square error (RMSE) percentage. The RMSE [6] is calculated as:

$$RMSE = \sqrt{\frac{1}{n}\sum_{i=1}^{n}(e_i - e'_i)^2}; \qquad (24)$$

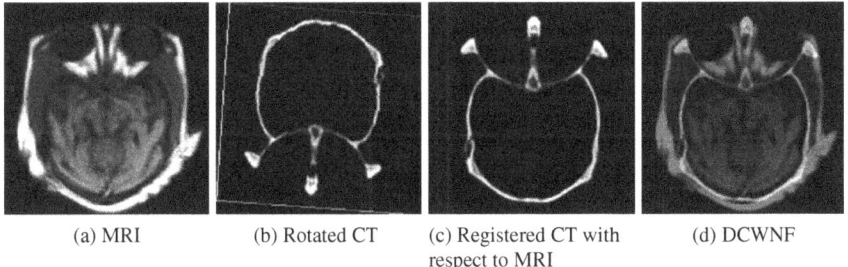

(a) MRI　　(b) Rotated CT　　(c) Registered CT with respect to MRI　　(d) DCWNF

Fig. 6. The fusion result of the proposed method (DCWNF) on data set 3

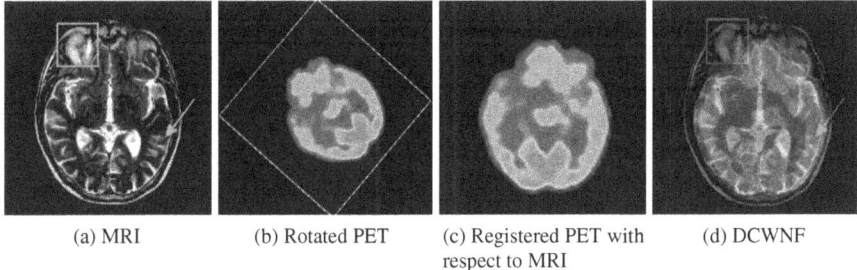

(a) MRI　　(b) Rotated PET　　(c) Registered PET with respect to MRI　　(d) DCWNF

Fig. 7. The fusion result of the proposed method (DCWNF) on data set 4

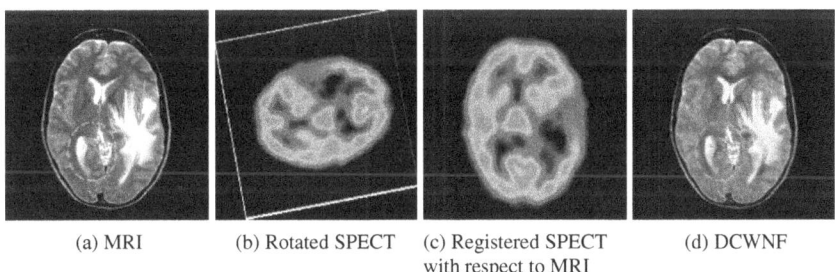

(a) MRI　　(b) Rotated SPECT　　(c) Registered SPECT with respect to MRI　　(d) DCWNF

Fig. 8. The fusion result of the proposed method (DCWNF) on data set 5

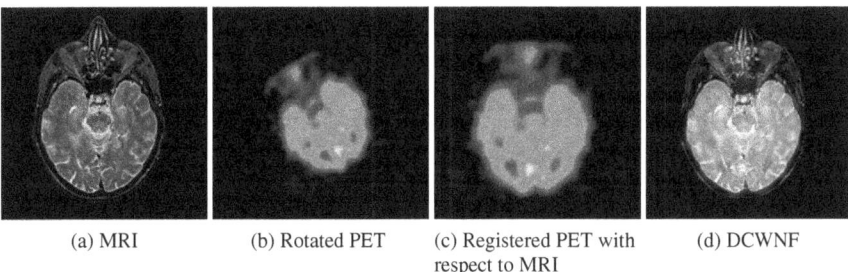

(a) MRI　　(b) Rotated PET　　(c) Registered PET with respect to MRI　　(d) DCWNF

Fig. 9. The fusion result of the proposed method (DCWNF) on data set 6

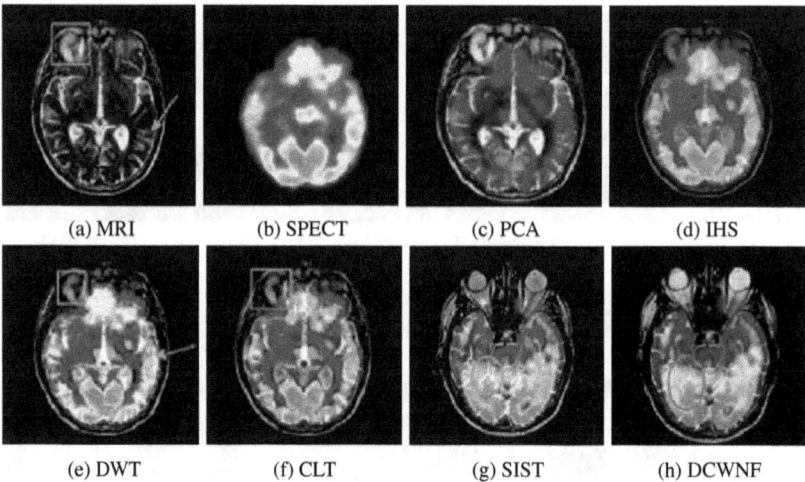

Fig. 10. Comparitive fusion results of the six methods on data set A

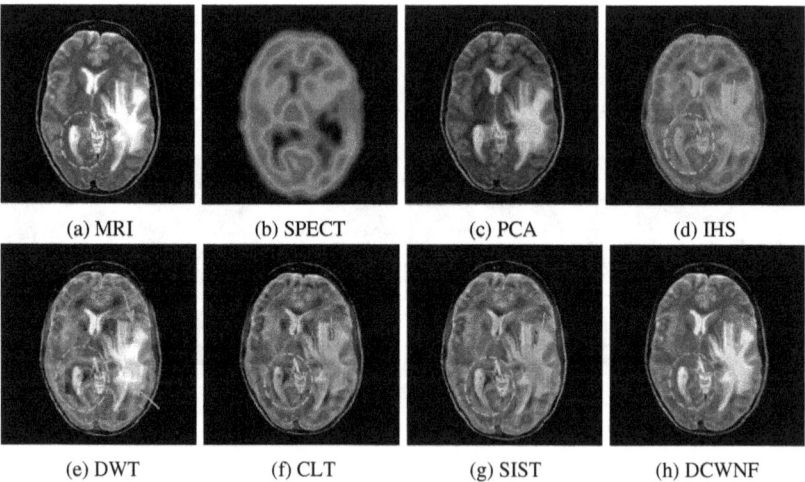

Fig. 11. Comparitive fusion results of the six methods on data set B

Here e_i is the root mean square of the source image and e'_i is the root mean square of the registered image. The smaller the RMSE is, the better the performance of the algorithm.

Entropy (EN): Entropy is used to measure the information content of an image [18]. The information content of an image can be expressed as:

$$EN = -\sum_{i=1}^{G} p(i) log_2 \{p(i)\} \qquad (25)$$

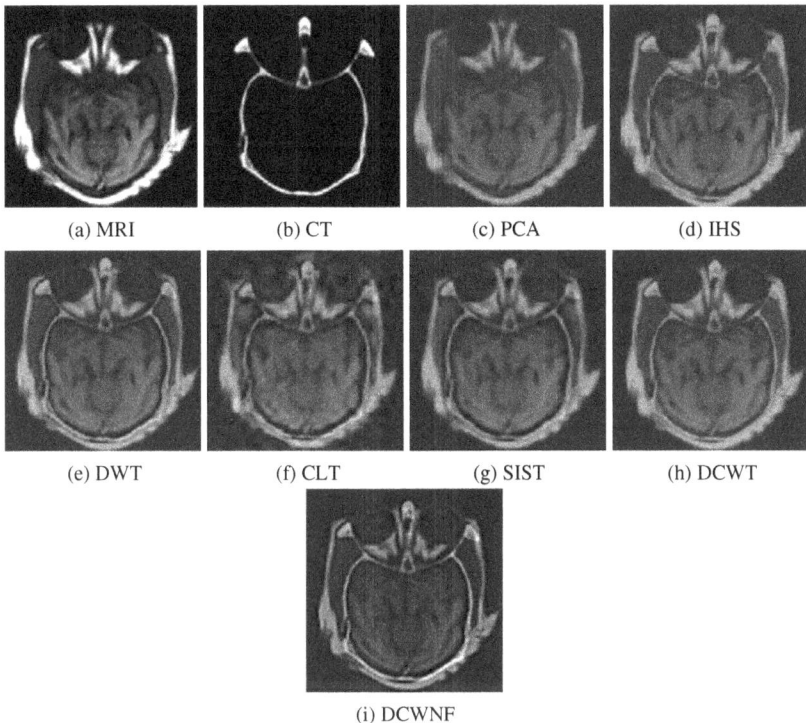

Fig. 12. Comparitive fusion results of the six methods on data set C

where G is the number of gray levels in the image histogram and $p(i)$ is the normalized frequency of occurrence of each gray level of the image. Entropy can be used to characterize the texture of the input image. The higher the entropy, the better is the performance of the fusion algorithm.

Spatial Frequency (SF): The average gradient of an image $g(I)$ is the measure of its sharpness in terms of gradient values [16], which is defined by:

$$SF = \frac{1}{XY} \sum_{x=1}^{X} \sum_{y=1}^{Y} \sqrt{(\frac{d}{dx}f_x)^2 + (\frac{d}{dy}f_y)^2} \qquad (26)$$

where f_x and f_y are horizontal and vertical pixel value of image. To have an enriched quality and visualization of an image it needs to have high spatial frequency content.

Mutual Information (MI): Mutual information is a quantitative measurement of information about one random variable (Y) with respect to another random variable (X). However, information is a reduction in the uncertainty of a variable. So, more the mutual information between X and Y, less is the uncertainty of X knowing Y or Y knowing X. For image fusion, mutual information (MI) is a comparative information estimator, which calculates the sum of mutual information between each source image and fused image [16]. Let A, F are source and fused images so mutual information I_{AF} between them is defined by:

$$I_{AF} = \sum_{af} p_{A,F}(a,f) \log \frac{p_{AF}(a,f)}{p_A(a)p_F(f)} \qquad (27)$$

where $p_{A,F}$ is jointly normalized histogram of A and F, p_a and p_f are normalized histogram of A and F, and a, f represent pixel value of image A and image F respectively. Similarly I_{BF} have defined mutual information between source image B and fused image F. Thus the mutual information MI between sources image A, B and fused image F defined as:

$$MI = I_{AF} + I_{BF} \qquad (28)$$

potentially large MI value of the fused image indicates effectiveness of fusion.

Edge Strength Metric($\mathbf{Q^{AB|F}}$): Edge strength metric $Q^{AB|F}$ is non-reference objective evaluation metric that estimates strength of edge information of image [17]. Let A, B and F are source images and fused image of size $M \times N$ respectively. $Q^{AB|F}$ estimates the amount of gradient information propagated from source images to the fused image. It is calculated with the help of the following equation:

$$Q^{AB|F} = \frac{\sum_{i=1}^{M} \sum_{j=1}^{N} \left(Q^{AF}(i,j) W^A(i,j) + Q^{BF}(i,j) W^B(i,j)\right)}{\sum_{i=1}^{M} \sum_{j=1}^{N} (W^A(i,j) + W^B(i,j))} \qquad (29)$$

where $Q^{AF}(i,j) = Q_g^{AF}(i,j) Q_\alpha^{AF(i,j)}$; $Q_g^{AF}(i,j)$ and $Q_\alpha^{AF(i,j)}$ are edge sensitivity and orientation values at location (i,j), respectively. Similarly $Q^{BF}(i,j)$ is equivalent to $Q^{AF}(i,j)$. $W^A(i,j)$ and $W^B(i,j)$ indicate the weighted magnitude

Table 1. Statistical Result Analysis for DNFR: original image (Figure number of the original rotated and or translated PET image), Degree of rotation for original image (the degree to which the PET image was rotated to check the performance of our algorithm), θ of Registered image (The degree to which the image has been rotated for registering it with the source MRI image after applying our registration algorithm), δ_x of Registered image & δ_y of Registered image gives the translation of the image after applying our proposed algorithm to get the registered image.

Original image	Degree of rotation of original image	θ of Registered image	δ_x of Registered image	δ_y of Registered image
Fig. 4(b)	39^0	39^0	193	192.36
Fig. 5(b)	95^0	95^0	25	25 6
Fig. 6(b)	176^0	176^0	22	22
Fig. 7(b)	49^0	49^0	175.98	175.72
Fig. 8(b)	100.5^0	100.5^0	65.53	65
Fig. 9(b)	30^0	30^0	113	113

Table 2. Quantitative evaluation of DCWNF fusion method for medical images

Data Set	Method	MRI Image	PET Image	Fused Image
Set 1	Mutual Information	*	*	**2.8774**
	Entropy	3.9509	4.2382	**4.4520**
	$Q^{AB \backslash F}$	*	*	**0.5863**
	Spatial Frequency	28.7412	29.1392	**31.4482**
Set 2	Mutual Information	*	*	**2.7392**
	Entropy	3.9808	4.0820	**4.2384**
	$Q^{AB \backslash F}$	*	*	**0.5863**
	Spatial Frequency	29.4372	30.1469	**32.1428**
Set 3	Mutual Information	*	*	**4.4524**
	Entropy	4.9328	6.0131	**6.3592**
	$Q^{AB \backslash F}$	*	*	**0.6432**
	Spatial Frequency	28.1385	30.7082	**31.8828**
Set 4	Mutual Information	*	*	**2.1727**
	Entropy	3.8964	4.0973	**4.1954**
	$Q^{AB \backslash F}$	*	*	**0.4938**
	Spatial Frequency	27.5930	29.3671	**30.8534**
Set 5	Mutual Information	*	*	**2.3225**
	Entropy	3.8237	4.1296	**4.3270**
	$Q^{AB \backslash F}$	*	*	**0.5427**
	Spatial Frequency	27.8392	29.3745	**30.8638**
Set 6	Mutual Information	*	*	**2.4390**
	Entropy	3.9632	4.1524	**4.2536**
	$Q^{AB \backslash F}$	*	*	**0.5120**
	Spatial Frequency	27.3913	29.8370	**31.2963**

of $Q^{AF}(i,j)$ and $Q^{BF}(i,j)$ respectively. The dynamic range of $Q^{AB|F}$ should be always normalized. More edge strength i.e. $Q^{AB|F}$ indicates better fusion scheme.

A group of medical images [22,34,35] were used for comparison of DCWNF with five existing fusion methods. Each data set has a pair of medical images from different capture devices such as PET and MRI, SPECT and MRI, CT and MRI images. In the experiment the corresponding pixels of the two input images have been rightly co-aligned. To evaluate our algorithm, we utilized MATLAB R2012b Image toolbox and a PC having Intel CPU 3.2 GHz and 2GB RAM.

For evaluating the performance of DCWNF, at first, we have used a number of benchmark medical images [22,34,35]. In Figs. 4, 5, 6, 7, 8 and, 9 we have presented the fusion results using six image data sets of benchmark medical images, which are taken from [22,26,34]. The geometrically transformed

Table 3. Quantitative evaluation of various fusion methods for medical images

Data Set	Metric Method	MI	Entropy	$Q^{AB\backslash F}$	Spatial Frequency
Set A	PCA	2.7351	3.7237	0.4384	30.1395
	IHS	2.7286	3.7678	0.3968	28.9940
	DWT	2.8364	4.2725	0.5273	30.3827
	CLT	2.8194	4.4362	0.5538	31.3968
	SIST	2.8717	4.4412	0.5827	31.4391
	DCWNF	**2.8774**	**4.4520**	**0.5863**	**31.4482**
Set B	PCA	2.2529	3.8416	0.4253	30.0264
	IHS	2.2645	3.9430	0.4617	29.0919
	DWT	2.2672	4.1853	0.4626	30.7477
	CLT	2.2727	4.2180	0.5068	30.8312
	SIST	2.3145	4.2955	0.5326	30.8541
	DCWNF	**2.3225**	**4.3270**	**0.5427**	**30.8938**

Table 4. Quantitative evaluation of various fusion methods for medical images on data set C

Metric Method	Entropy	$Q^{AB\backslash F}$
PCA	5.7415	0.6399
IHS	3.9543	0.5697
DWT	4.5351	0.6824
CLT	5.9507	0.5373
SIST	6.2310	0.5776
DCWT	5.9559	0.6386
DCWNF	**6.3592**	**0.6432**

PET/SPECT/CT images in Figs. 4, 5, 6, 7, 8 and, 9 are registered with the MRI images of the corresponding data sets. In Table 1 we have shown that the registration was carried out successfully by calculating θ, δ_x and δ_y for the registered images. Then we have applied DCWNF on the registered image and the source MRI image and it is observed that the proposed fusion technique indicates better results as shown in Table 2. Source images of Figs. 7 and 8 have also been used as source for the existing popular algorithms [15,33], and the results of fusion for the existing algorithms and also that of DCWNF are shown in Figs. 10 and 11 respectively. Source image from [22] is used to perform a comparison amongst the existing popular algorithms [22,33] and that of ours, the results are shown in Fig. 12. The merit of DCWNF is that it enhances edge and color information in fused images without any loss of information. The comparative results are shown in Table 4. The comparative statistical information is given in Tables 3 and 4 and the best results are in bold faced. We can conclude that

DCWNF provides excellent, promising and effective outcomes in comparison to the existing popular methods for multi-modal image fusion.

5 Conclusion

In this paper, we have proposed a new method for image fusion along with registration, involving positron emission tomography (PET), single-photon emission computerized tomography (SPECT), computerized tomography (CT) and magnetic resonance images (MRI), coined as DCWNF. We have also successfully implemented color image registration based on DNFR. The experimental results prove that performance of our proposed fusion technique (DCWNF) outperforms the existing state of the art research works in terms of quantitative measures like entropy, mutual information, average gradient and edge strength.

In future we plan to extend DCWNF to handle images in different noise models.

References

1. Bradski, G.: Introduction. In: Rusu, R.B. (ed.) Semantic 3D Object Maps for Everyday Manipulation in Human Living Environments. STAR, vol. 85, pp. 1–14. Springer, Heidelberg (2013)
2. Maes, F., Vandermeulen, D., Suetens, P.: Medical image registration using mutual information. Proc. IEEE **91**(10), 1699–1722 (2003)
3. Pajares, G., de la Cruz, J.M.: A wavelet-based image fusion tutorial. Pattern Recogn. **37**(9), 1855–1872 (2004). http://www.sciencedirect.com/science/article/pii/S0031320304001037
4. Gonzalez, R.C., Woods, R.: Digital image processing, 3rd edn. Pearson, Upper Saddle River (2008)
5. Karani, M.R.B., Kekre, H.B., Sarode, T.K.: A deviant transtorm based approach for color image registration (2012)
6. Wei Feng, C.Y., Hu, B.: A subpixel color image registration algorithm using quaternion phase-only correlation. In: International Conference on Audio, Language and Image Processing (2008)
7. Yang, B., Jing, Z.-L., Zhao, H.-T.: Review of pixel-level image fusion. J. Shanghai Jiaotong Univ. (Sci.) **15**(1), 6–12 (2010). http://dx.doi.org/10.1007/s12204-010-7186-y
8. Pohl, C., Van Genderen, J.L.: Review article multisensor image fusion in remote sensing: Concepts, methods and applications. Int. J. Remote Sens. **19**(5), 823–854 (1998). http://www.tandfonline.com/doi/abs/10.1080/014311698215748
9. Li, H., Manjunath, B.S., Mitra, S.K.: Multisensor image fusion using the wavelet transform. In: First International Conference on Image Processing (ICIP 1994), vol. 1, pp. 51–55, November 1994. http://vision.ece.ucsb.edu/publications/94ICIPWav.pdf
10. Liu, Z., Blasch, E., Xue, Z., Zhao, J., Laganiere, R., Wu, W.: Objective assessment of multiresolution image fusion algorithms for context enhancement in night vision: a comparative study. IEEE Trans. Pattern Anal. Mach. Intell. **34**(1), 94–109 (2012)

11. Lewis, J.J., O'Callaghan, R.J., Nikolov, S.G., Bull, D.R., Canagarajah, N.: Pixel- and region-based image fusion with complex wavelets. Inf. Fusion **8**(2), 119–130 (2007). http://dx.doi.org/10.1016/j.inffus.2005.09.006
12. Montagner, J., Barra, V., Boire, J.-Y.: A geometrical approach to multiresolution management in the fusion of digital images. In: Lévy, P.P., Le Grand, B., Poulet, F., Soto, M., Darago, L., Toubiana, L., Vibert, J.-F. (eds.) VIEW 2006. LNCS, vol. 4370, pp. 121–136. Springer, Heidelberg (2007)
13. Li, S., Yang, B.: Multifocus image fusion by combining curvelet and wavelet transform. Pattern Recogn. Lett. **29**(9), 1295–1301 (2008). http://dx.doi.org/10.1016/j.patrec.2008.02.002
14. Cao, Y., Li, S., Hu, J.: Multi-focus image fusion by nonsubsampled shearlet transform. In: 2011 Sixth International Conference on Image and Graphics (ICIG), pp. 17–21 (2011)
15. Po, D.D.-Y., Do, M.N.: Directional multiscale modeling of images using the contourlet transform. Trans. Img. Proc. **15**(6), 1610–1620 (2006). http://dx.doi.org/10.1109/TIP.2006.873450
16. Li, S., Yang, B., Hu, J.: Performance comparison of different multi-resolution transforms for image fusion. Inf. Fusion **12**(2), 74–84 (2011). http://dx.doi.org/10.1016/j.inffus.2010.03.002
17. Xydeas, C., Petrovic, V.: Objective image fusion performance measure. Electron. Lett. **36**(4), 308–309 (2000)
18. Pei, Y., Zhou, H., Yu, J., Cai, G.: The improved wavelet transform based image fusion algorithm and the quality assessment. In: 2010 3rd International Congress on Image and Signal Processing (CISP), vol. 1, pp. 219–223 (2010)
19. Nencini, F., Garzelli, A., Baronti, S., Alparone, L.: Remote sensing image fusion using the curvelet transform. Inf. Fusion **8**(2), 143–156 (2007). http://dx.doi.org/10.1016/j.inffus.2006.02.001
20. Yang, L., Guo, B.L., Ni, W.: Multimodality medical image fusion based on multi-scale geometric analysis of contourlet transform. Neurocomput. **72**(1–3), 203–211 (2008). http://dx.doi.org/10.1016/j.neucom.2008.02.025
21. Qu, X.-B., Xie, G.-F., Yan, J.-W., Zhu, Z.-Q., Chen, B.-G.: Image fusion algorithm based on neighbors and cousins information in nonsubsampled contourlet transform domain. In: International Conference on Wavelet Analysis and Pattern Recognition, ICWAPR 2007, vol. 4, pp. 1797–1802 (2007)
22. Singh, R., Khare, A.: Multimodal medical image fusion using daubechies complex wavelet transform. In: 2013 IEEE Conference on Information Communication Technologies (ICT), vol. 1, pp. 869–873 (2013)
23. Shahid, M., Gupta, S.: Image merging based on perceptual information. In: Singh, S., Singh, M., Apte, C., Perner, P. (eds.) ICAPR 2005. LNCS, vol. 3687, pp. 683–692. Springer, Heidelberg (2005)
24. Peters, J.F.: Near sets. special theory about nearness of objects. Fundam. Inf. **75**(1–4), 407–433 (2007). http://dl.acm.org/citation.cfm?id=1232299.1232323
25. Li, T., Wang, Y.: Multiscaled combination of mr and spect images in neuroimaging: a simplex method based variable-weight fusion. Comput. Methods Prog. Biomed. **105**(1), 31–39 (2012). http://dx.doi.org/10.1016/j.cmpb.2010.07.012
26. Bhatnagar, G., Wu, Q., Liu, Z.: Directive contrast based multimodal medical image fusion in nsct domain. IEEE Trans. Multimedia **15**(5), 1014–1024 (2013)

27. Khare, A., Tiwary, U.S., Pedrycz, W., Jeon, M.: Multilevel adaptive thresholding and shrinkage technique for denoising using daubechies complex wavelet transform. Imaging Sci. J. **58**(6), 340–358 (2010). 2010–12-01T00:00:00. http://www.ingentaconnect.com/content/maney/isj/2010/00000058/00000006/art00005
28. Lina, J.M., Mayrand, M.: Complexdaubechies wavelets. Appl. Comput. Harmonic Anal. **2**, 219–229 (1995)
29. Zhang, X.P., Desai, M.D., Peng, Y.N.: Orthogonal complex filter banks and wavelets:some properties and design. IEEE Trans. Sig. Proc. **47**(4), 1039–1048 (1999)
30. Dubois, D., Pradei, H.: Fuzzy Sets and Systems: Theory and applications. Academic Press, New York (1980)
31. Morvick, P.L.S.J., Shaw, J.: A fast, non-iterative and exact histogram matching algorithm. Pattern Recogn. Lett. **23**, 127–135 (2002)
32. Goshtas, A.A.: 2-D and 3-D Image Registration. Willey, Hoboken (2005)
33. Wang, L., Li, B., fang Tian, L.: Multi-modal medical image fusion using the inter-scale and intra-scale dependencies between image shift-invariant shearlet coefficients. Inf. Fusion **19**, 20–28 (2014). http://www.sciencedirect.com/science/article/pii/S1566253512000346
34. Medical image database. http://www.med.harvard.edu.aanlib
35. Daneshvar, S., Ghassemian, H.: Mri and pet image fusion by combining ihs and retina-inspired models. Inf. Fusion **11**(2), 114–123 (2010). http://dx.doi.org/10.1016/j.inffus.2009.05.003

Optimization and Networks

A Hybrid Method for Context-Based Gait Recognition Based on Behavioral and Social Traits

Shermin Bazazian[✉] and Marina Gavrilova

Computer Science Department, University of Calgary, Calgary, Canada
`sbazazia@ucalgary.ca, marina@cpsc.ucalgary.ca`

Abstract. With the increasing demand for automatic security systems capable of recognizing people from a far distance and with as little cooperation as possible, gait as a behavioral biometric has recently gained a lot of attention. It is a remotely observable and unobtrusive biometric. However, the complexity and the high variability of gait patterns limit the power of gait recognition algorithms and adversely affect their recognition rates in real applications. With the goal to improve the performance of gait recognition systems without investing into costly and complex algorithms, we introduce a novel multimodal gait recognition system that combines the gait behavioral patterns of the subjects with the social patterns of their activities. For this purpose, a standard gait recognition system is implemented. A novel context matcher module is added to the system that provides a framework for modeling, learning, extracting and matching the contextual behavioral patterns. The learning of gait and behavioral patterns and clustering of results is performed. This allows grouping the subjects into similar profiles for faster recognition and enrollment. The results from two modules: context matcher and gait recognition are fused in the multi-modal decision making. The experiments on HumanID Challenge dataset are performed to validate that recognition rate improves using the combination of video context and gait recognition method even in the presence of low quality data.

Keywords: Context-based model · Biometric security system · Gait recognition · Social profiles · Behavioral patterns

1 Introduction

Recently, there has been a surge in new developments in the area of context-aware computing systems [1]. In general, such systems are concerned with the acquisition of context from the environment, context processing and understanding, and subsequent application of obtained knowledge in decision-making systems. However, the application of context in biometric security systems has been scarce up to date. In this paper, we fill the niche by proposing a context-based gait biometric recognition system.

Gait analysis deals with analyzing the patterns of walking movement. Although gait analysis is most well-known for its application in access control, surveillance and activity monitoring, it can also be used in sports training and medical applications. The popularity of gait recognition in the field of biometrics is attributed to a couple of unique properties. This trait is unobtrusive and the attention or cooperation of the subject is not needed for collecting the data [1]. Furthermore, gait is remotely observable and, in fact, it is the most remotely observable biometric [1]. These properties make the data collection process of gait recognition more convenient compared to other biometrics. In addition to data collection convenience, imitating the walking style of another person is very difficult [1]. It is also not easy to conceal the way one walks [2]. These properties make gait forgery more tricky, which is an important advantage for security applications. Finally, gait recognition techniques usually do not need high resolution video sequences [4] and since they usually work based on binary silhouettes they are not extremely sensitive to illumination changes and they can be used at nights using infrared imagery [4]. Despite all these interesting properties, gait recognition suffers from some limitations and challenges. Since age, mood, illness, fatigue, drug or alcohol consumption, etc. can affect the walking style of a person, the gait patterns are not always reproducible [2]. Similarly, person's walking style might change by wearing a different kind of shoes, walking upon a different surface, etc. [5]. In summary, the main drawback of using gait for individual identification is its wide variability per subject.

The wide variability creates difficulty for extracting features that are robust enough to handle all the possible scenarios and are distinctive enough to distinguish the subject in a large population. Furthermore, even if such distinctive features exist, any factor that can change the appearance of the person like wearing a hat, carrying a suitcase, loose clothing, etc. can adversely affect the performance of gait recognition by obscuring the distinctive gait features [2]. This problem becomes more critical in the condition of low quality samples that is the case in a lot of security applications. Due to these limitations, it might not be possible to achieve high recognition rates using only the gait patterns. This paper overcomes the above problems by taking an alternative route. Instead of increasing gait recognition algorithm's complexity which might still not be good enough in case of poor quality samples, we propose an original way for improving the performance of the gait recognition systems through incorporating more knowledge about the subjects in the system and building a multimodal gait recognition system. Biometric area has just witnessed the incredible popularity of multi-modal systems being developed for increased person recognition rates. These systems consistently show advantages over single module (or traditional) biometric systems in both their recognition rates (as high as 99% for certain data samples), versatility and circumvention [6–8]. However, those systems usually consider biometric traits of the same class (i.e. face and fingerprint) or sometimes physiological and behavioral traits (i.e. fingerprint and signature). The novelty of our approach is that, for the first time to the best of our knowledge, we incorporate metadata based on social context into the standard gait recognition system.

The main purpose of this paper is to investigate the impact of using supplementary metadata about people's social life on the performance of gait recognition systems. At the preprocessing stage, image sequences of the probe are analyzed to extract metadata about context in which the gait samples were obtained. Afterwards, the extracted contexts are matched to behavioral profiles of subjects, identified either real-time or offline. Multimodal biometric information fusion technique is then used to improve the accuracy rate as compared to standard gait recognition methods [9]. Our experimental results demonstrate that incorporating knowledge about behavioral patterns improves the performance of gait recognition and it is even possible to achieve very high recognition having distinctive behavioral patterns. The method is especially effective in case of low quality data or insufficient accuracy of gait recognition algorithm. The main target applications for this work are the controlled environments where users provide information about their daily regulations when registering to the system and are obligated to be consistent with their schedules. In such environments, the proposed system can also be use for risk analysis and abnormal behavior detection. Since the system has information about the users' behavioral patterns, it is able to detect cases where users are violating their behavioral routines and can report such scenarios as suspicious activities.

In the following, Sect. 2 provides a brief overview of current gait recognition systems and their challenges. Section 3, discusses different steps of the used methodology in detail. Section 4, provides more implementation detail and the results of the proposed method. Section 5 concludes the paper by summarizing the proposed approach and its main advantages.

2 Related Work

The source of inspiration for a lot of gait analysis techniques is the work of Johansson in [10] that showed that people can quickly recognize the motion of walking only from the moving patterns of a few point lights attached to the human body. Inspired by Johansson's work, Cutting and Kozlowski in [11] performed some experiments to show that the same array of point lights can be used for recognizing friends even if they happen to have similar height, width and body shapes. Considering the wide variety of potential applications for gait analysis, these studies initiated an advanced research in this field.

There are mainly two approaches for gait recognition: model-based and model-free. The model-based approaches use an explicit model to model the human body. These methods estimate the parameters of the model in each frame. The value of these parameters and how they change over time is used for gait representation [3]. The model-based methods are generally computationally expensive and time consuming but they can to some degree handle view/scale changes, appearance changes and occlusions [12]. Model-free approaches, on the other hand, do not use a priori body model. Instead, they make a compact representation of walking motion by considering the silhouette as a whole [3]. These methods are simple, cheap and fast but having no knowledge about the human body and working only based on the shape of the silhouettes, they are more sensitive to appearance changes, view/scale changes, occlusions and every other factor that can change the shape of the silhouette [3]. Knowing both advantages and disadvantages of model-free and model-based approaches, the fact that model-free methods are cheap, fast and easy to understand has made them more popular and in fact most of gait recognition algorithms fall in this category. One of the most popular model-free approaches is the Gait Energy Image (GEI) introduced by Han and Bhanu [14]. GEI is one single image obtained by finding the average of all silhouette images for one single gait cycle. GEI is an efficient and compact representation of gait, despite of its simplicity it shows promising results and it also reduces the noise by averaging [15]. For all these reasons, we decided to use GEI as our gait feature in the proposed context-based gait recognition system. Although recent advanced gait recognition algorithms show promising results, the wide intraclass variability of gait patterns limited their power and application in real world scenarios. Attempting to solve this problem, recently multimodal gait recognition systems are introduced to improve the recognition rate by combining gait patterns with other sources of information. Multimodal biometric system is a biometric system that uses advanced information fusion technique to combine more than one source of information in the decision making process which normally results in better performance, more population coverage and harder forgery [16, 18]. The majority of existing multimodal gait recognition systems only use gait as their biometric trait but have different algorithms for extracting a variety of gait features that are then combined using information fusion techniques. As an example, Cuntoor et al. in [4] extract multiple gait features, match them separately and then combine the results of different matchers to make the final decision. Ma et al. in [18] introduce a multimodal gait recognition system that combines GEI with other gait features at feature level. F´elez et al. try to make GEI more efficient by finding more than one GEI for each gait cycle. Each GEI is classified separately using a nearest neighbor classifier and the final person identification is done by majority voting of the decisions of different classifiers. Although these systems achieve better performance by incorporating multiple feature extraction algorithms, they still suffer from the intrinsic limitations of the single biometric trait they use. Therefore, to get the most benefits from multimodal gait recognition including better coverage and harder forgery, it is more suitable to combine the gait patterns with other biometric information.

One of the systems developed in this direction is the combination of gait patterns and soft biometrics. The soft biometric characteristics have been very recently introduced as a subset of biometric characteristics representing information like gender, weight, height, ethnicity, age, eye color, etc. Moustakas et al. in [19] combine soft biometric features with gait features. In this work, they used the subject's height and the stride length as their soft biometric features. GEI and Radon transforms are used as geometric gait features. These features are combined using a probabilistic approach [19]. This system needs extra information for calculating the values of the soft biometrics. The datasets used in this work are captured with stereoscopic cameras so that the system can obtain the height of the subject.

Taking a look at the multimodal gait recognition systems that use more than one biometric trait, it seems that gait has most commonly been combined with face. Hossain and Chetty combine gait and face features in one feature vector and use Bayesian classifier for classifying the concatenated feature vectors [19]. Bhanu and Han in [20] use GEI as their gait feature and Enhanced Side Face Image as their face feature. They have two independent classifiers for finding the matching scores for face and gait that are combined using different match score level information fusion rules including sum, product and max [20]. The main problem with combining face and gait is that face is not as remotely observable as gait and it can easily get covered. Therefore, combining these two might reduce the remote observability and obtrusiveness of the system. Furthermore, face recognition algorithms are expensive and adding them to the system might add a lot of computation.

The multimodal gait recognition system that we introduce in this paper combines the gait patterns of the subjects with their behavioral patterns. Modeling and predicting human behavioral patterns is an emerging area of research that mostly has been explored in the domain of market analysis and customer profiling. Almost all major retail companies, travel agencies, car dealerships, and groceries stores have list of customers with very detailed information stored on their shopping preferences. The data is collected first time once person becomes a customer of a store or joins their loyalty program and usually includes name, address, phone numbers, gender, age, and birthday. It however becomes soon extended with specific shopping patterns: day of the week, time of transaction, average amount spent, family/friends affiliations, and goes to such details as predicting changes in marital status, loss of job, having a child, assuming a mortgage, moving to another part of the city etc. All this data is then used to effectively market product or service to a customer [13, 28–30]. With advent of web-based technologies, even more information from social networks becomes available for mining to add to the existing profile. Using social data and behavioral patterns has very recently started being explored in Biometric context [24, 25]. Our proposed system is one of the very first examples of using behavioral and social patterns in a multimodal gait recognition framework that shows the following unique advantages:

- Using context provides rich metadata for increased biometric recognition rate.
- The system is using more than one single biometric trait. Thus it shows better performance, it has more coverage and it is harder to fool.
- Matching the behavioral patterns with the context of the gait video does not add a lot of computations to the system.
- Extracting the context of the video does not need any special device and can be directly extracted from the gait sequence manually or using image processing techniques.
- Behavioral pattern matching does not need high quality data, does not need the subject to be close to the camera and does not need his/her cooperation. Therefore, involving context does not reduce the remote observability and unobtrusiveness of the overall multimodal gait recognition system while increasing recognition rate.

The methodology of the proposed context-based gait recognition system is described in details in the following section.

3 Methodology

In this paper we introduce a novel context-based multimodal gait recognition system that takes advantage of the behavioral habits and daily routines of the subjects. This results in a more accurate decision in comparison with applying the gait recognition algorithm alone. The block diagram of the proposed system is shown in Fig. 1.

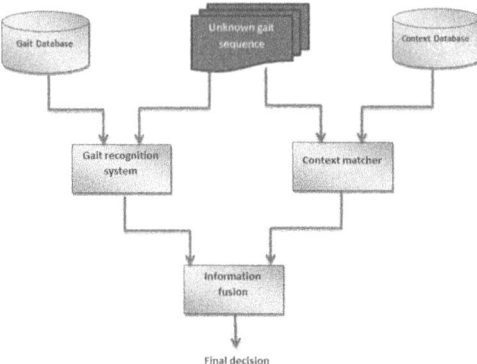

Fig. 1. Block diagram of the proposed multimodal gait recognition system

According to Fig. 1, the information about the subjects is represented via two main databases: the gait database that stores the gait patterns of the subjects and the context database which is a novel database introduced specifically to accommodate metadata in our gait recognition system and stores the behavioral patterns of the subjects. Having this information, the system is presented with a gait sequence of an unknown subject called the probe and it establishes the identity of this unknown subject using the three following main modules:

1. The gait recognition system: this module is responsible for finding the similarity of the subjects to the probe according to the gait patterns.
2. The context matcher: this original module is responsible for finding how well the context of the probe matches with the behavioral patterns of the subjects.
3. The information fusion: this module combines the output of the gait recognition system and context matcher into one final list and presents it to the user to be used for final identification.

These three main modules are explained in the following subsections.

3.1 Gait Recognition System

Preprocessing. We start by obtaining the binary silhouettes. Having the silhouettes, similar to the method used by Han and Bhanu [14], in each frame we perform the following preprocessing steps:

1. Noise removal: with an attempt to remove the noise we apply dilation and then find the largest connected component of the silhouette image and remove all the rest.
2. Scale normalization: for making the algorithm robust to scale changes we resize the silhouette so that its height is always 128 pixels.
3. Centralization: we find the centroid of the silhouette and we define a bounding box around the silhouette that is exactly 128*50 pixels using the centroid as the center of the bounding box.

At the end of these steps, all the frames will have the exact same size, they contain only the centralized silhouettes and a lot of extra background pixels have been removed.

For extracting the gait cycle, in each frame we count the number of pixels in the lower half of the silhouettes (leg region) to obtain a curve and then we find the local minima of this curve to find the beginning and ending frames of the cycles. We also compute the gait cycle as the average of distances between minima, skipping every other minimum.

Feature Extraction and Recognition. As mentioned in Sect. 2, GEI has been used as the gait signature in this paper. Gait Energy Image (GEI) is the average of all the binary silhouettes of a gait cycle and can be obtained using the following formula.

$$GEI = \frac{1}{C} \sum_{i=1}^{C} B_i \qquad (1)$$

C in Eq. (1) is the number of frames in a gait cycle and B_i is the ith normalized binary silhouette. Since all the normalized binary silhouettes are of size 128*50, the resulting GEI is also a 128*50 image. To make the method robust to the moving direction (left or right), we propose to use the centroid movement direction to flip the GEI when necessary.

For the final recognition, we find the Euclidean distance of the probe's GEI from all the GEI templates in the gait database to provide the user with a rank list of top N most similar subjects. We set N = 5 for the purpose of this paper.

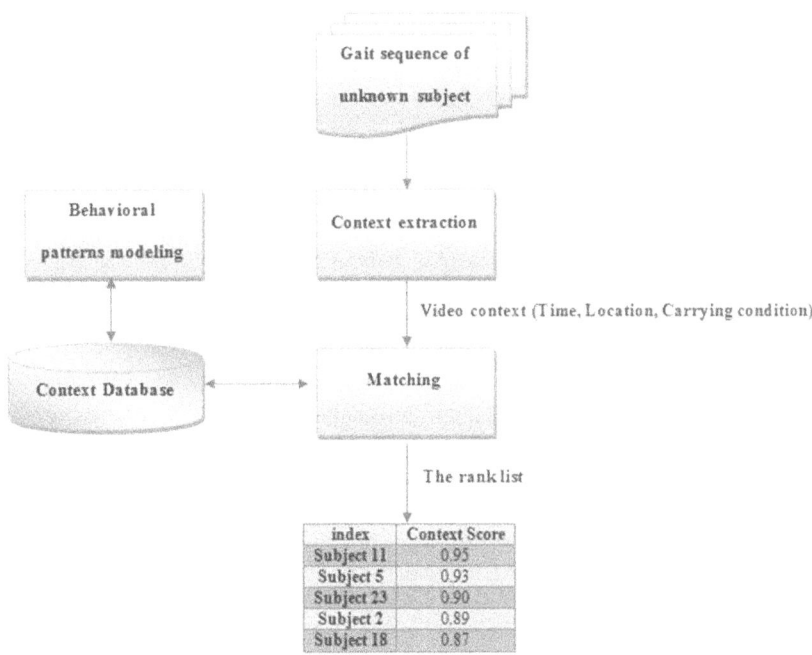

Fig. 2. The flow chart of the context matcher

3.2 The Context Matcher

In the same way that the gait recognition system is responsible for matching the gait patterns, the context matcher is responsible for matching the context of the probe with the behavioral patterns of the subjects. To the best of our knowledge, there are no similar systems developed for gait recognition with context matching and behavioral pattern analysis. The framework of our context matcher is shown in Fig. 2. One of the main modules of the context matcher is the behavioral patterns module which is responsible for modeling the behavioral patterns of the subjects and storing the resulting patterns in the context database. Having the context database, the context extraction module extracts the context of the probe and then the matching module matches how compatible the extracted context is with the behavioral patterns of the subjects stored in the context database and outputs a rank list of the subjects with their corresponding matching scores. The following subsections are dedicated to describing these main functionalities of the context matcher.

Behavioral Patterns Module. The main purpose of the behavioral patterns module is to provide a framework for defining and storing the behavioral patterns of the subjects. For this purpose, first a formal definition of a behavioral pattern should be established. Afterwards, a methodology for modeling the behavioral patterns of the subjects should be defined. Finally, the behavioral patterns should be stored in the context database to be used later by the context matcher. These steps are described in the following.

Behavioral Pattern Definition. The first step of modeling the behavioral patterns is to define what information do we want to capture by these patterns and which parameters do we want to use for representing this information. To make sure the method is computationally efficient and feasible to implement, mainly three issues should be considered in defining the behavioral patterns. First, the parameters that are used for modeling the behavioral patterns should be defined in a way that their values are extractable later from the gait sequence in an efficient way. Second, it is assumed that the subjects should be predictable according to the parameters, i.e. not deviate significantly from the expected behavior This has been supported by the recent psychological studies that normally people follow routine during their everyday activities [26]. Third, the behavioral patterns should be defined so that they can be stored, extracted and matched in an efficient manner both time-wise and space-wise. Considering the three mentioned factors, we decided to define the behavioral patterns of a subject in the following way: "at what time of the day, in which locations and in what conditions subject can usually be observed by the system". Consequently, for representing the behavioral patterns we use three parameters: time, location and carrying condition. To store the behavioral patterns of the subjects in an effective way and also to have an efficient matching mechanism, we decided to make all the parameters discrete. For some other applications and systems, there could be additional/other parameters defined. They are very easy to incorporate in the present system.

Behavioral Patterns Modeling. Having a formal definition for a behavioral pattern, the next step of creating a context database is to model the behavioral patterns of the subjects. The behavioral patters can be inputted in the system during user registration, as a series of answers on a given questionnaire. They can also be assigned according to the subject job description, social status or known everyday activities. Finally, they can be extracted from actual videos through semi-automated learning system. However, this approach is more time consuming and resource intensive than the first two.

To experiment with the above models, we have devised three approaches for modeling the behavioral patterns.

1. Random models

In this approach, as the simplest and most generic solution, a random model is used which assumes that there is no predefined distribution for the context parameter values and any parameter value for any subject is equally probable. This approach can easily be implemented in real applications by asking the users to fill in questionnaires during registration. Since the parameters of behavioral patterns are well defined and they only take discrete values, the questionnaires can simply be designed accordingly.

2. Behavioral profiles

In this approach, instead of modeling the behavioral patterns of each subject individually that can be quite time consuming, we define some groups of users based on the similarities in their behavior. Such similarities can be dictated by similar profession of the subject, similar environment in which behavior is observed, similar place where behavior is observed, etc. Then we place subjects with similar behavioral patterns in the same group. We model the behavioral patterns of the whole group all together and we call the resulting behavioral patterns the behavioral profiles.

This approach can also be easily implemented in real scenarios. The profiles of each environment correspond to working groups in that environment. The users can be assigned to their corresponding profile based on their job title.

3. Gaussian models

As an attempt to reduce the overlap in subjects' behavioral patterns, we researched into using Gaussian distribution for the distribution of each parameter. We discovered that Gaussian distributions have been commonly used in modeling and simulating real world processes and more precisely human behaviors [21–23]. Based on these observations, we propose to use Gaussian modeling as an alternative approach to the random modeling approach. In this approach the distribution of each parameter for each subject is assumed to be a Gaussian distribution.

The above three methods are generic methods that can be used for creating the behavioural models for any set of individuals. For each specific application, the most suitable method that is consistent with the behavioral patterns of that application should be applied.

Behavioral Patterns Learning. In real scenarios, there can be cases that there is no information available about the behavioral patterns of the users; for example the users do not officially register to the system or the environment is not fully known. For such cases, the system should still be able to learn the behavioral patterns of the subjects using their gait video samples. This is very important advantage of the system because it makes the system fully unobtrusive and capable of recognizing completely unknown subjects without their cooperation. Two following learning approaches have been proposed in this paper to enable the system to learn the behavioral patterns of the subjects from the context of gait samples.

1. Random behavioral patterns learning

In this approach, similar to random modeling, the behavioral patterns of each subject do not follow any particular distribution. However, since there is no information available about the behavioral habits of the subjects, this information is extracted from the context of gait samples. The proposed learning procedure for is to extract the value of the context parameters for all the training samples of each subject and tag the samples with the resulting context parameters. Having the tags, a parameter value is acceptable for a subject if the subject has a sample tagged with that parameter value.

2. Behavioral profiles learning

The purpose of this approach is to learn the behavioral profiles for each environment based on the available gait samples for the subjects.

The proposed learning approach is consisted of the following main steps:

- Learn the behavioral patterns of each subject using the approach described for random behavioral patterns learning. Since all the parameter values are discrete, the result of this step determines which parameter values are acceptable for each subject.
- Cluster the resulting behavioral profiles using k-means clustering algorithm.
- Extract the behavioral profiles from the output of the clustering algorithm. The corresponding profile for each subject is the cluster index for that subject. The behavioral patterns for each profile are the behavioral patterns of the resulting cluster centers.

Context Extraction. The context extraction module is responsible for extracting the context of the probe to be matched later with the behavioral patterns stored in the context database. Since this process requires advanced image processing techniques, it is beyond the scope of this paper. Therefore, in this work, it is assumed that the probe video has already been tagged with the context data.

Matching the Context. The final step of our context matcher is to match the context of the probe with the behavioral patterns of the subjects stored in the context database and generate a matching score for each subject accordingly.

In this section, we develop a method to assign context score to each subject by comparing the context of the probe video with the behavioral patterns of that subject. As a part of our context database, for each subject we have a list for each parameter that demonstrates which parameter values are acceptable. Having these lists for each subject and for each context parameter, we assign a score of one to the subject and that parameter if there is a match between the context of the probe and the subject's context for that parameter; otherwise the score is set to zero. A match corresponds to the case that the value of the parameter in the probe video is listed as one of the possible parameter values for the subject in the context database. After this calculation, for each subject we will have one separate score for each of the parameters. After obtaining the score for all the parameters, we add all the parameter scores together to obtain a single context score for each subject.

3.3 Information Fusion

The main purpose of information fusion block in our multimodal biometric system is to combine our two sources of information (gait patterns and behavioral patterns) and make the final decision. The information fusion technique used for this purpose is match score level information fusion. In this approach, each source of information has its own matcher which outputs a matching score for each subject [7]. In our proposed system, the gait recognition system is responsible for calculating gait scores. The gait score for each subject is the similarity of the candidate's gait feature (GEI) to that of the probe. Similarly, the context matcher is responsible for generating the context scores. The context score for each subject shows how well the context of the probe matches with the behavioral patterns for that subject. Having the gait scores and context scores, the information fusion block uses two following steps for finding the final scores:

1. Normalization: since the matching scores for two modalities can have different ranges and distributions, it is essential that we normalize them into a common domain before combining them. In this process, we find the minimum and maximum of the gait scores of all the subjects (min_{Gait} and max_{Gait} correspondingly) and normalize the gait score of subject "s" ($Gait\_score_s$) using the following equation.

$$Gait\_score\_normalized_s = \frac{Gait\_score_s - min_{Gait}}{max_{Gait} - min_{Gait}} \quad (2)$$

A similar procedure is applied on the context scores according to Eq. (3).

$$Context\_score\_normalized_s = \frac{Context\_score_s - min_{Context}}{max_{Context} - min_{Context}} \quad (3)$$

In Eq. (3), $min_{Context}$ and $max_{Context}$ are the minimum and maximum of the context scores of all the subjects correspondingly. In the same way, $Context\_score_s$ and $Context\_score\_normalized_s$ are the context score and the normalized context score of subject "s" accordingly.

2. Weighted combination: in this step we calculate the final score of each subject as the weighted combination of the normalized gait score and the normalized context score with the weights being the confidence of each database. The confidence of the context database shows how predictable the subjects are in their behavioral patterns or in other words, how reliable the behavioral patterns in the context database are. The confidence value of the gait database shows how well the gait recognition system works in identifying the subjects. The values of the confidence values can be determined by the system admin. If the quality of the gait samples is not acceptable and if for any other reasons the gait recognition system does not show good performance for a specific application, setting the confidence of the gait database to a small value can improve the performance and reliability of the system by putting more weight

on the behavioral patterns. In the same way, if the environment and its subjects are not predictable in their social behavior, the importance of the context data can be reduced by setting the confidence value of the gait database to a small number.

After calculating the final scores, the subjects are sorted based on their final scores and the user is presented with a rank list of top N subjects.

4 Results

The goal of this section is to validate the proposed methodology on examples of real publicly available video databases containing gait sequences. The questions we want to get answers on are: How the recognition rate of the system is affected after including the context data and how much performance gain can we obtain by fusing the context? How much overhead is associated with fusing the context data? How does the idea of learning the behavioral patterns work in practice with real data and how much improvement can we gain with this approach? We try to answer these questions through various experimental settings and conclude that the proposed method indeed offers benefits of increased recognition rate under less than ideal input data conditions with a very low overhead. The following subsections present the conducted experiments and the obtained results.

4.1 Experimental Data

The context-based gait recognition system uses two main databases: the gait database and the context database. The gait database is the database of the gait signatures of the system users. Similarly, the context database is the database of behavioral patterns of the system users. The HumanID Gait Challenge Dataset introduced by Sarkar et al. in [24] has been used as the gait database for evaluating the system. This dataset contains gait sequences for 122 subjects. Five covariates were taken into account: surface type, shoe type, carrying condition, viewpoint and time. This dataset is available online and can be downloaded from http://figment.csee.usf.edu/GaitBaseline/. The dataset is partitioned into a training set and 12 probe sets with different difficulties. More information about the twelve probe sets is provided in Table 1. The size of each probe set is the number of samples in the probe set and the factor shows in which factors the probe set is different from the training set.

Table 1. The twelve probe sets of the Human ID Gait Challenge dataset V: Viewing angle, Sh: Shoe, S: Surface, B: Briefcase, T: Time.

Probe	A	B	C	D	E	F	G	H	I	J	K	L
Size	122	54	54	121	60	121	60	120	60	120	33	33
Factor	V	Sh	V/Sh	S	S/Sh	S/V	S/V/Sh	B	B/S	B/V	T/Sh	T/S

Two approaches have been considered for creating the context database. First, the common approach in biometric community for creating virtual databases is used to create the context database virtually. In the second set of experiments, the context database is extracted from real data. These two approaches for creating context databases are described in the following.

Creating Virtual Context. The main step in creating a context database is to model the behavioral patterns of the subjects. For evaluating the performance of the three proposed methods of modeling the behavioral patterns (Random models, Behavioral Profiles and Gaussian models), a variety of virtual context databases have been created using each of these methods as discussed below.

1. Random models: In this approach, it is assumed that there is no limitation or condition for the values the parameters can take for each subject. Thus, for creating the behavioral patterns of each subject, a subset of possible parameter values is randomly assigned to that subject.
2. Behavioral profiles: In this approach, a user profile is generated which corresponds to similar behavioral patterns of users. We have chosen the university as our environment, and three profiles have been created: student, professor and staff. For each of these profiles, the behavioral patterns have been created. Having the profiles, each subject is randomly assigned a profile in our virtual database.
3. Gaussian models: In this approach, the distribution of each parameter for each subject is assumed to be a Gaussian distribution. The parameters of the Gaussian distributions (mean and variance) for each subject and each parameter are generated randomly. Having the mean and variance, the next step is to assign parameter values to the subject by drawing samples from the obtained Gaussian distribution.

Creating a Real Context Database Through Behavioral Patterns Learning. In this approach, we learn the behavioral patterns of the subjects and create a real context database from the HumanID challenge dataset. The five covariates of this dataset (viewpoint, shoe type, surface type, time and carrying condition) all represent contextual information and can be extracted from the gait video. Furthermore, for each of these covariates two values have been considered in this dataset. This implies that all the covariates have discrete values. Therefore, we can directly map the five covariates to context parameters. The gait sequences of this dataset are all labeled with the corresponding values for each of the five covariates. Thus, we can extract the value for each context parameter of a gait video by parsing its label. Therefore, we can tag all the gait sequence with the context data. Having the tagged silhouettes, we use the two approaches (Random behavioral patterns learning and Behavioral profiles learning) discussed in methodology section to learn the context database.

4.2 Performance Evaluation

For the experiments with virtual context database, the predefined sets of HumanID challenge database (introduced in Table 1) have been used as training and testing sets.

However, for real context database, two fold cross validation have been used for evaluating the performance of the system. The reason is that the standard training set for HumanID dataset contains only one sample for each subject which does not provide enough information for leaning the behavioral patterns. The performance of the system is reported using Rank k performance measures. Rank k performance represents the percentage of the times that the correct subject appeared as the first k subjects of the rank list.

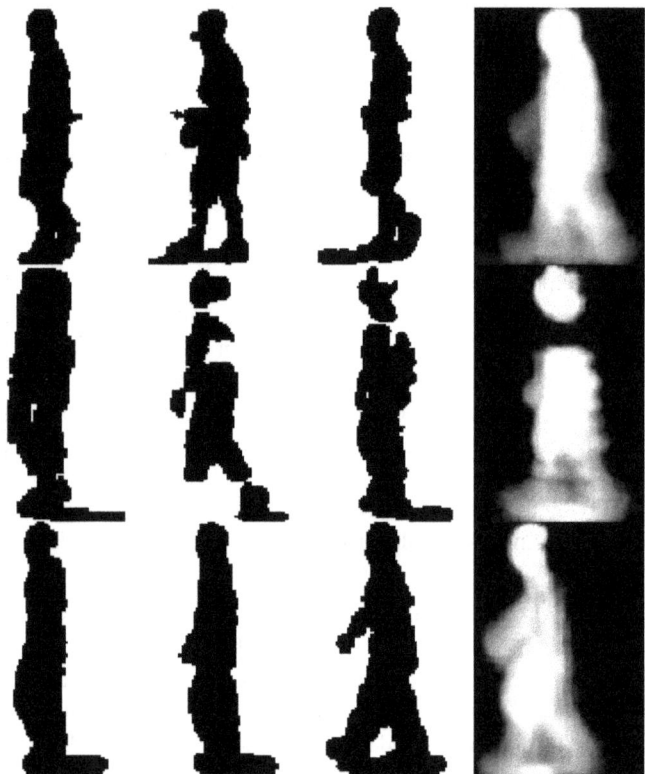

Fig. 3. The binary silhouettes and the resulting GEIs for 3 subjects of HumanID gait dataset.

4.3 Experiments

The binary silhouettes and the corresponding calculated GEIs for three subjects of the HumanID gait dataset is shown in Fig. 3. As can be seen, all the silhouettes have shadows. The silhouette of the second subject is disconnected and some parts of the human body are missing. As a result, the obtained GEI is also disconnected and not of satisfactory quality. In the last row, the subject is carrying a suitcase which resulted in a little bump appearing at the bottom of the silhouette. The drawback of having these troublesome cases is more noticeable in Fig. 4 which is showing different GEIs of the same subjects. Looking at the GEIs of the first and second subjects, we can see that the similarity between the GEIs of the two subjects in some cases is more than the similarity of the GEIs of the same subject. This is the result of recording the walking movement of each individual under different conditions and at different times. This wide variability is a source of trouble for the gait recognition module which works based on finding the similarities of GEIs.

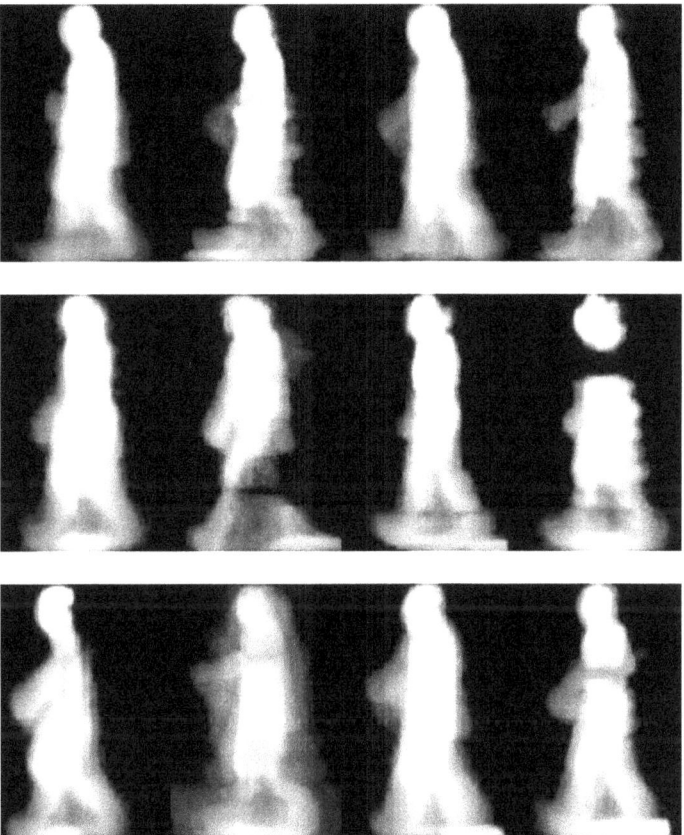

Fig. 4. Examples of the Gait Energy Images for three subjects of HumanID gait dataset. Each row: the Gait Energy Images for four different gait samples of the same subject.

Having seen these examples, it can be concluded that GEI alone does not seem to be powerful enough for reliable identification of the subjects, particularly if the gait samples are of low quality and are recorded under varying conditions. Therefore, there is a need to augment the GEIs with other sources of information to have a more accurate identification. The results of the rest of conducted experiments confirm this conclusion.

Table 2 presents the performance of the proposed context-based gait recognition system in identifying subjects from the twelve probe sets of HumanID gait dataset with and without involving the virtual context databases created using the three methods of modeling the behavioral patterns. According to this table, integrating context data always improves the recognition rate. Comparing different approaches for behavioral modeling, the Gaussian modeling is showing the best performance. Random behavioral modeling is the next best method and the behavioral profiling is the last one. In the Gaussian modeling of the behavioral patterns, the behavioral patterns of each individual follow unimodal narrow distributions; whereas in the random modeling and behavioral profiles, the distribution of the parameter values is completely random. As a result, the Gaussian modeling makes behavioral patterns more distinctive and there is less chance of having overlaps between the behavioral patterns of different subjects. Consequently, involving this information increases the discriminative power of the system which justifies why the system shows its best performance for this case. The reason behavioral profiles are falling behind is that the dataset has 122 subjects. Therefore, using only three behavioral profiles for this population might not provide a powerful mechanism for distinguishing the subjects. As a result, it can be concluded that it is a good idea to avoid using very general profiles. In fact, the number of profiles defined for each application should be based on the number of subjects and the variability of their behavioral patterns.

Table 2. The performance of the system in identifying subjects from the HumanID Challenge Gait dataset using virtual context database (NC = No Context, RC = Random Context, GC = Gaussian Context, PC = Profiles Context)

Probe set	Rank 1 performance				Rank 5 performance			
	NC	RC	GC	PC	NC	RC	GC	PC
A	47%	77%	82%	59%	76%	97%	98%	84%
B	80%	85%	91%	85%	89%	98%	98%	93%
C	44%	65%	67%	57%	65%	87%	94%	70%
D	17%	45%	46%	21%	32%	79%	87%	45%
E	16%	40%	40%	17%	36%	79%	93%	45%
F	3%	22%	34%	8%	17%	62%	77%	30%
G	9%	29%	36%	9%	17%	69%	78%	34%
H	46%	74%	74%	52%	69%	91%	97%	79%
I	41%	74%	69%	52%	67%	93%	95%	76%
J	21%	56%	59%	34%	53%	90%	92%	65%
K	93%	93%	93%	93%	93%	100%	100%	93%
L	11%	32%	47%	11%	32%	63%	89%	32%

Table 3 compares the performance of the proposed system on HumanID dataset and Gaussian virtual context database with three similar works in the same area. According to this table, the proposed context-based gait recognition system performs better than all other approaches based on Rank 5 performance for all the twelve probe sets. The proposed method also outperforms the baseline algorithm in Rank 1 performance on all the probe sets. However, the multimodal gait recognition system of Han and Bahnu [14] performs better than our system according to Rank 1 for a few of probe sets (A, C, D and E). Similarly, the work of Ma et al. in [18] achieves better Rank 1 performance for only probe sets A and C. For all other probe sets, the performance of the proposed context-based gait recognition is equal to or better than the other methods.

Table 3. Comparing the performance of the proposed system on HumanID challenge dataset and virtual Gaussian context database with similar gait recognition systems

Probe set	Rank 1				Rank 5			
	Baseline [24]	GEI [13]	GMI [17]	Our method	Baseline [24]	GEI [13]	GMI [17]	Our method
A	73%	**90%**	84%	82%	88%	94%	92%	**98%**
B	78%	91%	91%	**91%**	93%	94%	94%	**98%**
C	48%	**81%**	70%	67%	78%	93%	91%	**94%**
D	32%	**56%**	26%	46%	66%	78%	55%	**87%**
E	22%	**64%**	29%	40%	55%	81%	62%	**93%**
F	17%	25%	14%	**34%**	42%	56%	35%	**77%**
G	17%	36%	16%	**36%**	38%	53%	45%	**78%**
H	61%	64%	64%	**74%**	85%	90%	84%	**97%**
I	57%	60%	64%	**69%**	78%	83%	76%	**95%**
J	36%	60%	42%	**59%**	62%	82%	76%	**92%**
K	3%	6%	9%	**93%**	12%	27%	12%	**100%**
L	3%	15%	6%	**47%**	15%	21%	24%	**89%**

From the above table, it can be concluded that the most benefit of using context-based gait recognition is for the case that the gait recognition performance is very low. As can be seen in the table, the performance of the proposed context-based gait recognition system for these cases is a lot better than the other methods. The reason is that all the other methods are only using the gait features, however, our proposed system have extra information about the subjects in terms of their behavioral patterns that can help the system when the gait patterns are not distinctive or of low quality. This is one of the main advantages of using more than one biometric characteristic (gait patterns and behavioral patterns) in our multimodal gait recognition system. Since the gait recognition algorithm used in the proposed system is extremely simple, the overall system is really fast. However, using more complicated gait feature extraction algorithms in the proposed system might slightly improve the performance. In fact, the simplicity of the used gait matching mechanism can be the reason that two of the methods are performing slightly better than ours in the first few probe sets (Table 3). Based on this observation, to make the system faster, context can be applied as an advanced filter. If the performance of gait recognition algorithm is higher than a threshold, the system can proceed without involving context. However, if the system performance is less than a threshold, the context data can be integrated to improve the performance.

Table 4 presents the performance of the context based gait recognition with real context database obtained by learning approaches. This table compares the three following cases: having no context database, using context database learnt by random behavioral learning and using context database learnt by behavioral profiles learning.

Table 4. The performance of the system for the HumanID Challenge Gait dataset using real context information and two learning approaches (NC = No Context, RL: Random Behavioral Learning, PL: Behavioral Profiles Learning)

Rank 1			Rank 2			Rank 5		
NC	RL	PL	NC	RL	PL	NC	RL	PL
29%	32%	32%	36%	41%	41%	51%	56%	56%

As can be seen, involving the context data, when the behavioral patterns are obtained by learning, improves the performance of gait recognition. The amount of improvement is around 3 % to 5 %. It is not as noticeable as in the experiments with virtual context data mainly for two reasons. First, since the majority of the subjects have been recorded under only two possible values for each of the five covariates, the behavioral patterns of the subjects are very similar to each other. This reduces the discriminative power of the behavioral patterns. Second, because we are using the real data, we have no control over the testing set and there is a possibility that the context tags for a subject in the testing set do not follow the behavioral patterns learnt for that subject from the training set. To backup this argument, we took the subset of HumanID Challenge Gait dataset with more distinctive real behaviors of subjects. We ran the same experiment on the generated subset and measured the performance. The results of this experiment are presented in Table 5. As can be seen, more improvement is achieved for this case and the Rank 2 and Rank 5 performance measures are both increased by 10 %.

Table 5. The performance of the system for a subset of the HumanID Challenge Gait dataset using real context information and two learning approaches (NC = No Context, RL: Random behavioral learning, PL: behavioral profiles learning)

Rank 1			Rank 2			Rank 5		
NC	RL	PL	NC	RL	PL	NC	RL	PL
40%	45%	43	45%	55%	51%	59%	69%	64%

5 Conclusions and Future Work

Gait recognition has recently become a very attractive area of research in the field of biometrics. However due to the complexity of the problem and the wide variability of gait patterns, despite of the extensive research dedicated to this field in the past few decades, still most of the proposed systems work under very constrained conditions. The model based approaches are expensive, time consuming and sensitive to noise. On the other hand, the model-free approaches, although simple and fast, are not able to handle the unpredictable situations that can happen in real world scenarios. As an alternative route, we proposed to improve the performance of gait recognition by fusing behavioral models and we introduced a novel, fast and accurate multimodal gait recognition method based on information fusion and behavioral modeling.

Performance evaluation of the implemented system indicates that combining the gait method with social patterns always improves the performance of the system. The amount of improvement depends on the distinctiveness of the behavioral patterns and the original gait recognition rate. As a part of the experiments, it's been shown that the behavioral patterns of the subjects can successfully be learnt from the gait sequences and fusing the resulting behavioral patterns with gait recognition will result in more accurate identification. This is an important property of the proposed system that makes the system fully unobtrusive by enabling it to learn the behavioral patterns of the subjects without their cooperation.

The idea of involving the behavioral routines of the subjects in their identification is quite new and there is a lot of room for improvement. One of the most important future areas of research in this direction is to conduct studies for gathering extensive real data (both context data and gait patterns) from a large number of users and under different conditions and scenarios. This data can be used for investigating behavioral modeling methods and finding the optimized methods that can fit the context data and also efficiently be created, stored and matched. Investigating context parameters that can be used in the system is another area of future research.

Acknowledgements. Authors are grateful to NSERC for support of this project.

References

1. Vinh, P.C., Tung, N.T.: Coalgebraic aspects of context-awareness. Mob. Netw. Appl. **18**, 391–397 (2012). Springer
2. Wang, C.-H.: A literature survey on human gait recognition techniques. Directed Studies EE8601, Ryerson University, Toronto, Ontario, Canada (2005)
3. Liu, J., Zheng, N.: Gait history image: a novel temporal template for gait recognition. In: 2007 IEEE International Conference on Multimedia and Expo, Beijing, China (2007)
4. Wang, J., She, M., Nahavandi, S., Kouzani, A.: A review of vision-based gait recognition methods for human identification. In: 2010 IEEE International Conference on Digital Image Computing: Techniques and Application, Piscataway, NJ (2010)
5. Cuntoor, N., Kale, A., Chellappa, R.: Combining multiple evidences for gait recognition. In: 2003 International Conference on Multimedia and Expo. IEEE Computer Society, Washington, DC (2003)
6. Bashir, K., Xiang, T., Gong, S.: Gait recognition using gait entropy image. In: 2009 IEEE International Conference on Crime Detection and Prevention, London (2009)
7. Ross, A.A., Nandakumar, K., Jain, A.K.: Handbook of Multibiometrics. Springer, New York (2006)
8. Monwar, M., Gavrilova, M.: A multimodal biometric system using rank level fusion approach. IEEE Trans. Man Syst. Cybern. TMSC Part B Spec. Issue Cogn Inform. Cybern. **39**(5), 867–878 (2009)
9. Gavrilova, M., Ahmadian, K.: Dealing with biometric multi-dimensionality through novel chaotic neural network methodology. Int. J. Inf. Technol. Adv. Trends Biometrics **11**, 18–34 (2011)
10. Bazazian, S., Gavrilova, M.: Context based gait recognition. In: SPIE 8407, Baltimore, Maryland, USA (2012)

11. Joansson, G.: Visual perception of biological motion and a model for its analysis. Percept. Psychophys. **14**(2), 201–211 (1973)
12. Cutting, J., Kozlowsk, L.: Recognizing friends by their walk: gait perception without familiarity cues. Bull. Psychon. Soc. **9**(5), 353–356 (1977)
13. Wang, C., Zhang, J., Pu, J., Yuan, X., Wang, L.: Chrono-gait image: a novel temporal template for gait recognition. In: Daniilidis, K., Maragos, P., Paragios, N. (eds.) ECCV 2010, Part I. LNCS, vol. 6311, pp. 257–270. Springer, Heidelberg (2010)
14. Han, J., Bhanu, B.: Individual recognition using gait energy image. IEEE Trans. Pattern Anal. Mach. Intell. **28**(2), 316–322 (2006)
15. Yang, X., Zhou, Y., Zhang, T., Shu, G., Yang, J.: Gait recognition based on dynamic region analysis. Sig. Process. **88**(9), 2350–2356 (2008)
16. Mane, V., Jadhav, D.: Review of multimodal biometrics: applications, challenges and research areas. Int. J. Biometrics Bioinform. (IJBB) **3**(5), 90–95 (2009)
17. Tian, Y., Wang, Y., Gavrilova, M.L., Ruhe, G.: A formal knowledge representation system for the intelligent knowledge base of a cognitive learning engine. Int. J. Softw. Sci. Comput. Intell. IJSCCI, IGI **394**, 1–17 (2012)
18. Ma, Q., Wang, S., Nie, D., Qiu, J.: Recognizing humans based on gait moment image. In: 8th ACIS International Conference on Software Engineering, Artificial Intelligence, Networking, and Parallel/Distributed. IEEE Computer Society, Washington, DC (2007)
19. Moustakas, K., Tzovaras, D., Stavropoulos, G.: Gait recognition using geometric features and soft biometrics. IEEE Sig. Process. Lett. **17**(4), 367–370 (2010)
20. Hossain, E., Chetty, G.: Person identity verification based on multimodal face-gait fusion. IJCSNS Int. J. Comput. Sci. Netw. Secur. **11**(6), 77–86 (2011)
21. Bhanu, B., Han, J.: Match score level fusion of face and gait at a distance. In: Bhanu, B., Han, J. (eds.) Human Recognition at a Distance in Video, pp. 185–207. Springer, London (2011)
22. Linoff, G., Berry, M.: Data Mining Techniques: For Marketing, Sales, and Customer Support. Wiley, New York (2011)
23. Giudici, P., Figini, S.: Applied Data Mining for Business and Industry. Wiley, Chichester (2009)
24. Greengard, S.: Advertising gets personal. Commun. ACM **55**(8), 18–20 (2012)
25. Gavrilova, M.L., Yampolskiy, R.: Applying biometric principles to avatar recognition. In: Gavrilova, M.L., Tan, C., Sourin, A., Sourina, O. (eds.) Transactions on Computational Science XII. LNCS, vol. 6670, pp. 140–158. Springer, Heidelberg (2011)
26. Wang, Y., Berwick, R.C., Haykin, S., Pedrycz, W., Kinsner, W., Baciu, G., Zhang, D., Bhavsar, V.C., Gavrilova, M.: Cognitive informatics and cognitive computing in year 10 and beyond. Int. J. Cogn. Inform. Nat. Intell. **5**(4), 1–21 (2010)
27. Jiao, Y., Liu, Y., Wang J., Zhu, J.: Impact of habitual behaviors on human dynamics and spreading process In: 5th International ICST Conference on communications and networking, China (2010)
28. Wei, Y., Kalay, Y.: Simulating human behaviour in built environments. In: CAAD Futures, Vienna (2005)
29. Mith, J., Brokaw, J.: Agent-based simulation of human movements during emergency evacuations of facilities. In: Structures Congress, pp. 1–10 (2008)
30. Sarkar, S., Phillips, J., Liu, Z., Isidro, R.V., Patrick, G., Kevin, W.B.: The HumanID gait challenge problem: data sets, performance, and analysis. IEEE Trans. Pattern Anal. Mach. Intell. **27**(2), 162–177 (2005)

Cluster Head Selection Heuristic Using Weight and Rank in WSN

Gunjan Jain[1(✉)], S.R. Biradar[2], and Brijesh Kumar Chaurasia[1]

[1] ITM University Gwalior, Gwalior, India
{jgunjan.18,bkchaurasia.itm}@gmail.com
[2] MITS University, Sikar, India
srbiradar@gmail.com

Abstract. In this paper, clustering issue of sensor network is addressed. These types of network is a large wireless network, consisting of tiny, low cost sensors which senses phenomenal data, such as light, temperature, pressure, sound, etc. The sensors are small hardware devices, which sense using their sensing unit and measure physical conditions of the area being monitored. There are number of applications in which a hierarchical based network is highly demanded and key concept of such network is clustering. We have proposed clustering heuristic on the basis of ranks and weights assignment based protocol. This approach considers not only residual energy but also node's degree and distance of nodes with base station. The node which has higher weight will be chosen as a cluster head. The objective of this approach is to have balance distribution of clusters, enhance lifetime and better efficiency than traditional protocols. The same approach is also applied for multi hop clustering. Results show the efficacy of proposed approach in terms of energy consumption of the sensor nodes and longevity of the network.

Keywords: Sensor · Cluster head · Homogenous · Rank · Clusters

1 Introduction

Wireless sensor network (WSN) consists of sensor nodes with sensing and communication capabilities employed in a wide range of data gathering applications such as military, environmental monitoring and other fields [1]. WSN is composed of a large number of sensor nodes for gathering data and transmitting them to a processing center called base station [2]. The fundamental challenges of WSN have been the low data rate communications and limited lifetime of the sensor nodes. Other main constraints on WSNs, however, are finite and irreplaceable energy supply of sensor nodes. There are several applications in this field which require aggregation of data for their better performance. In such cases, the sensors node of different regions collaborate their information to provide more accurate reports about their local regions [3]. In order to support data aggregation efficiently clustering is performed in which nodes are partitioned into small number of groups according to specific criteria describe in the mechanism [4]. These small groups are called clusters and each cluster has a cluster head (CH) acting as a coordinator, the other nodes of that clusters are called member nodes. The cluster heads may be selected randomly or based on one or more criteria. However, selection of cluster head largely affects WSNs lifetime. CH collects the data from respective cluster's nodes and forwards the aggregated data to Base Station (BS) [5]. Clustering has proven to be an effective approach for organizing the network into a connected hierarchy. The challenges of clustering mechanism in WSN are which parameters to decide the role of sensor node, which sensor node initializes the cluster head selection, does the load is evenly distributed, does the network require single hop transmission or multi hop transmission. The main aim of clustering approaches is to reduce the number of nodes taking part in transmission, useful energy consumption, enhancement of network lifetime and to improve scalability. For balanced distribution, the protocol requires that after particular time interval the role of the cluster head is given to different sensor node and this term is called dynamic clustering.

2 Contributions of the Present Work

The contribution of the proposed work in this paper is rank and weight assignment based protocol for the WSN. Member nodes are assigned with ranks considering three descriptors *i.e.* node's degree, distance of nodes from base station and residual energy and the weight is calculated by summing the ranks. The node which is having highest weight is elected as a cluster head. Rank and weight based assignment is also applied on hierarchal multi hop network. An analysis to the disadvantages of conventional protocols to select the cluster head and comparison of network lifetime has been evaluated. The performance of the proposed clustering mechanism has been evaluated using simulation experiments for single and multi hop communication along with comparison of conventional clustering protocols.

The rest of the paper is organized as follows. In Sect. 3, related work is discussed. The problem formulation is depicted by Sect. 4. The proposed protocol is presented in Sect. 5. The performance results are discussed in Sect. 6 with conclusion of the work in Sect. 7.

3 Related Works

In existing literature, numbers of clustering protocols have been explored in order to obtain the effective energy usage in wireless sensor network. Low Energy Adaptive Clustering Hierarchy (LEACH) is presented in [6] in which the decision is made by choosing a random number between 0 and 1. LEACH is the most basic protocol, based on randomized rotation of the CHs to distribute the energy load among the sensor nodes evenly in the entire network. The dense network of sensor nodes are grouped in to clusters and utilizes randomized rotation of clusters. These local cluster heads act as a router to send information or knowledge to the base station. Other advantage of LEACH includes it incorporates data fusion into routing protocols; amount of information to the base station is reduced; more effective over direct communication in prolonging network lifetime; also the clusters forms grid like area. Reduces communication overhead both for single and multi hop. Although the complexity of LEACH is low, the algorithm is not energy efficient due to irregular distribution of the CHs. There is unreasonable cluster head selection while nodes have different energy; once the energy of the cluster head node depletes all other nodes fails to function; the algorithm does not take in to account location of nodes, residual energy and other information which may lead cluster head node rapidly fail. In order to further improve the performance of LEACH, a number of protocols are proposed to modify the selection criteria of cluster head like LEACH-C [7], LEACH-B [8], HEED [9], EECS [10], EAHC [11] etc. In [9], it works on the basis of cluster head probability which is the function of residual energy and neighbor proximity. The protocol aims to have balanced cluster, works better both for uniform and non-uniform node distribution; required low message overhead but increase in iterations results in complex algorithm. The decrease in residual energy leads to low cluster head probability. HEED outperforms several generic protocols but is deficit in some parameters. Multiple CHs are used for transferring the data to the base station using the concept of multi-hop communication. However, the protocol does not guarantee the optimum number of elected CHs. EECS [10] works by considering the distance of nodes from the base station. The node with the shortest distance is chosen as a cluster head. The EECS protocol is effective in balancing the energy among cluster head but not energy of the whole network. Energy aware hierarchal clustering (EAHC) algorithm [11] reduces message and time complexity in the network and selects the cluster head on the basis of highest residual energy and lowest communication cost. The cluster head selection is made dynamic to balance the load evenly. A shortcoming of EAHC is that it does not consider the issue of minimizing the number of cluster heads. Energy-efficient heterogeneous clustered (EEHC) scheme in heterogeneous environment in which a percentage of nodes are equipped with more energy than others is presented in [12]. The concept of heterogeneity is used; this protocol does not consider different parameters for the selection of CHs. Cluster head is based on the weighted election probabilities according to the residual energy. Other heterogeneous-aware protocol is discussed in [13]. SEP is based on weighted election probabilities of each node to become cluster head according to the remaining energy in each node. The average throughput in SEP is also greater than the conventional protocol. Distributed hierarchical agglomerative clustering (DHAC) is discussed in [14]. It classifies sensor nodes into appropriate groups instead of simply gathering nodes to some randomly selected CHs. The techniques such as SLINK, CLINK, UPGMA, and WPGAM, with quantitative and qualitative data, are demonstrated in this clustering method [15]. Similarly threshold sensitive energy efficient sensor network protocol is a hierarchical protocol designed to be responsive to sudden changes in the sense attribute. The cluster head broadcast two types of threshold; hard threshold to allow the nodes to transmit only when the sensed attribute is in the range of interest and soft threshold to reduce the number of transmission if there is little or no change in the sensed attribute. APTEEN [16] is an extension of TEEN [17] and captures both periodic data and time critical events. The energy dissipation and network life time is better than LEACH but the main drawback of TEEN and APTEEN are the overhead and complexity of forming cluster head at multiple levels and implementing threshold based function and dealing with attribute based naming of queries.

4 Problem Formulation

In WSN, sensor nodes have limited power and hence requires saving power of whole sensor network efficiently. It performs user task by utilizing the power of each sensor node deployed in the network. In a WSN, frequent failure, dynamic network topology and environmental condition etc. affect upon sensor nodes. Each sensor node is participating in transmitting or receiving data to or from the network that depletes the node energy, in turn, decreases the lifetime of the sensor network and degrades its performance. Clustering may be viable solution of these problems. Existing clustering approaches have its own limitations. Variable cluster size and unreasonable cluster head selection while the nodes have different energy, cluster member nodes deplete energy after cluster head was dead. The algorithm does not take into account the location of nodes, residual energy which may easily lead to cluster head node will rapidly fail. Some protocols probabilistically decides whether or not to become the cluster head, there might be cases when two cluster-heads are selected in close vicinity of each other increasing the overall energy depleted in the network. The number of cluster-head nodes generated is not fixed so in some rounds it may be more or less than the preferred value. The node selected can be located near the edges of the network, wherein the other nodes will expend more energy to transmit data to that cluster-head. While some protocol has to calculate the threshold and generate the random numbers in each round, consuming cycles. Similarly, in using heterogeneous environment has the drawback that the election of the cluster heads among the two types of nodes is not dynamic, which results that the nodes that are far away from the powerful nodes will die first. So, cluster size and cluster head should be needed variable and merge-able into each other small into big and vice versa before dead.

5 The Proposed Protocol

A WSN can be modeled as a set of nodes and identified by a unique identifier. The nodes are dispersed in a square unit region following a random distribution and interconnected by full-duplex wireless communication links. Since the network is mobile, the nodes may change their positions from time to time without any notice. However, the mobility of sensor node is very low. The base station (BS) is a node with no energy constraint and enhanced computation capabilities and placed at the center of the field. Nodes deployed in a square area are differentiated on the bases of grids and partitioned into disjoint clusters. A node can be a part of only one cluster at a time; it can communicate directly with its cluster heads. The initial number of clusters is fixed by taking the optimum value and keeps on varying with the node density once the nodes start dying. The smaller clusters may be merged with the bigger ones. For every round of transmission there will be assignment of weights to the nodes. We have considered three types of nodes in the network.

Base station nodes: The node is static and denoted by *BS* with no energy constraints.

Normal nodes: All those nodes that lie in the transmission range of a single cluster-head.

Cluster-heads: The nodes responsible for gathering data from ordinary or normal nodes.

The clustering problem is defined as the selection of cluster-heads, enough in number to completely cover the network. It should be fast, less complicated, and efficient in terms of the number of messages. The proposed protocol is based on energy and rank based heuristics. Similar to HEED, DECA and DEMC, the PCR and in [18], which first calculates its weight based on energy. The weight is calculated on the basis of node residual energy (E) and node identifier (I). It is a linear combination of E and I. Here, E is having greater proportion in weight calculation, in comparison to I. The weight of node is

$$weight = \alpha \times E + \beta \times I$$

Hence one can reasonably assume that $0 < \beta < \alpha < 1$.

Delay for broadcasting clustering message is

$$Delay = \frac{1}{weight}$$

However, energy measurement is an issue of WSN and it depends on so many components as node's degree, mobility of nodes, node's distance from base station. Here we are calculating weight as

$$weight(i) = \sum_{i=1}^{n} D(i) + N(i) + E(i)$$

Where, $D(i)$ = rank of node i based on distance of node from base station,
$N(i)$ = rank of node i based on degree,
$E(i)$ = rank of node i based on residual energy.

And cluster head selection is done by choosing the node which has maximum weight i.e.

$$Clusterhead = max(weight)$$

The proposed protocol focused on variable transmission power rather than small packets of fixed size, in order to minimize energy consumption. The efficacy of proposed protocol is verified in two conditions. First is one hop communication and second is multi-hop communication.

5.1 Single Hop Communication

For every round of transmission there will be assignment of *weights* to the nodes. Each node is given a *weight* on the basis of above parameters like node degree, distance and residual energy. These nodes are placed at different locations and have different energy level as the computation increases shown in Fig. 1. The *BS* in the figure is representing base station which is positioned in between the sensor nodes. The nodes belonging to one cluster or grid send their information regarding node's degree and its distance from base station to the base station (supervisor node). The base station on receiving the data assigns the rank. For example if there are n nodes in the grid then a rank for distance $D(i) = n$ is given to node which is most close to the base station. Similarly, $D(i) = 1$ if the node is farthest from the base station this is because more is the distance more will be the communication cost. Likewise the rank $N(i) = n$ having higher number of degree and $N(i) = 1$, having the least degree, since we require higher connectivity of the nodes with the cluster head. We know that for transferring the data some amount of energy is consumed in communication and computation processes therefore after this process the nodes send their residual energy status. The base station assigns the rank $E(i) = n$ to the node, which is having higher energy. In case if the nodes have the same value of parameter, the same rank is given to those nodes. After assignment of ranks the weight is calculated by summing up all the ranks.

$$W(i) = D(i) + N(i) + E(i)$$

Where, $1 \leq i \leq n$.

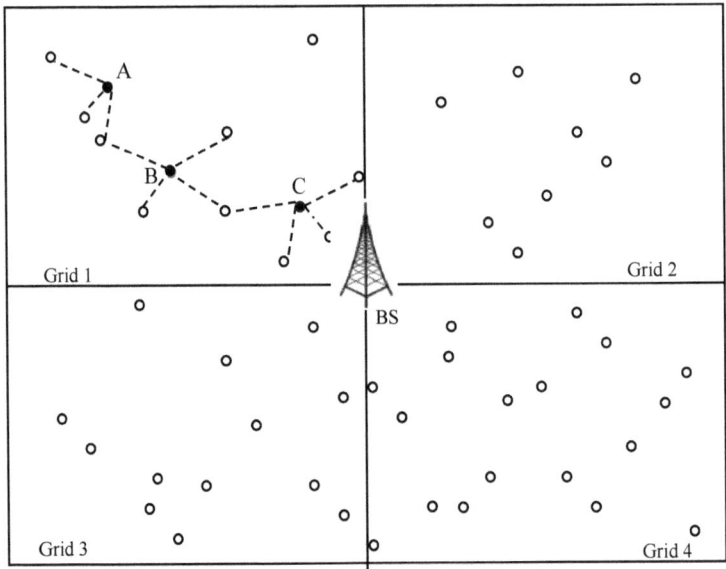

Fig. 1. Simulation scenario for single hop communication

For example, In Fig. 1, if we have to consider only three nodes A, B and C that are competing for cluster head selection in grid 1 that is having total 13 nodes then distance from *BS* and calculation of rank is given as:

$$\text{Node A} = 11\text{m} \quad [\text{Rank} = D(A) = 13]$$
$$\text{Node B} = 7\text{ m} \quad [\text{Rank} = D(B) = 12]$$
$$\text{Node C} = 6\text{ m} \downarrow [\text{Rank} ==D(C) = 11]$$

Similarly, the degrees of nodes are

$$\text{Node A} = 3 \uparrow \quad [\text{Rank} = N(A) = 12]$$
$$\text{Node B} = 4 \quad [\text{Rank} = N(B) = 13]$$
$$\text{Node C} = 4 \quad [\text{Rank} = N(C) = 13]$$

Similarly, based on the residual energy:

$$\text{Node A} = 0.4 \quad [\text{Rank} = E(A)13]$$
$$\text{Node B} = 0.3 \quad [\text{Rank} = E(B) = 12]$$
$$\text{Node C} = 0.2 \downarrow [\text{Rank} = E(C) = 11]$$

From the rank equation the weight can be calculated as:

$$\text{For node } A = w(A) = 13 + 12 + 13 = 38$$
$$\text{For node } B = w(B) = 12 + 13 + 12 = 37$$
$$\text{For node } C = w(C) = 11 + 13 + 11 = 35$$

Since the resultant weight of A is higher than B and C i.e. $w(C) < w(B) < w(A)$, Node A is selected as cluster head for the current round. The same process is repeated for every round. However in this example, only three nodes are being considered but in simulation the same process is applied on all the nodes of each cluster for cluster head selection.

5.2 Multi Hops Communication

The proposed approach has also been verified for multi-hop communication in which each grid is further divided into two areas i.e. grid1a and grid1b. Grid1a and grid1b will elect cluster head with the same procedure used in rank and weight proposed mechanism. The cluster head of grid1a which is far away from *BS* will aggregate all the data of its member nodes and fuse the data collected by cluster head of grid1b which reduces redundancy. The cluster head of grid1b will send the combination of grid1a and grid1b data to the *BS*. Thus the data of grid1a will reach indirectly and data of grid1b will reach directly to the base station shown by Fig. 2. In multi-hop communication, the proposed protocol has two advantages. First, if cluster nodes are died then cluster may be merged

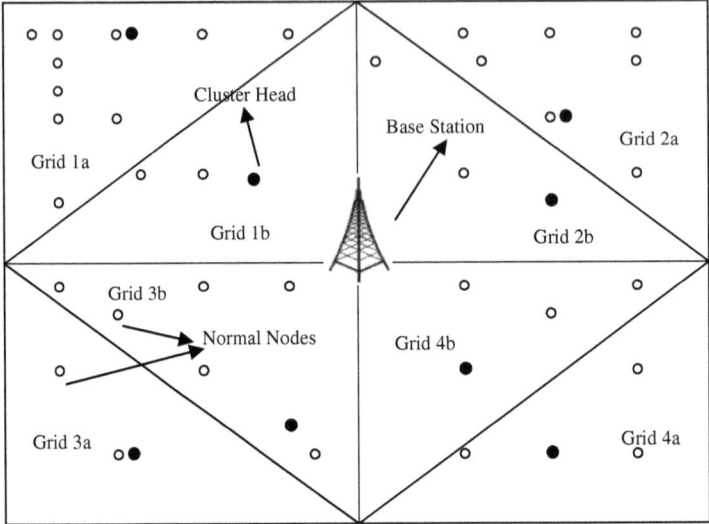

Fig. 2. Simulation scenario for multi hop communication

in another cluster. Secondly, if cluster head died then grid1b can directly communicate with *BS* and vice versa.

The two areas of grid 1 are distinguished on the basis of line, which can be computed as

$$y - y_1 = \frac{y_2 - y_1}{x_2 - x_1}(x - x_1)$$

Thus proposed protocol in multi hopped communication is using hierarchal clustering and each grid has a two level cluster. The technique helps to reduce the communication cost.

Moreover, the fact is considered that there may be a case when all the nodes of grid1b will die thus this region will become bottleneck, as the nodes of grid1a also become fail to pass their data since cluster head of grid1b was an intermediate. In such case the cluster head of grid1a will start transmitting to the base station directly.

6 Simulation and Result Discussion

In this section, the proposed protocol has been simulated using MATLAB. The nodes in the network are randomly deployed in a $100 \times 100 = m^2$ area and those nodes are differentiated on the basis of grids. Figure 3 shows the simulation scenario for homogeneous networks for a multi hop communication. For every round of transmission there will be assignment of weights to the nodes. Each node is given a weight on the basis of three parameters and the process described above. Network parameters are shown by Table 1.

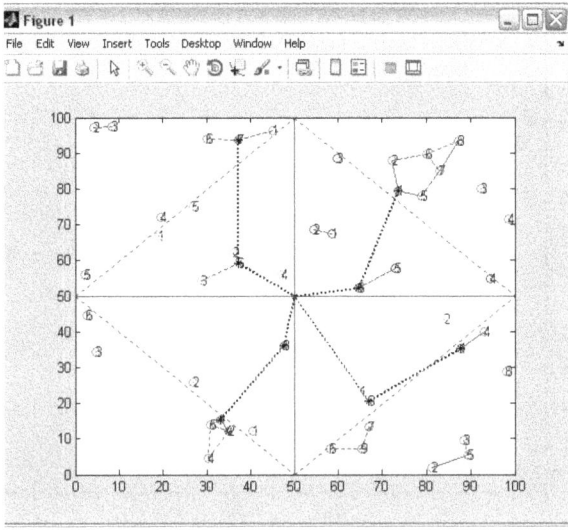

Fig. 3. Simulation scenario

Table 1. Network simulation parameters

Simulation parameters	Values
Network size	100 * 100 m
Location of sink	(50, 50)
Data packet length	4000 bit
Initial energy of nodes	0.5 Joule
Transmitter/receiver electronic	50 nj/bit
Aggregation energy, E_{DA}	5 nj/bit
Transmit amplifier, $\in_{fs}$, if $d_{toBS} < d_0$	10 pj/bit/m^2
Transmit amplifier, $\in mp$, if $d_{toBS} \geq d_0$	0.0013 pj/bit/m^2

Figure 4 shows the results of proposed protocol in terms of dead nodes. The simulation runs multiple times upon one grid of the network. Random number of nodes deployed in grid1. This experiment is done for 2000 rounds. The proposed protocol verified on SEP and LEACH. Result shows that proposed protocol is better in one hop communication scenario.

The same experiment when performed for all grids shows that total dead node in Proposed Heuristic is less as compared to LEACH and SEP. Figure 5 shows the calculation of total nodes die in 2000 rounds and Table 2 presents the calculation of time step of first node die. The network lifetime can also be evaluated by examining that at which time step (round) the first node of the network will die. Table 2 shows that the first node die more early in LEACH than SEP and the first node dead in SEP is earlier than Proposed Heuristic. It also evaluates that the results of Proposed Heuristic is at least 2 times better than LEACH and SEP for total dead nodes.

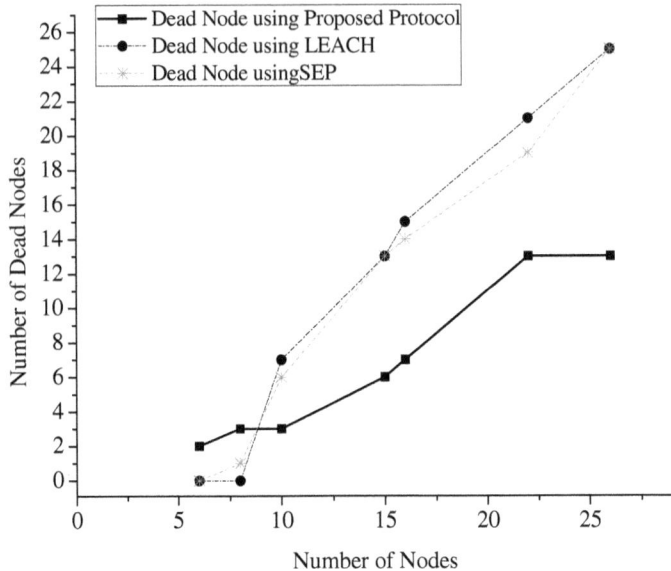

Fig. 4. Simulation scenario of grid1 for single hop communication

Table 2. Comparison of dead nodes and first node dead in proposed heuristics with LEACH and SEP

Total nodes	For all grids		
	Proposed heuristic	LEACH	SEP
	First node dead in number of round		
50	1226	833	1047
75	1171	806	943
100	1244	803	1077

However, in less number of nodes, number of dead nodes is more than SEP and LEACH. Network life time for all grids in terms of number of dead nodes is depicted by Fig. 5.

Stability period is defined as the region up to which all nodes are alive. This period lies between round 1 to round at which the first node dies. Figure 6 is the evaluation of stability period and the duration that how much the network is active. The simulation is done with 50 nodes and other parameters are listed in Table 1.

The comparison of proposed protocol for single hop and multi hop communication for WSN is shown by Fig. 7. It is observed that number of alive node is more in multi hop communication than in single hop communication when simulated with 2000 rounds. The overall resultant of the proposed protocol is upon dense network and

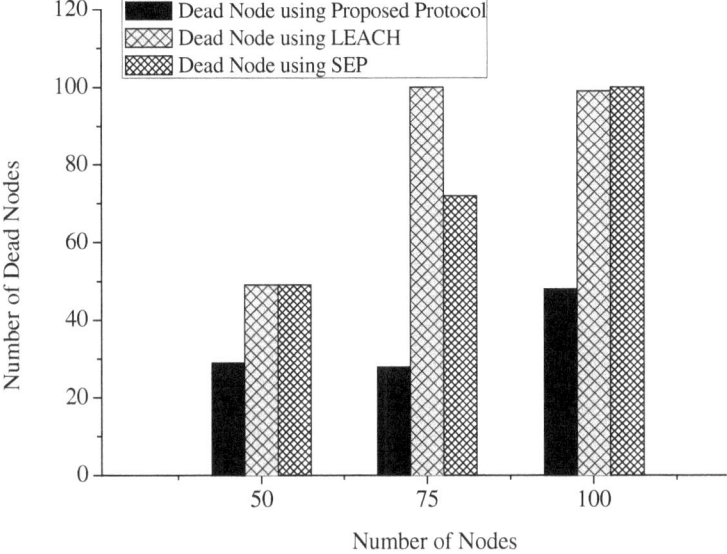

Fig. 5. Simulation scenario of all grids for single hop communication

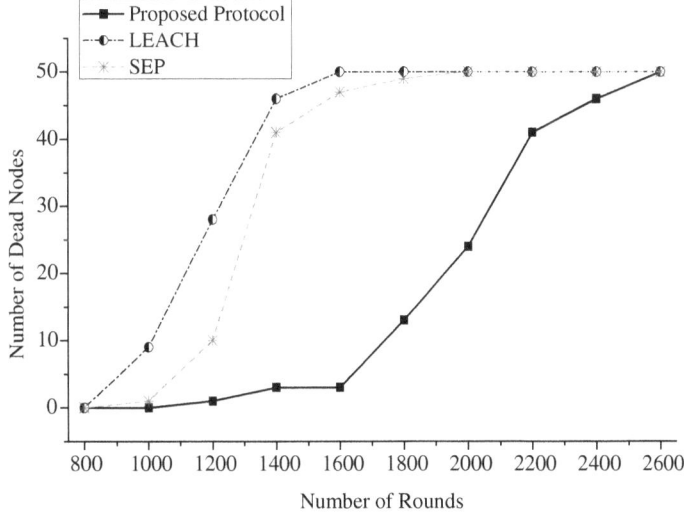

Fig. 6. Number of nodes v/s rounds using in protocols

multiple hop communication is better than single hop communication in showing better stability periods than conventional protocols. Furthermore, it is also observed that result shows that efficacy of proposed is also better than SEP and LEACH protocol in grid environment of WSN.

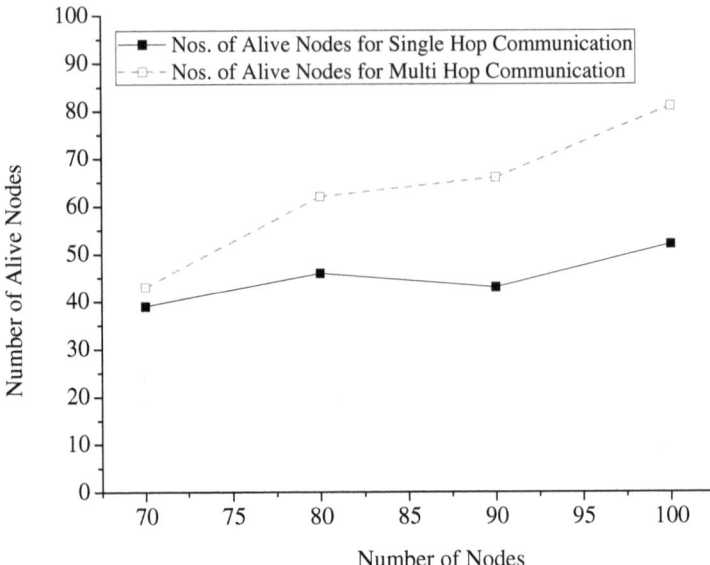

Fig. 7. Network life time of all grids for WSN

7 Conclusion

In this paper, a rank and weight based clustering protocol for WSN is presented. Cluster forming is a method that minimizes energy consumption and communication latency in WSN. We have resolved the limitations of conventional approaches using of weights and rank assignment to the nodes. The cluster head which will have higher weight will be chosen as cluster head. The efficacy of the proposed protocol is suitable and viable for WSN. It is adaptive in nature, not at every round cluster head changes like LEACH in which there was unreasonable cluster head selection while the nodes have different energy. In some conventional protocols like MTE if the cluster head dies all remaining nodes become fail to send data to base station instead in proposed protocol they elect a new cluster head in such condition. So cluster head is not a bottleneck here. Moreover, the protocol is able to achieve better performance upon dense and multi hop communication network in WSN (2nd level hierarchy is maintained in multi-hop). However, each round the data has to modify with new residual energy and keep checking to view the maximum weighted node which is time consuming. In comparison to other clustering based protocols, the proposed protocol has minimal overheads and maximizing life time of WSN.

References

1. Akyildiz, L., Su, W., Sankarasubramanian, Y., Cayirci, E.: A survey on sensor networks. IEEE Commun. Mag. **40**(8), 102–114 (2002)

2. Chen, G., Zhang, X., Yu, J., Wang, M.: An improved LEACH algorithm based on heterogeneous energy of nodes in wireless sensor networks. In: International Conference on Computing, Measurement, Control and Sensor Network, pp. 101–105 (2012)
3. Younis, O., Krunz, M., Ramasubramanian, S.: Node clustering in wireless sensor networks: recent developments and deployment challenges. IEEE Netw. **20**, 20–25 (2006)
4. Wang, P., Sun, Z., Vuran, M.C., Al-Rodhaan, M.A., Al-Dhelaan, A.M., Akyildiz, I.F.: On network connectivity of wireless sensor networks for sandstorm monitoring. Comput. Netw. **55**(5), 1150–1157 (2011)
5. Abbasi, A.A., Younis, M.: A survey on clustering algorithms for wireless sensor networks. Comput. Commun. **30**(14–15), 2826–2841 (2007)
6. Heinzelman, W., Chandrakasan, A., Balakrishnan, H.: Energy-efficient communication protocol for wireless microsensor networks. In: Proceedings of the 33rd Hawaii International Conference on System Sciences (HICSS 2000), pp. 1–10 (2000)
7. Heinzelman, W.B., Chandrakasan, A.P., Balakrishnan, H.: An application-specific protocol architecture for wireless microsensor networks. IEEE Trans. Wirel. Commun. **1**(4), 660–670 (2002)
8. Tong, M., Tang, M.: LEACH-B: an improved LEACH protocol for wireless sensor network. In: 6th WiCOM, pp. 1–4 (2010)
9. Younis, O., Fahmy, S.: HEED: a hybrid energy-efficient distributed clustering approach for ad hoc sensor networks. IEEE Trans. Mob. Comput. **3**(4), 366–379 (2004)
10. Ye, M., Lil, C., Chenl, G., Wu, J.: EECS: an energy efficient cluster scheme in wireless sensor networks. In: Proceedings of the IEEE IPCCC 2005, pp. 535–540 (2005)
11. Yan, X.F., Sun, Y.G., Zhao, C.L.: Energy-aware hierarchical clustering algorithm for wireless sensor networks. J. Tianjin Univ. **38**(12), 1106–1110 (2005)
12. Kumar, D., Aseri, T.C., Patel, R.B.: EEHC: energy efficient heterogeneous clustered scheme for wireless sensor networks. Comput. Commun. **32**(4), 662–667 (2009)
13. Smaragdakis, G., Matta, I., Bestavros, A.: SEP: a stable election protocol for clustered heterogeneous wireless sensor networks. In: 2nd SANPA 2004, pp. 1–11 (2004)
14. Lung, C.H., Zhou, C.: Using hierarchical agglomerative clustering in wireless sensor networks: an energy-efficient and flexible approach. Ad Hoc Netw. **8**(3), 328–344 (2010)
15. Akkaya, K., Younis, M.: A survey on routing protocols for wireless sensor networks. Ad Hoc Netw. **3**, 325–349 (2005)
16. Manjeshwar, A., Agrawal, D.P.: TEEN: a routing protocol for enhanced efficiency in wireless sensor networks. In: 15th International Parallel and Distributed Processing Symposium, pp. 2009–2015 (2000)
17. Manjeshwar, A., Agrawal, D.P.: APTEEN: a hybrid protocol for efficient routing and comprehensive information retrieval in wireless sensor networks. In: Proceedings International Parallel and Distributed Processing Symposium, IPDPS 2002, pp. 195–202 (2002)
18. Khan, A.R., Madani, S.A., Hayat, K., Khan, S.U.: Clustering-based power-controlled routing for mobile wireless sensor networks. Int. J. Commun Syst **25**(4), 529–542 (2012)

An FPGA-Based Multiple-Weight-and-Neuron-Fault Tolerant Digital Multilayer Perceptron (Full Version)

Tadayoshi Horita[✉], Itsuo Takanami, Masakazu Akiba, Mina Terauchi, and Tsuneo Kanno

Polytecnic University, 2-32-1, Ogawanishimachi,
Kodaira-shi, Tokyo 187-0035, Japan
horita@uitec.ac.jp
http://www.uitec.jeed.or.jp/english/index.html

Abstract. A method to implement a digital multilayer perceptron (DMLP) in an FPGA is proposed, where the DMLP is tolerant to simultaneous weight and neuron faults. It has been shown in [1] that a multilayer perceptron (MLP) which has successfully trained using the deep learning method is tolerant to multiple weight and neuron faults where the weight faults are between the hidden and output layers, and the neuron faults are in the hidden layer. Using this fact, a set of weights in the trained MLP is installed in an FPGA to cope with these faults. Further, the neuron faults in the output layer are detected or corrected using SECDED code. The above process is done as follows. The generator developed by us automatically outputs a VHDL source file which describes the perceptron using a set of weight values in the MLP trained by the deep learning method. The VHDL file obtained is input to the logic design software Quartus II of Altera Inc., and then, implemented in an FPGA. The process is applied to realizing fault-tolerant DMLPs for character recognitions as concrete examples. Then, the perceptrons to be made fault-tolerant and corresponding non-redundant ones not to be made fault-tolerant are compared in terms of not only reliability and fault rate but also hardware size, computing speed and electricity consumption. The data show that the fault rate of the fault-tolerant perceptron can be significantly decreased than that of the corresponding non-redundant one.

This paper is the full version of [2].

Keywords: Multilayer perceptron · Fault-tolerance · Weight fault · Neuron fault · VHDL · FPGA

1 Introduction

Feedforward neural networks, including multilayer perceptrons ("MLPs" for short), are widely tried to be used in computational or industrial fields.

Itsuo Takanami—Retired.

Furthermore, as VLSI technology has developed, the interest in implementing them in hardware is growing. For the case, there is the possibility of low yield and/or reliability of the system if there is no strategy for coping with defects or faults. Various studies concerning their fault-tolerances are described in the literature, e.g., [3–18] for the interested readers.

We have proposed another simple method called the "deep learning method" for making MLPs fault-tolerant to multiple weight-and-neuron faults in [1]. The idea is based on making a learning error smaller in learning phase than one in practical use. The analytical result shows that the MLP has the complete (100 %) fault-tolerant to multiple weight-and-neuron faults decided by the learning errors.

By the way, one of attractive features in the MLP is the massively parallel computation. However, this feature is not realized without its hardware implementation. Various studies concerning neural hardware architectures and/or implementations are described in the literature, e.g., [19–26]. Most of them deal with analog or mixed signal architectures and their fabrication costs seem high.

In this paper, we introduce a method of a multiple weight as well as neuron fault-tolerant digital MLP implementation using the deep learning method, SECDED (Single Error Correction, Double Error Detection) codes, the VHDL (VHSIC Hardware Description Language) notation, and the logic design software Quartus II. A VHDL source file which denotes a fault-tolerant digital MLP is automatically generated via our method, thus it can easily be implemented on FPGA (Field Programmable Gate Array) devices which are not so expensive via our method, and the hardware size is small because its architecture is so simple. Note that the easiness of the FPGA implementation implies the easiness of the speed-up of neural computations in the future where the higher-speed FPGA devices are produced via the VLSI technology development.

The works of [27–29] deal with digital MLP architectures, but their fault-tolerance and FPGA implementations are not considered, and moreover, their hardware sizes are larger than ours. The work of [30] deals with a fault-tolerant digital MLP architecture where the fault-tolerance is not realized via a learning method, but via the concept of digital error detection circuits. The neural computation might be faster than ours, but the hardware size is larger than ours. The work of [31] deals with a fault-tolerant digital MLP architecture on FPGAs using the VHDL notation and Max+Plus II. The weight training is so fast because it is executed on the hardware itself using genetic algorithms. The fault-tolerance is not based on a learning method, but on the concept of spare neurons and their replacements. The neural computation seems to be slower than ours, because selectors are used between layers of neurons whereas complete connections are used in our method.

In Sect. 2, the digital MLP is denoted. In Sect. 3, two fault models are defined and the fault-tolerances of digital MLPs in both models are defined. In Sect. 4, the properties of digital MLPs in both models concerning their fault-tolerances are shown. In Sect. 5, the process which generates fault-tolerant digital MLPs is denoted. In Sect. 6, the fault-tolerant digital MLPs are compared to the corresponding non-redundant digital MLPs by simulations of concrete examples of character recognitions, in terms of not only reliability and fault rate but also hardware size, computing speed and electricity consumption. The data show that the fault rate of the fault-tolerant perceptron can be significantly decreased than that of the corresponding non-redundant one. Finally in Sect. 7, this paper is concluded.

This paper is the full version of [2].

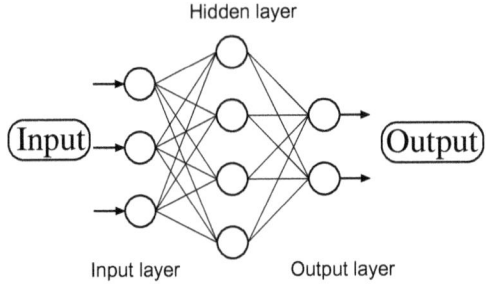

Fig. 1. 3-layer digital MLP

2 Digital MLP

Figure 1 shows a digital MLP (which is shortly denoted as a "DMLP" in the following). Each neuron in a layer is connected to all neurons in the adjacent layers through uni-directional links (synaptic weights). The first and the last layers are called the input and output layers respectively, and one between them is called a hidden layer. In this paper, we deal with only MLPs which have one hidden layer. The output of each neuron (o_i) is given by

$$o_i = f(X_i) \tag{1}$$

$$X_i = \sum_{j=0}^{N_{pre}} w_{ij} \cdot u_j \tag{2}$$

where w_{ij} is the synaptic weight from the j-th neuron in the preceding layer to the i-th neuron whose value is an integer, N_{pre} is the number of the neurons in the preceding layer connected to the i-th neuron, u_j is the output of the j-th neuron in the preceding layer whose value is 0 or 1, w_{i0} is the synaptic weight connected to the input $u_0 = 1$ corresponding to the threshold, X_i is called the "inner potential" of the neuron, and f is the activation function (the step function) of a neuron defined by

$$f(x) = \begin{cases} 1 & (x \geq 0) \\ 0 & (x < 0) \end{cases} \tag{3}$$

Let O be a set of indices of the neurons in the output layer, and let P be a set of indices of the learning examples consisting of pairs of input and output examples. Let $t_i^p (= 0 \text{ or } 1)$ and o_i^p be the learning output example and the output of the i-th neuron ($i \in O$) in the output layer for the p-th learning input example ($p \in P$) for a DMLP. If o_i^p is equal to t_i^p for any $i \in O$ and $p \in P$, the DMLP is called to work properly and denoted as wp-DMLP.

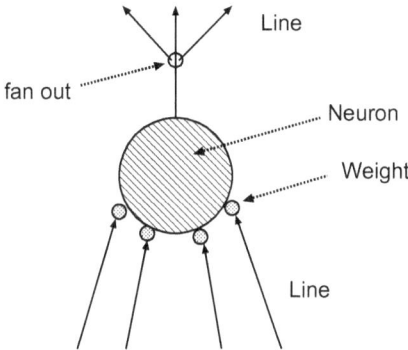

Fig. 2. Elements constructing a neuron

3 Fault Model and Fault-Tolerance in DMLPs

It is assumed that faults may occur at the neurons, weights and interconnection links (see Fig. 2). Then, it can be considered as a weight or a neuron fault that a link snaps or is stuck to some value. Then, we define the following.

Definition 1 *(Multiple fault)*. *A weight fault is a pair (i, x), where i and x denote the index and the value of the faulty weight. A neuron fault is a pair $[j, y]$, where j and y denote the index and the output value of the faulty neuron. A wp-DMLP is said to have a weight fault (i, x) if the value of the weight with index i is stuck to x. Similarly, a wp-DMLP is said to have a neuron fault $[j, y]$ if the output of the neuron with index j is stuck to y. A set of faults F is called a multiple fault if all the faults in F occur simultaneously. Let $\hat{N}_h^F = \{j \mid [j, y] \in F$ is a neuron fault in the hidden layer\}, let $\hat{N}_o^F = \{j \mid [j, y] \in F$ is a neuron fault in the output layer\} and let $\hat{W}^F = \{i \mid (i, x) \in F\}$. Then, $(\hat{N}_h^F, \hat{N}_o^F, \hat{W}^F)$ is called the index set of F.* □

The following are assumed on faults.

Assumption 1 *(the range of faults)*

– *Neuron fault*
  Neurons in the hidden layer may be faulty. Neurons in the input layer are assumed to be fault-free because they are only input terminals, that is, so

simple. Concerning neurons in the output layer, two cases are assumed. One is the case where they are fault-free, and denoted as model FM_{free-o}. Another is the case where they may be faulty, and denoted as model FM_{total}.
- Weight fault
  Any weight may be faulty. However, a weight fault between the input and the hidden layers is treated as a fault of the neuron in the hidden layer to which the line with the faulty weight is connected.

Assumption 2 *(the values of a weight).* The value of either healthy or faulty weight is finite and represented as an integer in the range from $-w_{max}$ to w_{max} ($w_{max} > 0$). This assumption is considered to be reasonable in a real world or hardware realization. The value of a weight is represented as an N_{bw} bit binary number in the range from $-(2^{N_{bw}-1}-1)$ to $(2^{N_{bw}-1}-1)$ in Sect. 5.3.

Assumption 3 *(the output value of a neuron).* The output value of a neuron is 0 or 1 which is the same as the output value of the neuron defined by it's activation function,

3.1 Model FM_{free-o}

In this model, in addition to Assumptions 1, 2 and 3, all neurons in the output layer are assumed to be fault-free. Under the assumption, the fault-tolerance is defined as follows.

Definition 2 *(Fault-tolerance of FM_{free-o}).* When F with index set $(\hat{N}_h^F, \phi, \hat{W}^F)$ occurs in a wp-DMLP, if it works properly, it is called to be fault-tolerant to F. □

3.2 Fault Model FM_{total}

In this model, in addition to Assumptions 1, 2 and 3, it is assumed that neurons in the output layer may be faulty. Such faults are fatal and some scheme such as error correcting or detecting code should be used to recover the fault. Then the original learning output examples are converted to proper code words, extra neurons may be added in the output layer of the original DMLP and the code words become the new learning output examples. Then, the DMLP with extra neurons added is called to be the extension of the original DMLP and denoted as EX-DMLP. Under the consideration above, fault-tolerance of FM_{total} is defined as follows.

Definition 3 *(Fault-tolerance of FM_{total}).* When F with index set $(\hat{N}_h^F, \hat{N}_o^F, \hat{W}^F)$ occurs in a wp-EX-DMLP, if it is fault-tolerant to the sub-fault of F with index set $(\hat{N}_h^F, \phi, \hat{W}^F)$ and the sub-fault of F with index set $(\phi, \hat{N}_o^F, \phi)$ is corrected or detected, the wp-EX-DMLP is called to be fault-tolerant to F. □

In the following, an error correcting and detecting code SECDED is used to detect or correct the values of faulty neurons in the output layer. Then, a wp-EX-DMLP is fault-tolerant to a multiple fault F with index set $(\hat{N}_h^F, \hat{N}_o^F, \hat{W}^F)$ if it is fault-tolerant to the sub-fault of F with index set $(\hat{N}_h^F, \phi, \hat{W}^F)$ and $|\hat{N}_o^F| \leq 2$.

4 Fault-Tolerant DMLPs

The following is called "deep learning condition with a parameter of non-negative integer N_d" which is denoted as $DL\text{-}cond(N_d)$ for a DMLP.

- $DL\text{-}cond(N_d)$

$$\min_{p \in P, i \in O, t_i^p = 1} (s_i^p) \geq w_{max} \cdot N_d$$
$$\max_{p \in P, i \in O, t_i^p = 0} (s_i^p) < -w_{max} \cdot N_d \tag{4}$$

where s_i^p is the value of the inner potential of the i-th neuron in the output layer for the learning example p. □

Note that a DMLP (EX-DMLP) which satisfies $DL\text{-}cond(N_d)$ is a wp-DMLP (EX-DMLP). Further, a DMLP (EX-DMLP) which satisfies $DL\text{-}cond(N_d)$ satisfies $DL\text{-}cond(N)$ for any N ($N \leq N_d$).

4.1 Fault-Tolerant DMLP in FM_{free-o}

We have the following.

Theorem 1. *A DMLP which satisfies $DL\text{-}cond(N_d)$ is fault-tolerant to any multiple fault with index set $(\hat{J}, \phi, \hat{L})$ if the following inequality is satisfied.*

$$|\hat{J} \cup \hat{L}| + |\hat{L}| \leq N_d \tag{5}$$

The proof is detailed in Appendix A. □

4.2 Fault-Tolerant DMLP in FM_{total}

Theorem 2. *An EX-DMLP which satisfies $DL\text{-}cond(N_d)$ is fault-tolerant to any multiple fault with index set $(\hat{J}, \hat{K}, \hat{L})$ if the following inequality is satisfied.*

$$|\hat{J} \cup \hat{L}| + |\hat{L}| \leq N_d \quad \text{and} \quad |\hat{K}| \leq 2 \tag{6}$$

Proof: From Theorem 1, an EX-DMLP which satisfies $DL\text{-}cond(N_d)$ is fault-tolerant to any multiple fault with index set $(\hat{J}, \phi, \hat{L})$. Further, since the number of faulty neurons in the output layer is less than or equal to 2, the values of faulty neurons in the output layer are detected or corrected using SECDED code. □

Here, some terms are defined as follows.

- FTDMLP
  A DMLP or EX-DMLP which satisfies $DL\text{-}cond(N_d)$ for some $N_d \geq 1$ is called a fault-tolerant DMLP or EX-DMLP and denoted as an "FTDMLP". If it should explicitly be indicated that an FTDMLP is an EX-DMLP, it is denoted as an "FTDMLP$_{total}$".

154 T. Horita et al.

- Degree of fault-tolerance (DFT)
  If an FTDMLP which satisfies $DL\text{-}cond(N_d)$ but not $DL\text{-}cond(N_d+1)$, N_d is called "degree of fault-tolerance" (simply, DFT) of that.
- An FTDMLP with DFT $N_d \geq 1$ is denoted as an FTDMLP(N_d).
- A DMLP which satisfies $DL\text{-}cond(0)$ but not $DL\text{-}cond(1)$, is called a non-redundant DMLP.

From Theorems 1 and 2, it is seen that an FTDMLP with a bigger DFT can cope with a multiple fault with an index set of bigger size.

5 Process to Realize Fault-Tolerant DMLPs

The outline of the process to implement FTDMLPs on FPGAs is described. This process is named "FTDMLP-gene-proc" which consists of three parts, that is, the deep learning method ("Deep-LM" for short), the VHDL source file generator named "VHDL-gene-func" and the outline of VHDL notation which describes an FTDMLP.

5.1 Deep Learning Method (Deep-LM)

The Deep-LM introduced in [1] is basically the same algorithm as the normal back-propagation one and is used to make a DMLP satisfy $DL\text{-}cond(N_d)$ for a set of learning examples. To do so, using an MLP defined below, a set of weights in the MLP which has successfully finished learning, is installed to a DMLP via the VHDL-gene-func. Here, an MLP with N_h neurons in the hidden layer is denoted as MLP(N_h) if N_h must be explicitly denoted.

1. The values of weights and the output of neurons are real numbers.
2. The sigmoid function f_o of a neuron in the output layer is $f_o = 1/(1 + \exp(-x/T))$ and $T = N_{lm}/\ln 9$, where N_{lm} is a parameter of positive integer and note that $f(N_{lm}) = 0.9$.
3. The sigmoid function f_h of a neuron in the hidden layer is $f_h = 1/(1 + \exp(-x))$.
4. The MLP defined above is made learn so as to satisfy the condition of $\max_{p \in P, i \in O}(t_i^p - o_i^p)^2 < e_a^2$ (here, e_a is set to 0.1), using the normal back propagation algorithm.
5. During the iteration of weight modification, if the condition of $\max_{p \in P, i \in O}(t_i^p - o_i^p)^2 < e_a^2$ is satisfied, the learning process is stopped and the learning is called to be "successful". Otherwise, if the times of the iteration reaches the maximum weight updates, the learning is called to be "failed".
6. If the value of a weight to be modified is greater (less) than $1(-1)$, it is set to $1(-1)$ so as to make it in the range from -1 to 1. This is called "$W_{|1|}$-process".

Then, since $f(N_{lm}) = 0.9$ and f is monotonically increasing, the following holds for the MLP defined above.

Property 1. *If the learning is successful, that is, $\max_{p \in P, i \in O}(t_i^p - o_i^p)^2 < e_a^2$ $(= 0.1^2)$,*

(1) $\min_{p \in P, i \in O, t_i^p = 1}(x_i^p) > N_{lm}$
(2) $\max_{p \in P, i \in O, t_i^p = 0}(x_i^p) < -N_{lm}$

where x_i^p is the value of the inner potential of the i-th neuron in the output layer for the learning example p. □

5.2 VHDL-gene-func

This function generates a VHDL source file whose outline is shown in the next section. This function uses a set of weight values in a successful MLP in Sect. 5.1 above. This function consists of the standard C functions such as fopen(), fprintf(), and fclose(). Inside this function, each weight value obtained by applying the Deep-LM is multiplied by w_{max}, and then, it is made an integer as $\lfloor$ (the value + 0.5) $\rfloor$, and is used as the new value of the weight, where $\lfloor x \rfloor$ is the maximum integer which is not greater than x. The detail of this function is not shown.

```
-- Some libraries are included

entity DigitalNeuralNetwork is
        port(I:in std_logic_vector(1 to 4);
              O:out std_logic_vector(1 to 4));
end DigitalNeuralNetwork;
                      :
-- signals are defined.

begin
WI11 <= "1001" when I(1)='1' else "0000";
WI21 <= "0101" when I(2)='1' else "0000";
WI31 <= "0001" when I(3)='1' else "0000";
WI41 <= "1101" when I(4)='1' else "0000";
WI12 <= "0011" when I(1)='1' else "0000";
WI22 <= "1111" when I(2)='1' else "0000";
                      :
H1J11 <= ( WI11(3) & WI11 ) + ( WI21(3) & WI21 );
H1J12 <= ( WI31(3) & WI31 ) + ( WI41(3) & WI41 );
HP1   <= ( H1J11(4) & H1J11 ) + ( H1J12(4) & H1J12 );

H1 <= not HP1(5);
                      :
```

Fig. 3. Outline of VHDL notation

5.3 Outline of the VHDL Notation

Figure 3 shows the outline of the VHDL notation which the VHDL-gene-func generates and a sample where the number of neurons in the input layer (neurons in the output layer) is 4 (4) and the bit width of a weight N_{bw} is 4.

The explanation of the outline of the VHDL notation:

- In the "entity" declaration, the "port" "I" ("O") is the 4 (4) bit input (output) bus signal, and each bit represents a neuron in the input layer (neuron in the output layer).
- Each weight value is represented as an N_{bw} bit binary number. A positive value is represented as a normal N_{bw} bit binary number, but a negative one is represented as an N_{bw} bit 2's complement binary number.
- "WIij" (i and j are integer) is (the weight value between the i-th neuron in the hidden layer and j-th neuron in the output layer) times (the value of the i-th neuron in the hidden layer).
- The inner potential of the 1st-neuron in the hidden layer "HP1" is coded as
    signal H1J11, H1J12 : std_logic_vector(4 downto 0);
    signal HP1 : std_logic_vector(5 downto 0);
    H1J11 <= (WI11(3) & WI11) + (WI21(3) & WI21);
    H1J12 <= (WI31(3) & WI31) + (WI41(3) & WI41);
    HP1 <= (H1J11(4) & H1J11) + (H1J12(4) & H1J12);
    but not as
    HP1 <= "000000" + WI11 + WI21 + WI31 + WI41;
    so that the hardware size and the delay time from the inputs to the outputs (that is, the neural computing time) are both reduced.
- The output value of the 1st-neuron in the hidden layer "H1" is calculated as the inversion of the most significant bit of "HP1". By this expression, H1 becomes 1 when HP1 $\geq$ 0, 0 otherwise. Note that in this paper, the "step function" indicates this function.
- The inner potential of each neuron in the output layer and its output value are calculated likewise. (The detail is not shown.)

5.4 FTDMLP-gene-proc

The FTDMLP-gene-proc is executed as follows.

1. The C language simulation program for the *Deep-LM* is executed on MLP M defined in the *Deep-LM*.
    (a) Each weight value in M is initialized using a pseudo random number.
    (b) The execution is judged to be successful or failed, but go to the next step without reference to the judgment.
2. The VHDL-gene-func generates a VHDL source file which describes an FTDMLP.
3. The logic design software QuartusII compiles the generated VHDL source file, and generates the binary object file which should be downloaded to an FPGA.

When Step 1 has been executed on M, if the learning is successful, the values of the inner potentials of the neurons in the output layer satisfy (1) and (2) in Property 1. Then, the MLP M_a which is obtained by multiplying the value of each weight in M satisfies $DL\text{-}cond(N_{lm})$. However, the values of weights and the output values of neurons in the DMLP to which the values of weights in M_a are copied in Step 2 are restricted in bit width. In addition, the activation function in the DMLP is the step function. Then, in common cases, the DMLP cannot satisfies $DL\text{-}cond(N_{lm})$ but $DL\text{-}cond(N_d)$ for some $N_d < N_{lm}$. Considering these, FTDMLP-algo which is the extension of FTDMLP-gene-proc will be described in Sect. 6.4. It generates FTDMLPs from the point of view of increasing their reliabilities.

6 Simulation Results

The process to realize FTDMLPs for pattern recognitions is illustrated in detail and the FTDMLPs realized are evaluated in terms of hardware size, computing speed and electricity consumption, comparing with those of the corresponding non-redundant DMLPs.

6.1 Environments and Tools

The simulations for FTDMLPs are executed using two tools mainly, where one is the gcc-4.4.4 compiler and the GNU OpenMP Library (libgomp-4.5.1-4) on a PC which has an AMD PhenomII X6 2.8 GHz CPU, 2 GB RAM, and Fedora 13 x86_64 version linux OS, and the other is the logic design software Quartus II 9.1 subscription web of Altera Inc. on the other PC with Windows XP professional OS, an Intel 2.0-MHz Core 2 CPU, and 1.5 G-byte RAM. The target FPGA device family in the Quartus II is assigned cyclone III. The Quartus II automatically chooses the smallest device on which an FTDMLP can be realized among the family devices.

6.2 Learning Examples

Figures 4 and 5 show each 20 and 40 examples in the two sets of learning input examples called *Set*-1 and -2, respectively. Each example in *Set*-1 consists of 100 pixels (black = 1 and white = 0), while each example in *Set*-2 consists of 225 pixels. Table 1 shows the original learning output examples when the number of examples is 40. In case where it is less than 40, necessary and sufficient bits should be used to express all the examples. For example, in case where only ten learning examples are used, four bits from zeroth to third bits in Table 1 should be used, and fourth and fifth bits must not be used. For an EX-DMLP, each one in Table 1 is encoded to a SECDED code using the H matrix (H_4, H_5 or H_6) which corresponds to its bit width.

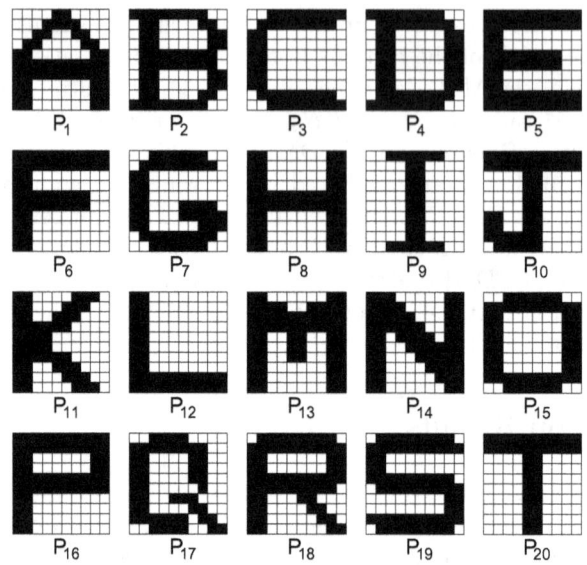

Fig. 4. Learning input examples (*Set*-1)

Table 1. Original learning output examples (*Set*-1 and -2)

Input	Output $t_5^p t_4^p t_3^p t_2^p t_1^p t_0^p$
P_1	000000
P_2	000001
P_3	000010
omitted	
P_{39}	100111
P_{40}	101000

$$H_4 = \begin{bmatrix} 1 & 1 & 1 & 0 & 1 & 0 & 0 & 0 \\ 1 & 1 & 0 & 1 & 0 & 1 & 0 & 0 \\ 1 & 0 & 1 & 1 & 0 & 0 & 1 & 0 \\ 0 & 1 & 1 & 1 & 0 & 0 & 0 & 1 \end{bmatrix} \quad (7)$$

$$H_5 = \begin{bmatrix} 1 & 1 & 0 & 1 & 1 & 1 & 0 & 0 & 0 & 0 \\ 1 & 0 & 1 & 1 & 0 & 0 & 1 & 0 & 0 & 0 \\ 0 & 1 & 1 & 1 & 0 & 0 & 0 & 1 & 0 & 0 \\ 0 & 0 & 0 & 0 & 1 & 0 & 0 & 0 & 1 & 0 \\ 1 & 1 & 1 & 0 & 1 & 0 & 0 & 0 & 0 & 1 \end{bmatrix} \quad (8)$$

Fig. 5. Learning input examples (*Set*-2)

$$H_6 = \begin{bmatrix} 1 & 1 & 0 & 1 & 1 & 0 & 1 & 0 & 0 & 0 & 0 \\ 1 & 0 & 1 & 1 & 0 & 1 & 0 & 1 & 0 & 0 & 0 \\ 0 & 1 & 1 & 1 & 0 & 0 & 0 & 0 & 1 & 0 & 0 \\ 0 & 0 & 0 & 0 & 1 & 1 & 0 & 0 & 0 & 1 & 0 \\ 1 & 1 & 1 & 0 & 1 & 1 & 0 & 0 & 0 & 0 & 1 \end{bmatrix} \qquad (9)$$

The number of neurons in the input layer is set to 100 (225) when Set-1 (-2) is used. The number of neurons in the output layer is set to the bit width of encoded learning output examples.

6.3 How to Evaluate the Reliability of DMLPs

Here, the reliability of an $FTDMLP(N_d)$, named R_{ft} is considered where it has N_h neurons in the hidden layer and N_o neurons in the output layer. First, let $IH_{FT}(p_{h_{ft}})$ be the reliabilities of the part between input and hidden layer of the $FTDMLP(N_d)$, where $p_{h_{ft}}$ is the reliability of the neuron in the hidden layer of the $FTDMLP(N_d)$. From Theorem 1, $IH_{FT}(p_{h_{ft}})$ can be calculated by the following equation.

$$IH_{FT}(p_{h_{ft}}) = \sum_{k=0}^{N_d} {}_{N_h}C_k \cdot p_{h_{ft}}^{N_h-k} \cdot (1-p_{h_{ft}})^k \qquad (10)$$

Next, let $HO_{FT}(p_{o_{ft}})$ be the reliabilities of the part between hidden and output layer of the $FTDMLP(N_d)$, where $p_{o_{ft}}$ is the reliability of the neuron in the output layer. From Sect. 3.2, $HO_{FT}(p_{o_{ft}})$ can be calculated by the following equation.

$$HO_{FT}(p_{o_{ft}}) = \sum_{k=0}^{2} {}_{N_o}C_k \cdot p_{o_{ft}}^{N_o-k} \cdot (1-p_{o_{ft}})^k \qquad (11)$$

From the above, R_{ft} can be calculated by the following equation.

$$R_{ft} = IH_{FT}(p_{h_{ft}}) \cdot HO_{FT}(p_{o_{ft}}) \qquad (12)$$

On the other hand, the reliability of a non-redundant DMLP, named R_{nr}, can be calculated by the following equation.

$$R_{nr} = p_{h_{nr}}^{sz\_total/sz\_h_{nr}} \qquad (13)$$

where $p_{h_{nr}}$ is the reliability of a neuron in the hidden layer of the non-redundant DMLP, sz_total and sz_h_{nr} are the hardware sizes (the number of logic elements) of the total non-redundant DMLP and a neuron in the hidden layer, respectively. For comparison between R_{ft} and R_{nr} to be mentioned later, R_{ft} is calculated based on $p_{h_{nr}}$ using the equations $p_{h_{ft}} = p_{h_{nr}}^{sz\_h_{ft}/sz\_h_{nr}}$ and $p_{o_{ft}} = p_{h_{nr}}^{sz\_o_{ft}/sz\_h_{nr}}$, where sz_h_{ft} and sz_o_{ft} are the hardware sizes of the neurons in the hidden and the output layers of the $FTDMLP(N_d)$, respectively.

Here, the hardware sizes such as sz_total and sz_h_{nr} are evaluated as follows. Let NN.vhd be the VHDL source file which is generated by the VHDL-gene-func. We have developed another generator which generates a part between the input and hidden layers of an NN.vhd as a VHDL source file, by modifying the VHDL-gene-func. The generated file is named "IH.vhd". The IH.vhd has the same input signals as those of the NN.vhd. However, it outputs the output signals of neurons in the hidden layer of the NN.vhd. Likewise, we have developed the other generator for a part between the hidden and output layers of an NN.vhd. The generated file is named "HO.vhd". Let sz_NN, sz_IH and sz_HO be the numbers of logic elements in FPGAs as the Quartus II compilation results of NN.vhd, IH.vhd and HO.vhd, respectively. We have checked that $(sz\_IH + sz\_HO - sz\_NN)/sz\_NN$ is less than 0.053 in several cases, even though the Quartus II works some optimization processes. This means that the circuit structures of the IH.vhd and the HO.vhd in an FPGA are almost the same as those of the parts between the input and hidden layers and between the hidden and output layers of NN.vhd, respectively. From the above, sz_total, (sz_h_{ft} or sz_h_{nr}) and sz_o_{ft} are estimated as sz_NN, (sz_IH/N_h) and (sz_HO/N_o), respectively.

6.4 Algorithm to Generate DMLPs

The following FTDMLP-Algo which is the extension of the FTDMLP-gene-proc generates FTDMLPs from the point of view of increasing their reliabilities R_{ft}s in terms of N_h, N_d and N_{bw}. In the following, a learning using the deep-LM is denoted as a deep-LM learning.

[FTDMLP-Algo]

1. To find the minimum N_h so that a deep-LM learning for an MLP(N_h) is successful, named $N_{h_{min}}$, the following process is done.
   (a) A positive integer is set to $N_{h_{alg}}$ so that the deep-LM learning for MLP (N_{alg}) is successful.
   (b) 100 deep-LM learning trials are done, where the parameters in each trial are as follows.
      i. The maximum weight update is 5×10^5.
      ii. e_a is 0.1.
      iii. The learning constant η is 0.02 if $N_{lm} < 3$, 0.1 otherwise.
      iv. Weight values are initialized by -0.1 to 0.1 random numbers.
      v. Output examples are SECDED codes.
   (c) If one or more deep-LM learnings are successful, the value of $(N_{h_{alg}} - 1)$ is set to $N_{h_{alg}}$ and go to the step 1b. Otherwise, the value of $N_{h_{min}}$ is found and the value of $(N_{h_{alg}} + 1)$ is set to $N_{h_{min}}$ and go to the next step.
2. The digitization in Step 3 of the FTDMLP-gene-proc is executed on MLP ($N_{h_{min}}$) for each case of N_{bw} being 2, 3, ... and 10, and the maximum value of N_d for which the $DL\text{-}cond(N_d)$ is satisfied is calculated using the Eq. (4). In the following, N_d means this maximum value.
3. For only the case of N_{bw} for which N_d is greater than 0 in the previous step, the VHDL source files of IH.vhd, HO.vhd and NN.vhd are generated by their generators using the set of digitized weight values. These files are compiled by the Quartus II, and sz_NN, sz_IH and sz_HO are obtained as their compilation results.

Note that FTDMLP-Algo is executed for the cases of N_{lm} being 3, 4, ... and 18 to obtain the data in the next section.

On the other hand, the algorithm to generate non-redundant DMLPs, named "nrDMLP-algo", is almost the same as FTDMLP-Algo. The difference is as follows: In nrDMLP-algo, (1) Output examples are not SECDED coded, and (2) the non-redundant DMLP is obtained as the case of the minimum $size\_NN$, among the trials which N_{lm} is 1 to 4.

6.5 Results Concerning Reliability

The case of simulation is denoted as "n_N_p", where n and N_p are the set number and the number of used examples ($n = 1$ or 2), respectively.

In the following, the four cases of 1_10, 1_20, 2_20 and 2_40 are considered.

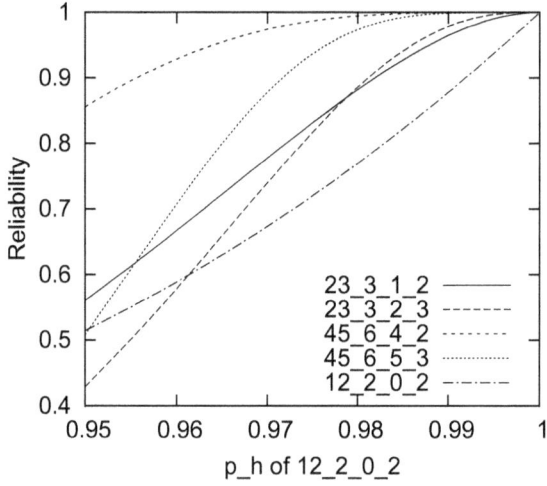

Fig. 6. The relation between $\{R_{ft}$ or $R_{nr}\}$ and $p_{h_{nr}}$ (1_10, $N_{lm} = 3$ and 6)

Figures 6 and 7 show the relation between $\{R_{ft}$s or $R_{h_{nr}}\}$ and $p_{h_{nr}}$ for the case of 1_10, where $N_{lm} = \{3$ and $6\}$ and $\{9$ and $12\}$, respectively. The meaning of labels in these figures is $N_{h_{min}}\_N_{lm}\_N_d\_N_{bw}$. The case where N_{lm} is the other value is omitted because the data shown in these figures are sufficient to give considerations in the following. Further, The other cases, such as 23_3_2_4, are omitted because they are clearly inferior to the cases shown in the figures in terms of reliability. The reason of this omitting is denoted as follows.

- Concerning the FTDMLPs for which (N_h, N_{lm} and N_d) are the same with each other, an FTDMLP with bigger N_{bw} is clearly inferior to an FTDMLP with smaller one in terms of reliability, because the bigger N_{bw} requires the more its hardware size.
- Concerning the FTDMLPs for which (N_d and N_{bw}) are the same with each other, an FTDMLP with bigger N_h is clearly inferior to an FTDMLP with

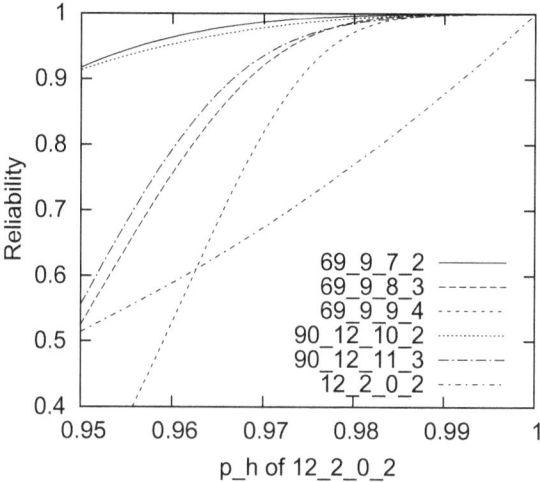

Fig. 7. The relation between $\{R_{ft}$ or $R_{nr}\}$ and $p_{h_{nr}}$ (1_10, $N_{lm} = 9$ and 12)

smaller one in terms of reliability, because the bigger N_h requires the more its hardware size.

From these figures, the following are seen.

– In a group of FTDMLPs for which (N_h and N_{lm}) are the same with each other, the FTDMLP M for which N_{bw} is 2 is superior to the FTDMLP(s) for which N_{bw} is bigger than 2 and N_d is bigger than that for M, especially for the cases where $N_{lm} \geq 6$. Therefore in the following, the only FTDMLPs for which N_{bw} is 2 are considered.
– The bigger N_d brings the higher reliability one way, but on the other hand, the bigger N_d (which is greater than 9 in the figures) brings the lower reliability. Therefore in the following, the case with the highest reliability is searched for each n_N_p case.

Figure 8 shows the relation between $\{R_{ft}$ or $R_{nr}\}$ and $p_{h_{nr}}$ for the case of 1_10 where N_{bw} is 2. The meaning of labels in these figures is, $N_{h_{min}}$_N_{lm}_N_d. From this figure, the following are seen.

– The reliability of the FTDMLP for the case of 61_8_6 is the highest in the case of 1_10.
– The reliabilities of the FTDMLPs, including the case of 61_8_6, are much higher than that of the non-redundant DMLP 12_2_0.

Figures 9, 10 and 11 show the similar relations for the cases of 1_20, 2_20 and 2_40 ($N_{bw} = 2$), respectively. The meaning of labels in these figures is the same as in the previous one. From these figures, the following are seen.

– The reliabilities of the FTDMLPs for the cases of 102_11_8, 72_9_8, and 108_12_10 are the highest in the cases of 1_20, 2_20 and 2_40, respectively.

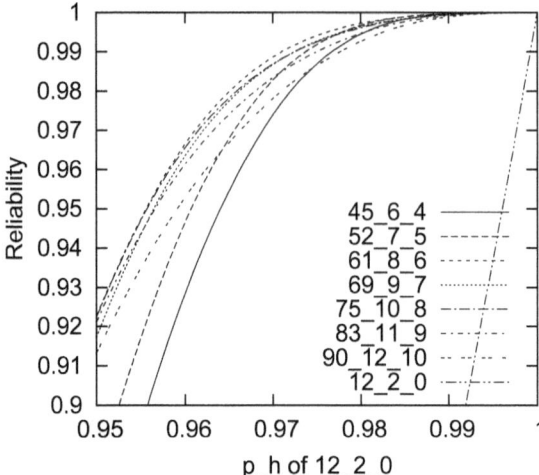

Fig. 8. The relation between $\{R_{ft}$ or $R_{nr}\}$ and $p_{h_{nr}}$ (1_10, $N_{bw} = 2$)

– The reliabilities of the FTDMLPs are much higher than those of the non-redundant DMLPs in the cases of 1_20, 2_20 and 2_40, respectively.

6.6 Consideration About Fault-Tolerance in Terms of FIT Rate

Here, as further consideration from the previous section, the fault-tolerance of DMLPs in terms of FIT is considered.

Let the reliability of an FPGA device be given in an exponential distribution. Then, let r, λ and T be the reliability of the FPGA device, the failure rate, and the device hours, respectively. The following equation holds.

$$r = e^{-\lambda T} \tag{14}$$

From this equation,

$$\lambda = -\frac{1}{T}ln(r) \tag{15}$$

and the FIT rate is $\lambda \cdot 10^9$.

From the above and the data in Figs. 8, 9 and 10, for the FPGA devices of the cyclone III family in the case of $T = 87,600$ (h) (=10 years), Fig. 12 shows the relations between the FIT rates of the $FTDMLP_{total}$ with the highest reliability and non-redundant one, for each n_N_p case, via the same value of $p_{h_{nr}}$.

Table 2 shows the relation between the FIT rate in Fig. 12 and the reliability r.

Reference [32] reports that the FIT rate of a cyclone III family device is 42.8 at a typical use condition of Vcc nominal in a 55 °C still-air ambient. However, this value is calculated using seven kinds of 65 nm products where the hardware complexity of a product is more than ten times that of the other, under 60 % confidence level. The FIT rate in [32] becomes 3.27 times under 95 % confidence level.

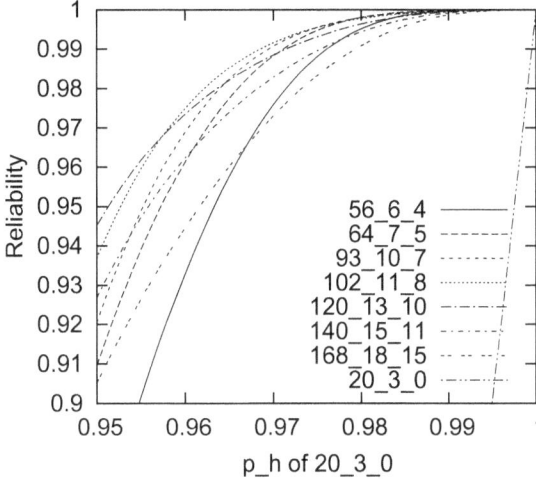

Fig. 9. The relation between $\{R_{ft}$ or $R_{nr}\}$ and $p_{h_{nr}}$ (1_20, $N_{bw} = 2$)

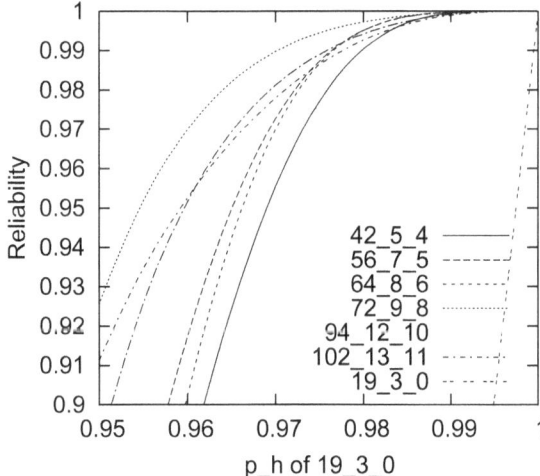

Fig. 10. The relation between $\{R_{ft}$ or $R_{nr}\}$ and $p_{h_{nr}}$ (2_20, $N_{bw} = 2$)

Therefore, we consider that the true FIT rate value might be about five times the value in [32] or more especially for a complicated 65 nm product. From Table 2, if the true FIT rate of an FPGA is $42.8 \cdot 5 = 214$, the reliability of a non-redundant DMLP is about 0.98 and this failure rate is not small in some cases. However, even in this case, Fig. 12 shows that the FIT rate of the $FTDMLP_{total}$ remarkably decreases to less than 1 and this failure rate is so small in common cases.

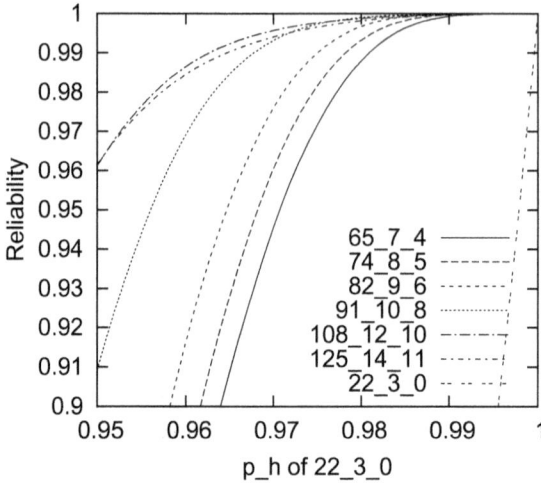

Fig. 11. The relation between $\{R_{ft} \text{ or } R_{nr}\}$ and $p_{h_{nr}}$ (2_40, $N_{bw} = 2$)

6.7 The Data Concerning Hardware Size, Computing Time and Electricity Consumption

Table 3 shows the data for the $FTDMLP_{total}$ with the highest reliability and non-redundant one, for each n_N_p case. Concerning the labels in these tables, "(ns)" indicates the neural computation time (computing speed) (nano sec.) which is equal to the delay time of the critical path obtained by the "Timing Analyzer" tool in the Quartus II, and "(mW)" indicates the electricity consumption (milli watt) obtained by the "PowerPlay Power Analyzer" tool in the Quartus II, using the input file for the logic simulation called the "vector waveform file", in which input signals are randomly changed per 100 (ns) during 2.0 (us).

From these data, the following are seen.

- (Hardware size) the sz_NN of the $FTDMLP_{total}$ is 4.9 to 6.1 times that of non-redundant one in each n_N_p case. This shows that the hardware overhead of the $FTDMLP_{total}$ is very high.
- (Computing speed) Concerning "(ns)", the value for the $FTDMLP_{total}$ is 1.4 to 1.5 times that of non-redundant one for each n_N_p case. In addition, the

Table 2. The relation between the FIT rate and the reliability r ($T = 87,600\,(\text{h})$)

FIT	20	40	60	80	100
r	0.9998	0.9965	0.9948	0.9930	0.9913
FIT	200	500	1000	1500	2000
r	0.9826	0.9571	0.9161	0.8769	0.8392

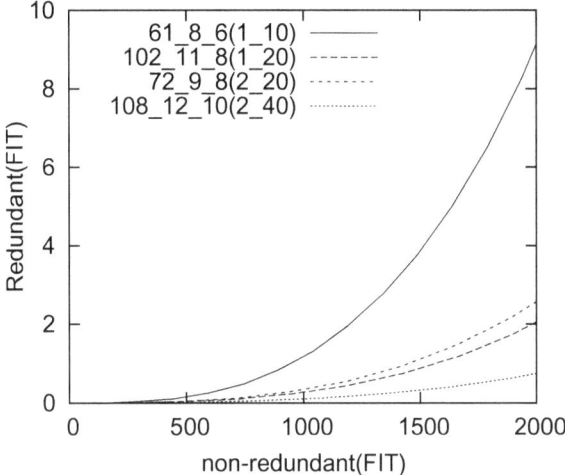

Fig. 12. The relation of the FIT rates between $FTDMLP_{total}$s and non-redundant DMLPs ($T = 87,600\,(\text{h})$)

Table 3. Data concerning hardware size, computing time and electricity consumption

Case	DMLP	sz_NN	(ns)	(mW)
1_10	61_8_6	6379	31.1	198
	12_2_0	1052	22.3	81
1_20	102_11_8	16000	40.7	533
	20_3_0	3273	29.4	118
2_20	72_9_8	11137	37.5	323
	19_3_0	2165	26.0	117
2_40	108_12_10	30202	39.9	774
	22_3_0	5827	27.5	163

data show that the neural computation time is less than 40.7 (ns) and very short even when the MLP is realized as an $FTDMLP_{total}$.
- (Electricity consumption) Concerning "(mW)", the value of the $FTDMLP_{total}$ is 2.4 to 4.7 times that of non-redundant one for each n_N_p case. However, the value is less than 800(mW) and this is much less than that of a PC.

7 Conclusion

A method to realize weight as well as neuron fault-tolerant digital MLPs on FPGAs is proposed. The properties concerning their fault-tolerances are shown. By simulations, The process to realize FTDMLPs for pattern recognitions is illustrated in detail and the FTDMLPs realized are evaluated in terms of not only reliability and FIT rate but also hardware size, computing speed and electricity consumption, comparing with those of the corresponding non-redundant DMLPs. From the above, it is seen that the method proposed is useful to design FPGA-based FTDMLPs for MLPs.

As future works, we will apply our method to the other learning algorithm which realize the fault-tolerant such as the fault injection one proposed in [18], and compare the results with ones in this paper.

Acknowledgment. This research is supported by the university program of Altera Inc., a nice idea of a prototype FTDMLN VHDL notation created by Y. Nishimura, and other preliminary works by H. Sudo, T. Kanda, T. Murata and K. Takeuchi.

Appendix A: Proof of Theorem 1

Let X ($\hat{X}$) be the weighted sum of inputs to a neuron in the output layer when the MLP is fault free (the MLP has faulty neurons in the hidden layer and/or faulty weights). X and $\hat{X}$ are given as follows.

$$X = \sum_{i \in I_M} w_i h_i \tag{16}$$

where I_M is the set of neurons in the hidden layer indices. Note that the index of the weight which is connected to the target neuron in the output layer is also represented as i.

$$\hat{X} = \sum_{k \notin \hat{L}, k \notin \hat{J}} w_k \cdot h_k + \sum_{k \in \hat{L}, k \notin \hat{J}} w'_k \cdot h_k$$
$$+ \sum_{k \notin \hat{L}, k \in \hat{J}} w_k \cdot h'_k + \sum_{k \in \hat{L}, k \in \hat{J}} w'_k \cdot h'_k \tag{17}$$

where w_i (w'_i) is the value of the i-th weight when it is healthy (faulty) and h_i, (h'_i) is the value of the i-th neuron in the hidden layer when it is healthy (faulty).

From the Eqs. (16) and (17),

$$\hat{X} - X = \sum_{k \in \hat{L}, k \notin \hat{J}} (w'_k - w_k) \cdot h_k \tag{18}$$

$$+ \sum_{k \notin \hat{L}, k \in \hat{J}} w_k \cdot (h'_k - h_k) \tag{19}$$

$$+ \sum_{k \in \hat{L}, k \in \hat{J}} (w'_k \cdot h'_k - w_k \cdot h_k) \tag{20}$$

In addition, the following equations are true because of Assumptions 2 and 3, and h_k being 0 or 1.

$$-2 \cdot w_{max} \leq (w'_k - w_k) \cdot h_k \leq 2 \cdot w_{max}$$

$$-w_{max} \leq w_k \cdot (h'_k - h_k) \leq w_{max}$$
$$-2 \cdot w_{max} \leq (w'_k \cdot h'_k - w_k \cdot h_k) \leq 2 \cdot w_{max}$$

Furthermore,
$$N_{18} + N_{20} = |\hat{L}|,$$
$$N_{19} + N_{20} = |\hat{J}|,$$

and
$$N_{20} = |\hat{J} \cap \hat{L}|,$$

where N_{18}, N_{19}, and N_{20} are the number of the terms in the summations of Eqs. (18), (19), and (20), respectively. Therefore,
$$2N_{18} + N_{19} + 2N_{20} = |\hat{J}| + 2|\hat{L}| - |\hat{J} \cap \hat{L}|$$
$$= |\hat{J} \cup \hat{L}| + |\hat{L}|$$

Thus,
$$-w_{max} \cdot (|\hat{J} \cup \hat{L}| + |\hat{L}|) \leq (\hat{X} - X) \leq w_{max} \cdot (|\hat{J} \cup \hat{L}| + |\hat{L}|).$$

Then
$$X - w_{max} \cdot (|\hat{J} \cup \hat{L}| + |\hat{L}|) \leq \hat{X} \leq X + w_{max} \cdot (|\hat{J} \cup \hat{L}| + |\hat{L}|).$$

From this equation and the $DL\text{-}cond(N_d)$,
$$\hat{X} \geq w_{max} \cdot (N_d - (|\hat{J} \cup \hat{L}| + |\hat{L}|)) \geq 0 \text{ (if } t_p = 1),$$
$$\hat{X} < -w_{max} \cdot (N_d - (|\hat{J} \cup \hat{L}| + |\hat{L}|)) < 0 \text{ (if } t_p = 0).$$

From these equations, the Eq. (5), and the use of the step function for calculating the output of each neuron, the theorem is proved. □

References

1. Horita, T., Takanami, I., Mori, M.: Learning algorithms which make multilayer neural networks multiple-weight-and-neuron-fault tolerant. IEICE Trans. Inf. Syst. **E91-D**(4), 1168–1175 (2008)
2. Horita, T., Takanami, I.: An FPGA-based multiple-weight-and-neuron-fault tolerant digital multilayer perceptron. Neurocomputing **99**, 570–574 (2013). Elsevier
3. Phatak, D.S., Koren, I.: Complete and partial fault tolerance of feedforward neural nets. IEEE Trans. Neural Netw. **6**(2), 446–456 (1995)
4. Fahlman, S.E., et al.: Neural nets learning algorithms and benchmarks database. Maintained by Fahlman, S.E., et al. at the Computer Science Department, Carnegie Mellon University
5. Nijhuis, J., Hoefflinger, B., van Schaik, A., Spaanenburg, L.: Limits to the fault-tolerance of a feedforward neural network with learning. In: Proceedings of International Symposium on FTCS, pp. 228–235 (1990)
6. Tan, Y., Nanya, T.: A faut-tolerant multi-layer neural network model and its properties. IEICE D-I **J76-D-I**(7), 380–389 (1993). (in Japanese)

7. Murray, A.F., Edwards, P.J.: Synaptic weight noise during multilayer perceptron training: fault tolerance and training improvement. IEEE Trans. Neural Netw. **4**(4), 722–725 (1993)
8. Hammadi, N.C., Ohmameuda, T., Kaneko, K., Ito, H.: Dynamic constructive fault tolerant algorithm for feedforward neural networks. IEICE Trans. Inf. Syst. **E81-D**(1), 115–123 (1998)
9. Takase, H., Kita, H., Hayashi, T.: Weight minimization approach for fault tolerant multi-layer neural networks. In: Proceedings of International Joint Conference on Neural Networks, pp. 2656–2660 (2001)
10. Kamiura, N., Taniguchi, Y., Hata, Y., Matsui, N.: A learning algorithm with activation function manipulation for fault tolerant neural networks. IEICE Trans. Inf. Syst. **E84-D**(7), 899–905 (2001)
11. Clay, R.D., Séquin, C.H.: Fault tolerance training improves generalization and robustness. In: Proceedings of International Joint Conference on Neural Networks, pp. I-769–I-774 (1992)
12. Cavalieri, S., Mirabella, O.: A novel learning algorithm which improves the partial fault tolerance of multilayer neural networks. Neural Netw. (Pergamon) **12**(1), 91–106 (1999)
13. Demidenko, S., Piuri, V.: Concurrent diagnosis in digital implementations of neural networks. Neurocomputing **48**(1-4), 879–903 (2002)
14. Zhanga, Y., Guoa, L., Yua, H., Zhao, K.: Fault tolerant control based on stochastic distributions via MLP neural networks. Neurocomputing **70**(4–6), 867–874 (2007)
15. Ho, K., Leung, C.S., Sum, J.: Training RBF network to tolerate single node faults. Neurocomputing **74**(6), 1046–1052 (2011)
16. Maka, S.K., Sum, P.F., Leung, C.S.: Regularizers for fault tolerant multilayer feedforward networks. Neurocomputing **74**(11), 2028–2040 (2011)
17. Takanami, I., Sato, M., Yang, Y.P.: A fault-value injection approach for multiple-weight-fault tolerance of MNNs. In: Proceedings of International Joint Conference on IJCNN, p. III-515 (2000)
18. Takanami, I., Oyama, Y.: A novel learning algorithm which makes multilayer neural networks multiple-weight-fault tolerant. IEICE Trans. Inf. Syst. **E86-D**(12), 2536–2543 (2003)
19. Massengill, L.W., Mundie, D.B.: An analog neural hardware implementation using charge-injection multipliers and neuron-specific gain control. IEEE Trans. Neural Netw. **3**(3), 354–362 (1992)
20. Frye, R.C., Rietman, E.A., Wong, C.C.: Back-propagation learning and nonidealities in analog neural network hardware. IEEE Trans. Neural Netw. **2**(1), 110–117 (1991)
21. Holt, J.L., Hwang, J.N.: Finite precision error analysis of neural network hardware implementations. IEEE Trans. Comput. **42**(3), 281–290 (1993)
22. Mauduit, N., Duranton, M., Gobert, J., Sirat, J.A.: Lneuro 1.0: a piece of hardware LEGO for building neural network systems. IEEE Trans. Neural Netw. **3**(3), 414–422 (1992)
23. Murakawa, M., Yoshizawa, S., et al.: The GRD chip: genetic reconfiguration of DSPs for neural network processing. IEEE Trans. Comput. **48**, 628–639 (1999)
24. Brown, B.D., Card, H.C.: Stochastic neural computation I: computational elements. IEEE Trans. Comput. **50**(9), 891–905 (2001)
25. Card, H.C., McNeal, D.K., McLeod, R.D.: Competitive learning algorithms and neurocomputer architecture. IEEE Trans. Comput. **47**(8), 847–858 (1998)
26. Ninomiya, H., Asai, H.: Neural networks for digital sequential circuits. IEICE Trans. Fundam. **E77-A**(12), 2112–2115 (1994)

27. Aihara, K., Fujita, O., Uchimura, K.: A sparse memory access architecture for digital neural network LSIs. IEICE Trans. Electron. **E80-C**(7), 996–1002 (1997)
28. Morishita, T., Tamura, Y., et al.: A digital neural network coprocessor with a dynamically reconfigurable pipeline architecture. IEICE Trans. Electron. **E76-C**(7), 1191–1196 (1993)
29. Fujita, M., Kobayashi, Y., et al.: Development and fabrication of digital neural network WSIs. IEICE Trans. Electron. **E76-C**(7), 1182–1190 (1993)
30. Bettola, S., Piuri, V.: High performance fault-tolerant digital neural networks. IEEE Trans. Comput. **47**(3), 357–363 (1998)
31. Sugawara, E., Fukushi, M., Horiguchi, S.: Self reconfigurable multi-layer neural networks with genetic algorithms. IEICE Trans. Inf. Syst. **E87-D**(8), 2021–2028 (2004)
32. Altera reliability report homepage. http://www.altera.com/literature/rr/rr.pdf

Performance Analysis of Coded Cooperation and Space Time Cooperation with Multiple Relays in Nakagami-m Fading

Sindhu Hak Gupta[1](✉), R.K. Singh[2], and S.N. Sharan[3]

[1] Department of Electronics and Communication Engineering,
ASET, Amity University, Noida, UP, India
sindhugupta09@rediffmail.com
[2] Uttarakhand Technical University, Dehradun, India
rksinghkec12@rediffmail.com
[3] Department of Electronics and Communication Engineering, GNIT,
Greater Noida, India
snathsharan@gmail.com

Abstract. In this paper expressions of outage probability under Nakagami-m fading for Coded Cooperative Communication have been developed. Performance of outage has been simulated for various factors such as allocated Rate, cooperation level, mean channel SNR and number of relays. Diversity order has been calculated for Coded Cooperative Communication with multiple relays. Outage probability expression for Space Time Cooperation with multiple partners under Nakagami-m have also been developed and analyzed. A critical comparative analysis is done for No Cooperation, Coded Cooperation and Space Time Cooperation. Simulation results highlight the benefits of Coded Cooperation over the other two schemes under the slow fading circumstances.

Keywords: MIMO · Coded Cooperation · Space Time Cooperation · Diversity order · Outage · Nakagami-m

1 Introduction

Fading affects wireless communication badly. MIMO offers data throughput and that also without additional burden of transmit power or bandwidth. MIMO achieves these qualities, primarily because of diversity technique. All wireless devices cannot support transmit diversity mainly because of limitation of transreceivers. Cooperative Communication helps in creating virtual MIMO. It enables single antenna mobiles to share their antennas in a multiuser environment and achieve transmit diversity.

Put on air nature of wireless communication is the basic building block for Cooperative Communication. It works on the principle that the signal which is broadcast between source and destination can be overheard at the neighboring nodes. The fundamental concept behind Cooperative Communication is the relay channel model which was presented by Laneman and Wornell [1]. Various cooperative protocols such as Amplify and Forward, Detect and Forward and Coded Cooperative protocol were proposed. Their performance and behaviour was analyzed in detail under various channel models [2–5]. For Coded Cooperative Communication, cooperative signaling is incorporated with channel coding. It works by transmitting different fraction of information of each user via two self regulating independent fading paths [6,7]. Each user, instead of repeating the received bits tries to broadcast incremental redundancy for its collaborator, whenever it is not feasible, the user routinely by design reverts to non cooperation mode. Space Time Cooperation can be described as an extended version of Coded Cooperations, certain attributes and advantages are associated with it in comparison to Coded Cooperation.

Figure 1(a), (b) and (c) illustrates No Cooperation, Cooperative Communication and Space Time Cooperation. These figures highlight the difference of Space Time Cooperation with Coded Cooperation and No Cooperation. Space Time Cooperation as was explained in [8] is illustrated by Fig. 1. Each user in the first frame transmits its data where as the power of the second frame is divided between the users bits and its partners bits.

In [9,10] Sharma first analyzed the outage behaviour and then analyzed the complete performance of Decode and Forward dual hop cooperative system; and behaviour of Full Duplex Relaying was compared with Half Duplex Relaying. In [12] Hunter has analyzed the outage behaviour of Coded Cooperation with multiple Relays under Rayleigh fading. In this paper the same frameworks as in [11,12,14] have been used but with channel fading statistics as Nakagami-m which is more comprehensive and general form of statics. Detailed outage analysis of Coded Cooperative Communication has been done and diversity order under Nakagami-m fading channel has also been calculated. Outage probability of Space Time Cooperation with multiple partners has also been calculated and simulated under Nakagami-m fading. Comparative analysis of No Cooperation, Coded Cooperation and Space Time Cooperation has been carried out. The further paper is organized as follows: System description is given in Sect. 2, in Sect. 3 we analyze the performance of Coded Cooperation over slow fading channels. For it, the fading coefficients stay constant through every frame transmission period. In Sect. 4 we will be calculating diversity order for Coded Cooperation, in Sect. 5 we analyze the performance of Space Time Cooperation, under slow fading channel. In Sect. 6 we discuss the Numerical Results and lastly in Sect. 7 we conclude.

2 System Description

We consider a model in which we have one Source (S) and Multiple relays (M) as shown in Fig. 2. This source along with multiple relays will form a cluster. When a particular user will transmit, all other existing users of the cluster will listen to this transmitted packet of the particular user. The wireless link between these two nodes is modelled as Nakagami-m fading channel. There will be either of

174   S.H. Gupta et al.

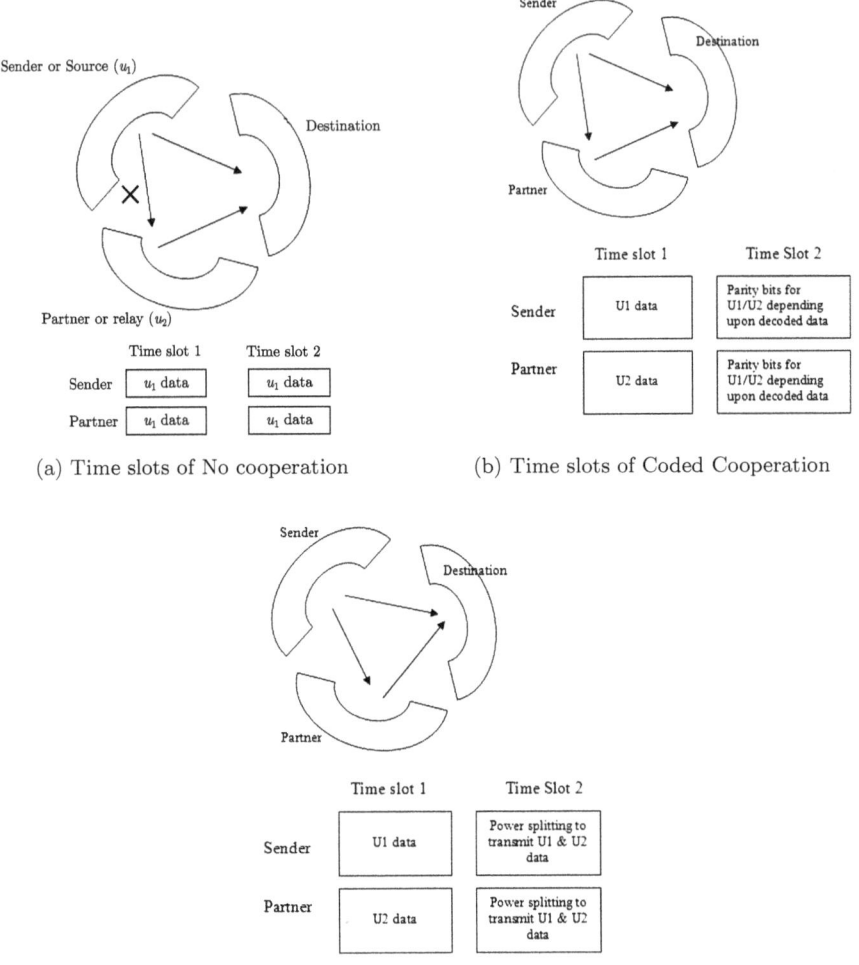

Fig. 1. Non-cooperation, Cooperative Communication and Space Time Cooperation

the two situations now. Situation 1, is that no neighbouring relay will be able to correctly decode, hence it is similar to Non Cooperative mode of communication. Situation 2 is that some (let us assume K numbers of relays) or all of the neighbouring relays (M) will be able to decode.

In the first situation as described above Non Cooperative models will be considered and in the second situation only those relays which are able to correctly interpret/translate data, will be considered, as they will send extra information or the redundant bits about source's packet to the destination D. r_i denotes the r_ith relay. We will analyze Coded Cooperation and Space Time Cooperation separately.

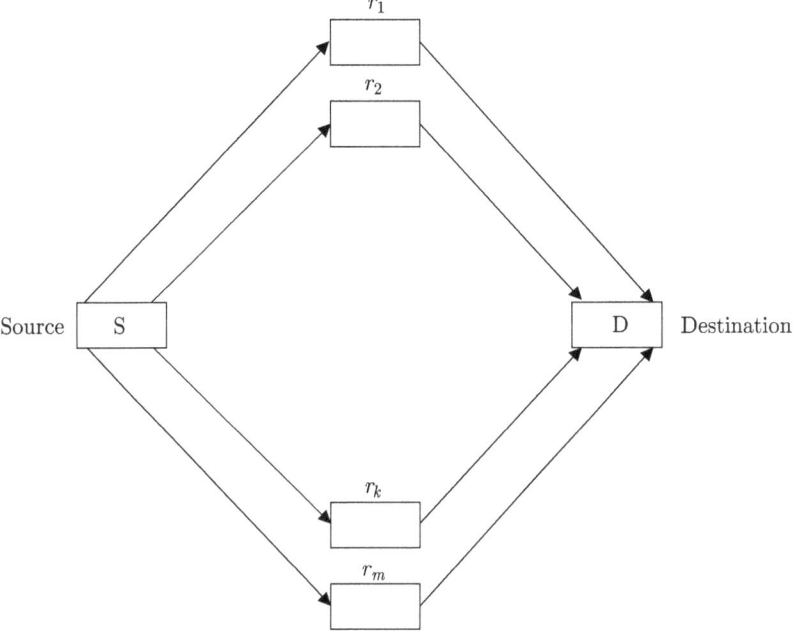

Fig. 2. Information is sent from S to D with the help of r

For Coded Cooperative Communication each user transmits an overall of N bits per source block over the two frames and N_1 is the number of bits transmitted by the user in the first frame, then cooperation ratio

$$\alpha = \frac{N_1}{N} = \frac{R}{R_1}. \qquad (1)$$

The second frame $N_2 = N - N_1$ contains left over remaining parity bits of the codeword. The N bits are transmitted at an overall rate R, R_1 is the rate at which N_1 bits will be transmitted and R_2 is the rate at the which N_2 bits will be transmitted. Both the users transmit source data containing N bits in each block code. To begin with, source will transmit its own N_1 bits. If r_ith successfully decodes the information from the source (S) it will calculate and transmit source N_2's remaining bits otherwise it will revert to No Cooperation mode and will transmit its own parity bits.

For Space Time Cooperation as was explained earlier, in the first frame each user will transmit its own data bits whereas for the second frame the power of it is divided between the user information and the relay information. The users own supplementary parity symbols are transmitted with power β_i (P_T) and the supplementary parity symbols of the relay is transmitted with power $(1-\beta_i)P_T$, where P_T denotes the users total average transmitted power. If the relay is not able to successfully decode all the power is allocated to the users total average power [8].

The strategy of Space Time Cooperation is highly effective in fast fading channel, as user's reverse channel sees independent fading between the first and the second frames. Therefore, by utilizing neighbouring partners channel for the second frame will not be providing any additional benefit or improvement. Thus, destination receives a part of data from source or user 1 (u_1) and other part of the user's data from relay or user 2 (u_2) which it combines together. The path chosen for transmission of data by both the users have different SNR (signal to noise) ratio and varying fading levels. Thus, power of partial frames is shared by the user and user's relay to transmit bits in this scheme.

In this cooperation scheme, the second frame by itself enjoys the diversity as each user transmits both users parities during the second frame [8]. The diversity which is offered in case of Space Time Cooperation is path diversity [$\beta_1 = \beta_2 = 0.5$].

3 Performance Analysis of Coded Cooperation

In order to make performance analysis simpler we will have to make following assumptions. Firstly no node can transmit or receive simultaneously and secondly each device whether it is a source, destination or a relay, it is equipped with single antenna transmitter and receiver. As mentioned in previous section there are two situations. Accordingly, we will evaluate the performance. Firstly, we consider Non Cooperative direct transmission between source (S) and destination (D) with Quasi static fading. The capacity conditioned on channel realization characterized by the instantaneous SNR can be given by Shannon's theorem [8,12,13].

$$C(\gamma) = \log_2(1+\gamma) \text{ in b/s/hz}. \tag{2}$$

The channel is said to be in outage if the conditional capacity $C(\gamma)$ drops below a certain evaluated threshold R and the corresponding outage event is

$$C(\gamma) < R \tag{3}$$

$$\gamma < 2^R - 1 \tag{4}$$

where
P_{out} = Outage Probability

$$P_{out} = P_r(\gamma < 2^R - 1) = \int_0^{2^R-1} P_\gamma(\gamma)d\gamma. \tag{5}$$

where $P_\gamma(\gamma)$ is the Probability density function (p.d.f) of random variable. The outage probability for Nakagami-m fading can be evaluated as:

$$P_{out} = \frac{1 - \Gamma\left(m, m\frac{(2^R-1)}{\Gamma}\right)}{\Gamma(m)}. \tag{6}$$

For case of Nakagami-m fading γ, has a gamma distribution p.d.f. Γ denotes the mean value of SNR over Nakagami-m fading and accounts for the combination of transmitted power and received noise which accounts for large scale path loss and shadowing effects. We will re-parametrize it in future when we will be calculating the diversity order. $\Gamma(m)$ is the gamma function defined as $\Gamma(m) = \int_0^\infty t^{m-1} e^{-1} dt$ and $\Gamma(m,\xi)$ is the upper incomplete Gamma function defined as $\Gamma(m,\xi) = \int_\xi^\infty t^{m-1} e^t dt$ [12,14].

As discussed in Sect. 2 we will consider a practical situation where some relays will not be able to decode N_1 frame of the source and hence they will switch to Non Cooperative mode where as some of the frames from the cluster will be able to decode N_1 and hence they will be computing and transmitting the N_2 frame for the source. The number of the cooperating relays range from 0 to K denoted by Ω the set of indices of the cooperating relays.

$$\Omega = \{(i_1, i_2, \ldots, i_K)\} \subset \{(1, 2, \ldots, M)\}. \tag{7}$$

Cardinality of Ω is K [12].

In Coded Cooperation, user data are transmitted over two successive frames. In the first frame each user transmit at a rate $R_1 = R/\alpha$ codeword. There are two possible cases for the second frame transmission as discussed above, accordingly two situations will arise.

Situation 1

When frame will be transmitted from source to destination none of the neighbouring relays from the cluster will decode the source frame successfully. This failed decoding leads to the following event.

$$C_{s,r_i}(\gamma_s, r_i) = \log_2(1 + \gamma_{s,r_i}) < \frac{R}{\alpha}. \tag{8}$$

Since, relay is unable to decode, in the second frame the source will transmit its own additional parity bits. Destination in this case will receive first as well as second frame from the source itself, this is somewhat similar to non-Cooperative Communication α fraction of total allocated N bits are occupied by the first frame where as remaining $(1-\alpha)$ fraction of total allocated bits are occupied by second frame. These two transmissions i.e. transmission of first frame with and transmission of second frame with $(1-\alpha)$ can be viewed as time sharing between two independent channels, where the first channel uses the fraction of time. Thus, we can write the outage event as

$$C_{s,d}(\gamma_{s,d}) = \alpha \log_2(1 + \gamma_{s,d}) + (1-\alpha)\log_2(1+\gamma_{s,d}) < R. \tag{9}$$

Situation 2

When frame will be transmitted from source to destination some or all of the neighbouring relays from the cluster will decode the source frame successfully. This successful decoding means that

$$C_{s,r_i}(\gamma_s, r_i) = \log_2(1 + \gamma_{s,r_i}) > \frac{R}{\alpha}. \tag{10}$$

This will lead to the corresponding outage event given by:

$$C_{s,d}(\gamma_{s,d}) = \alpha \log_2(1 + \gamma_{s,d}) + (1-\alpha)\log_2\left(1 + \gamma_{s,d} + \sum_{i=\Omega}\gamma_{r_i,d}\right) < R. \tag{11}$$

Since, the above two cases are disjoint we can write for Nakagami-m fading.

$$P_{\text{out}} = \prod_{i=1}^{M} P_r\{\gamma_{s,r_i} < 2^{\frac{R}{\alpha}} - 1\} \cdot P_r\{\gamma_{s,d} < 2^R - 1\}$$

$$+ \sum_{K=1}^{M}\binom{M}{K}\left\{\prod_{i\notin\Omega} P_r\{\gamma_{s,r_i} < 2^{\frac{R}{\alpha}} - 1\} \prod_{i\notin\Omega} P_r\{\gamma_{s,r_i} > 2^{\frac{R}{\alpha}} - 1\}\right.$$

$$\left. \cdot P_r\left\{(1+\gamma_{s,d})^{\alpha}\left(1 + \gamma_{s,d} + \sum_{i\in\Omega}\gamma_{r_i,d}\right)^{1-\alpha} < 2^R\right\}\right\} \tag{12}$$

$$= \prod_{i=1}^{M}\left[1 - \Gamma(m,m)\frac{(2^{\frac{R}{\alpha}}-1)}{\Gamma_{s,r_i}}\right]\left[1 - \Gamma(m,m)\frac{2^{\frac{R}{\alpha}}-1}{\Gamma_{s,r_i}}\right]$$

$$\cdot \left[\int_0^{2^{\frac{R}{\alpha}}-1}\frac{1}{\Gamma(m)^2}\left(\frac{m}{s,d}\right)^m \gamma_{s,d}^{m-1}\exp\left(-m\frac{\gamma_{s,d}}{\Gamma_{s,d}}\right)\right]$$

$$\cdot \left[1 - \Gamma\left(m, \frac{ma}{\Gamma_{r_i,d}}\right)\right]d\gamma_{r_i,d} \tag{13}$$

$$= \left[1 - \Gamma\left(m, \frac{m(2^{\frac{R}{\alpha}}-1)}{\Gamma_{s,r}}\right)\right]^{M}\left[1 - \Gamma\left(m, \frac{m(2^R-1)}{\Gamma_{s,d}}\right)\right]$$

$$+ \sum_{K=1}^{M}\frac{M!}{K!(M-K)!}\left[1 - \Gamma\left(m, \frac{m(2^{\frac{R}{\alpha}}-1)}{\Gamma_{sr}}\right)\right]^{M-K}$$

$$\cdot \Gamma\left[m, \frac{m(2^{\frac{R}{\alpha}}-1)}{\Gamma_{s,r}}\right]^{K}\int_0^{2^{\frac{R}{\alpha}}-1}\frac{1}{\Gamma(m)^2}\left(\frac{m}{s,d}\right)^m\left[1 - \Gamma m, \frac{ma}{\Gamma_{s,d}}\right] \tag{14}$$

Observations which can be made from Eq. (7) is that Coded Cooperation with multiple relays under Nakagami-m fading is a function of α the cooperation level, the rate R and most importantly mean channel SNR values $\{\Gamma_{s,d}, \Gamma_{s,r_i}, \Gamma_{r_i,d}\}$. As we know $\Gamma_{s,d}, \Gamma_{s,r_i}, \Gamma_{r_i,d}$ and R are constrained by communication channels. The only free parameter is α which can be varied in order to achieve optimal performance.

4 Asymptotic Analysis and Diversity Order for Coded Cooperation [12, 14]

In order to determine the diversity order we will observe and investigate the behavior of outage probability under high SNR regime. To achieve this we reparameterize the mean SNR as mentioned in previous section

$$\Gamma_{s,d} = \Gamma_T \overline{\Gamma}_{s,d}.$$

where Γ_T is the ratio of the user transmit power to the received noise. $\overline{\Gamma}_{s,d}$ is the finite constant which accounts for large scale path loss to shadowing effects. Expressing outage probability as a function of $1/\Gamma_T$ and then approximating Γ_T tends to infinity. The diversity order can be calculated and, is given by smallest exponent of $1/\Gamma_T$. To obtain the outage probability as a function of $1/\Gamma_T$ for the case of independent inter user channels, we expand each exponential term in final expression of P_{out} using the equivalent Taylor's series representation and collect like order terms:

$$\prod_{i=1}^{M}\left[1-\Gamma\left(m,\frac{m(2^{\frac{R}{\alpha}}-1)}{\Gamma_{s,r_i}}\right)\right]\left[1-\Gamma\left(m,\frac{m(2^{\frac{R}{\alpha}}-1)}{\Gamma_{s,d}}\right)\right]$$

$$= O\left(\frac{1}{\Gamma_T^M+1}\right)\prod_{i\notin\Omega}\left[1-\Gamma\left(m,\frac{m(2^{\frac{R}{\alpha}}-1)}{\Gamma_{s,r_i}}\right)\right]\prod_{i\in\Omega}\left(m,m\frac{2^{\frac{R}{\alpha}}-1}{\Gamma_{s,r_i}}\right)$$

$$= O\left(\frac{1}{\Gamma_T^{M-K}}\right) \tag{15}$$

$$\frac{1}{\Gamma_T^{L+1}}\frac{1}{\Gamma_{s,d}}\frac{1}{\Gamma(m)^2}\prod_{i\in\Omega}\frac{1}{\Gamma_{r_i,d}}\int_0^{2^{\frac{R}{\alpha}}-1}\left(\frac{m}{s,d}\right)^m \gamma_{s,d}^{m-1}\left(-m\frac{\gamma_{s,d}}{\Gamma_{s,d}}\right)$$

$$\cdot \exp\prod_{i\in\Omega}\left[1-\Gamma\left(m,\frac{ma}{\Gamma_{r_i,d}}\right)\right]d\gamma_{r_i,d}$$

$$< \frac{1}{\Gamma_T^{K+1}}\cdot\frac{1}{\Gamma_{s,d}}\cdot\frac{1}{\Gamma(m)^2}\prod_{i\in\pi}\frac{1}{\Gamma_{r_i,d}}\left[1-\Gamma\left(m,\frac{ma}{\Gamma_{r_i,d}}\right)\right]d\gamma_{r_i,d}$$

$$= O\left(\frac{1}{\Gamma_T^{M+1}}\right). \tag{16}$$

For (12) using the basic mathematical fact that $\exp(-X) \leq 1$ for all $x \geq 0$, we have (10). With this we conclude that each individual term in (16) behaves as $O(1/\Gamma_T^{M+1})$ [13].

Thus for Coded Cooperation full diversity order is achieved.

5 Space Time Cooperation

For Space Time Cooperation under Nakagami-m fading we have two situations similar to Coded Cooperation. Accordingly, the outage event will become [13].

$$C_{s,r_i}(\gamma_{s,r_i}) = \alpha \log_2(1+\gamma_s d) + (1-\alpha)\log_2[1+\beta_s\gamma_{s,d}$$
$$+ \sum_{i=\Omega}(1-\beta r_i \gamma_{r_i} d)] < R$$

$$P_{\text{out}} = \prod_{i=1}^{M} \Pr\{\gamma_{s,r_i} < 2^{R/\alpha} - 1\} \cdot \Pr\{\gamma_{s,d} < 2^R - 1\}$$
$$+ \sum_{N=1}^{M} \binom{M}{K}\left[\prod_{i \notin \Omega} \Pr\{\gamma_{s,r_i} < 2^{R/\alpha}-1\} \prod_{i \in \Omega} \Pr\{\gamma_{s,r_i} > 2^{R/\alpha}-1\}\right]$$

$$\Pr\{(1+\beta_s\gamma_{s,d})^\alpha \cdot (1+\beta_s\gamma_s d + \sum_{i=\Omega}(1-\beta r_i\gamma r_i d)^{1-\alpha})\} < 2^R$$

$$P_{\text{out}} = \prod_{i=1}^{M}\left[1-\Gamma(m,m)\frac{(2^{R/\alpha}-1)}{\Gamma_{s,r_i}}\right]\left[1-\Gamma(m,m)\frac{2-1^{R/\alpha}}{C_{s,r_i}}\right]$$
$$\times \left[\int_0^{2^{R/\alpha}-1} \frac{1}{\Gamma(m)^2}\frac{(m)^m}{C_{s,d}}\beta\gamma_{s,d}^{m-1}\right.$$
$$\left.\cdot \exp\left(-m\beta\frac{\gamma_{s,d}}{\Gamma_{s,d}}\right)\right]\left[1-\Gamma\left(m,\frac{mb}{\Gamma r_{i,d}}\right)\right]\partial\gamma r_i d$$

$$b = \frac{2^{R/1-\alpha}}{(1+\gamma_{i,d})^{\alpha/1-\alpha}} - 1 - \beta\gamma_{i,d}$$

$$P_{\text{out}} = \left[1-\Gamma\left(m,m\frac{(2^{R/\alpha}-1)}{\Gamma_{s,r}}\right)\right]^M \left[1-\Gamma\left(m,m\frac{(2^R-1)}{\Gamma_{s,d}}\right)\right]$$
$$+ \sum_{K=1}^{M} \frac{M!}{K!(M-K)!}\left[1-\Gamma\left(m,m\frac{(2^{R/\alpha}-1)}{\Gamma_{s,r}}\right)\right]^{M-L}$$
$$\cdot \int_0^{2^{R/\alpha}-1} \frac{1}{\Gamma(m)^2}\left(\frac{m}{\Gamma_{s,d}}\right)^m \left[1-\Gamma\left(m,\frac{mb}{\Gamma_{s,d}}\right)\right] \quad (17)$$

6 Numerical Results

This section represents the numerical results. In order to make calculations simple and approximate, the channels between S to D, r to S and S to r are assumed to be Nakagami-m fading channels.

Figure 3 depicts the plot between the outage probability as evaluated in Eq. (12) versus SNR. Rate is kept constant at 0.5 b/s/hz. All channels are assumed to have a mean equal SNR of 10 dB. As is observed from the figure that gain with Coded Cooperation is much more in comparison with No Cooperation. A very interesting property of Coded Cooperation is that it always performs better than No Cooperation.

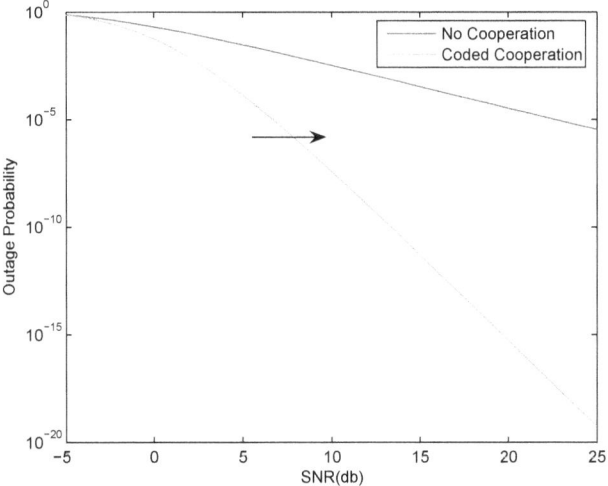

Fig. 3. SNR vs. outage probability for No Cooperation and Coded Cooperation

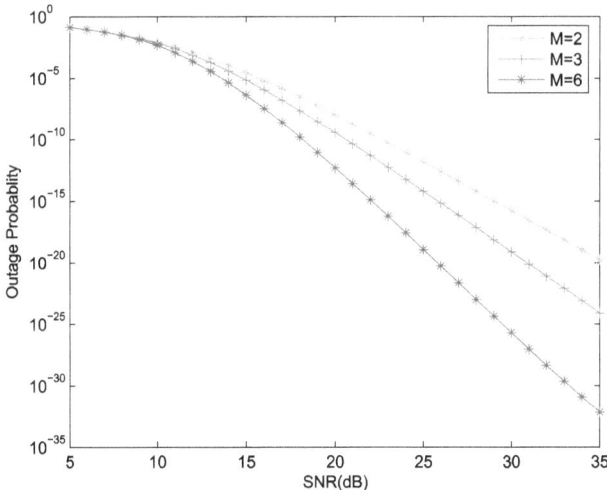

Fig. 4. SNR vs. outage probability for $M = 2, 3$ and 6 relay channels

As seen in Fig. 4, for Coded Cooperation with multiple relays M the coding gain improves as we increase the value of M. To present a clear variation in outage probabilities, three different values of M are considered ($M = 2, M = 3, M = 6$). In this analysis α has been kept constant at 0.25 and the information rate (R) has been fixed at 0.5 bits/sec/hz. As seen from the illustration that for Coded Cooperative Communication with multiple relays, at lower values of SNR (<10 db) there is no effect on outage probability as the number of relays are varied; but the variation becomes prominent as the SNR increases. As is seen the coding

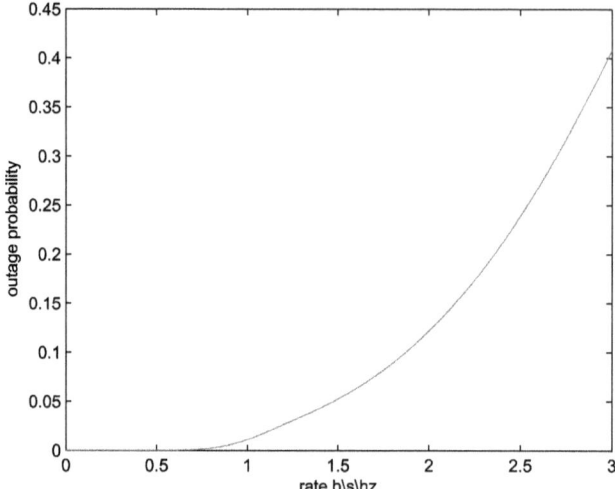

Fig. 5. Outage propagability vs. rate for Coded Cooperative Communication

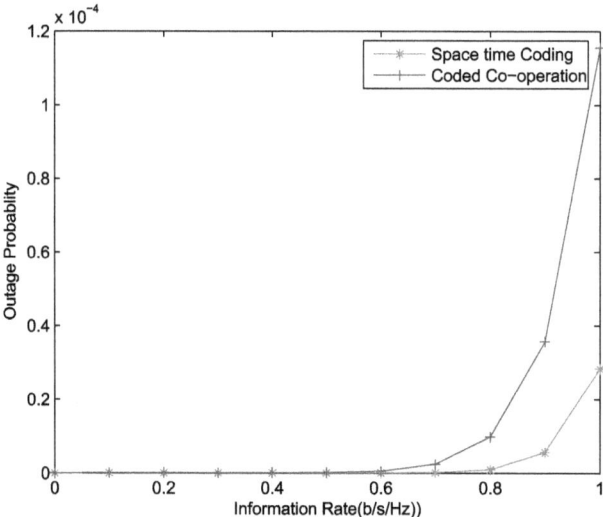

Fig. 6. Outage probability vs. rate for Coded Cooperative Communication and Space Time Cooperation

gain for $M = 6$ is much higher in comparison to the coding gain for $M = 2$. It can be concluded that the coding gain increases with increases in the number of relays.

Figure 5 shows the curve between rate and outage probability. It is assumed that all channels have a mean equal SNR of 10 db. We observe that as the

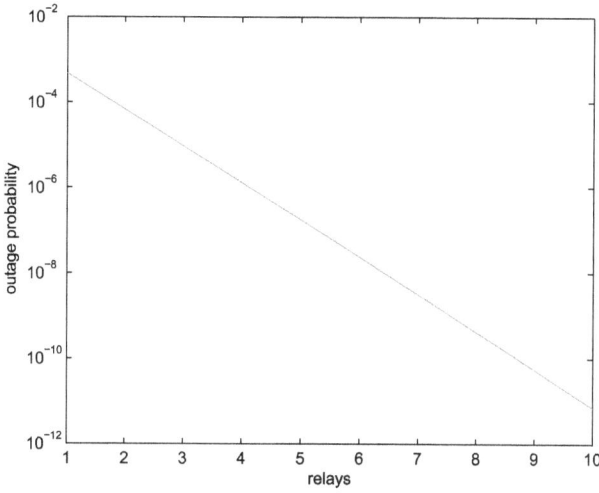

Fig. 7. Outage probability vs. number of relays for Coded Cooperative Communication

rate increases, outage probability increases exponentially, which concludes that higher the rate, higher will be the probability of signal to be in outage. As mentioned in Sect. 3 rate is constrained by channel parameters. As illustrated by the graph we cannot choose a high value for rate as it will deteriorate the performance of Coded Cooperative system. Figure 6 shows the comparative curves of rate vs outage probability for Space Time Cooperation with multiple relays and Coded Cooperation with multiple relays. For this analysis α is kept at 0.25 and number of cooperating relays are 3 from the graph that at the lower values (≤ 0.8 bits/s/hz) of Information rate the behavior of Coded as well as Space Time Cooperation is same. As the information rate increases the difference becomes evident. The further increase in information rate results in prominent difference in outage probabilities of Coded and Space Time Cooperation.

Figure 7 shows the outage probability versus number of relays at constant rate for Coded Cooperative Communication. It can be observed that as the number of relays increases the outage probability decreases significantly. This is due to increase in diversity gains.

Figure 8 shows the comparative analysis of outage probability versus SNR for No Cooperation, Coded Cooperation and Space Time Cooperation. For No Cooperation since there is no relay, so the value of $M = 0$, where as for both Space Time Cooperation and Coded Cooperation, multiple relays have been considered. For them we have kept $M = 3$. The analysis is done in the slow fading scenario. The graph illustrates that Cooperative Communication is showing an improvement in comparison to the Space Time Cooperation. Space Time Cooperation provides an improved performance over Coded Cooperation in fast fading environment. This advantage of Space Time Cooperation over Coded Cooperation is illustrated in [8].

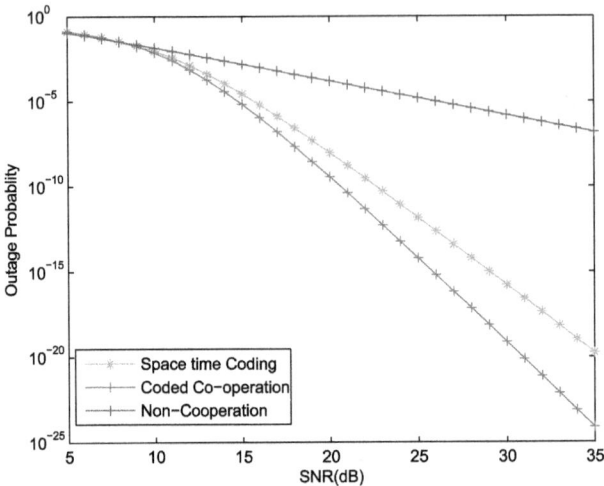

Fig. 8. SNR vs. outage probability for No Cooperation, Coded Cooperation and Space Time Cooperation

7 Conclusion

The outage probability of Coded Cooperative Communication and Space Time Cooperation with multiple relays in Nakagami-m fading channel model have been examined in this work. Mathematical expressions have been derived and simulations have been carried out for outage probability of Coded Cooperation and Space Time Cooperation. Derived mathematical expressions demonstrated the dependence of outage probability on various factors such as SNR, number of relays etc. using these mathematical expressions diversity order for Coded Cooperative Communication was derived and calculated. It was observed that it achieves full diversity. Same analysis has been carried out for Space Time Cooperation with Multiple partners/relays under Nakagami-m fading. Simulation of Numerical results depict that Coded Cooperative Communication achieves a very high gain in comparison to Space Time Cooperation under slow fading scenario. The gain starts falling as the rate increases. Performance is good at low rates ($R \leq .8$ b/s/hz). Results highlight the dependance of gain on number of cooperating relays (M). As the number of cooperating partners (M) increases coding gain also increases, for outage probability of 10^{-25} the gain is more than 20 dB for $M = 6$ in comparison with $M = 2$. As the numbers of relays increases outage reduces. This is more because relays will provide more diversity complexity of the system. We conclude that Coded Cooperation and Space Time Cooperation always perform better than No Cooperation. Increase in number of relays at low rates will always increase the performance of the system provided complexity is taken care off.

References

1. Laneman, J.N., Wornell, G.W., Tse, D.N.C.: An efficient protocol for realizing cooperative diversity in wireless networks. In: Proceedings of the IEEE International Symposium on Information Theory, Washinton DC, pp. 294–305, June 2001
2. Sendonaris, A., Erkip, E., Aazhang, B.: User cooperation diversity – part I: system description. IEEE Trans. Commun. **51**(11), 1927–1938 (2003)
3. Hunter, T.E., Nostratinia, A.: Cooperative diversity through coding. In: Proceedings of the IEEE International Symposium on Information Theory, Laussane, Switzerland, pp. 220–232, June 2002
4. Sendonaris, A., Erkip, E., Aazhang, B.: User cooperation diversity part II: implementation aspects and performance analysis. IEEE Trans. Commun. **51**(11), 1939–1948 (2003)
5. Laneman, J.N., Tse, D.N.C., Wornell, G.W.: Cooperative diversity in wireless networks: efficient protocol and outage behavior. IEEE Trans. Inf. Theory **50**(12), 3062–3080 (2004)
6. Laneman, J.N.: Cooperative diversity in wireless networks: algorithm and architectures. Ph.D. dissertation, MIT, Cambridge, MA (2002)
7. Nostratinia, A., Hunter, T.E., Hedayat, A.: Cooperative communication in wireless networks. IEEE Commun. Mag. **42**, 74–80 (2004)
8. Janani, M., Hedayat, A., Hunter, T.E., Nostratinia, A.: Coded cooperation in wireless communications: space-time transmission and iterative decoding. IEEE Trans. Sig. Process. **52**(2), 362–371 (2004)
9. Sharma, P., Garg, P.: Performance analysis of full duplex decode and forward cooperative relaying over Nakagami-m fading channels. Trans. Emerg. Telecommun. Technol. **25**(9), 905–913 (2013)
10. Sharma, P., Garg, P.: Outage analysis of full duplex decode and forward relaying over Nakagami-m channels. In: IEEE National Conference on Communications (NCC), pp. 1–5, February 2013
11. Hagenauer, J.: Rate-compatible punctured convolutional codes (RCPC codes) and their applications. IEEE Trans. Commun. **36**(4), 389–400 (1988)
12. Hunter, T.E., Sanayei, S., Nosratinia, A.: Outage analysis of coded cooperation. IEEE Trans. Inf. Theor. **52**(2), 375–391 (2006)
13. Li, C., Wang, Y., Xiang, W., Yang, D.: Outage probablity analysis of coded cooperation with multiple relays. In: Proceedings of the IEEE Vehicular Technology Conference, pp. 1–5, June 2011
14. Bansal, A., Garg, P.: Performance analysis of coded cooperation under Nakagami-m fading channels. In: IEEE International Conference on Communications (ICC), pp. 1–5, May 2010

Urban Railway Operation Plan Subject to Disruption

Amin Jamili[✉]

School of Industrial Engineering, College of Engineering,
University of Tehran, Tehran, Iran
a_jamili@ut.ac.ir

Abstract. The life cycle of an urban railway system is about thirty years, and therefore, any small improvement in operation, results huge savings. The daily operation follows a headway distribution, which itself computed based on the traffic volume. Passing the block sections and stopping in stations are always contaminated with disruptions. The disruptions affect the traffic especially when the headway is in minimum. In this paper, computing the exact practical travel and dwell times is studied. At the first stage a formula is proposed to compute the remained disruptions at the end of the last period in minimum headway. It is supposed that the travel and dwell times take values according to a symmetric distribution. The amount of supplementary times to reach the desired reliability is defined based on the probability of non-absorbed disruptions at the end of the last period. It is concluded that as the number of disrupted travel and dwell times increases the amount of required supplementary times to reach the same level of reliability, increases but in a descending rate. This finding improves the current method to reach the reliability in urban railway operation plans. Finally, the Karaj Metro Line 2 is studied and analyzed as the case study.

Keywords: Operation plan · Urban railway · Uncertainty · Disruption · Supplementary times

1 Introduction

One of the primary studies in constructing EPC urban railway projects such as Monorail, LRT, Subway, Tramway, etc., is to study the operation plan. The structure of this study is shown in Fig. 1. As shown in Fig. 1, one of the outputs of operation plan is computing the travel times. The travel times are used as an input to compute the number of trains in operation. In practical cases, when trains pass block sections and stations and during mounting and dismounting the passengers, as well as shunting operations, different kinds of disruptions may occur. These disruptions can be categorized in two classes.

First Class: Those which result huge effects on operation, and require a long time to be settled down, such as train failures, route failures, signaling system failures. In these situations, the operation switches to a more restricted mode based on the track plan.

Second Class: Those which are minor and just result a few seconds delays, such as increase of travelling times, increase of dwell times, increase of shunting times.

The second class repetitively happens during operation and therefore should be managed in planning stage. The method to manage the second class is considering supplementary times in primary travel and dwell times.

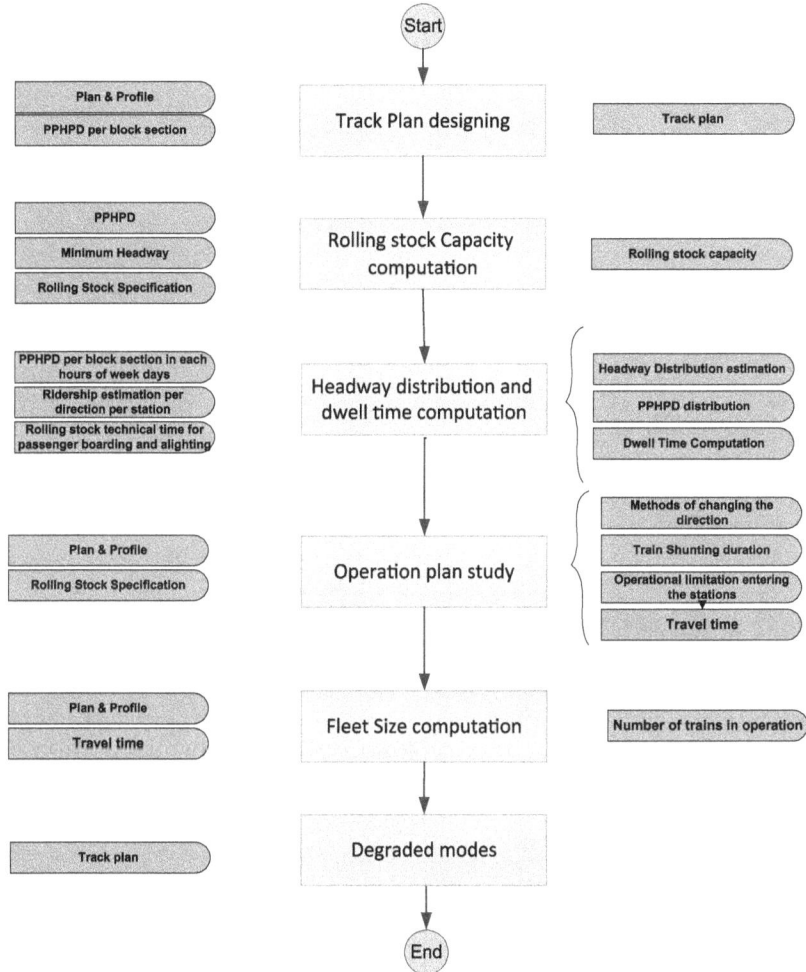

Fig. 1. The structure of operation plan study

Remark 1. The scope of this paper contains only the second kind of disruptions.

To absorb the second class of disruptions, and preventing propagation of delays among trains, some supplementary times are added to travel times and dwell times. Increase of travel times and dwell times leads to reduction of commercial speed. It is worth to mention that, as the commercial speed reduces the amount of required train increases. On the other hand, passengers always look for the transportation modes which offer services with shorter amount of time. These effects are shown in Fig. 2.

188   A. Jamili

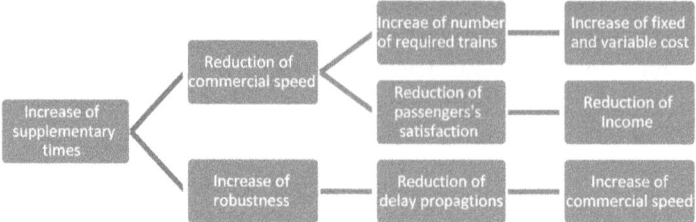

Fig. 2. The structure of operation plan study

Considering Fig. 2, it is easily understood that the tradeoff between increase of supplementary times and reduction of commercial speed should be managed precisely.

1.1 Previous Works

It is worth to mention that all practical problems are always contaminated with uncertainty. In transportation systems, travel times, dwell times, etc., are disrupted in practical cases. In main line railways, Shafia et al. [1] proposed a robust timetabling model based on Bertsimas and Sim approach [2], as well as a robustness index to compute the required buffer intervals for branch and bound algorithm. Khan and Zhou [3] proposed a two-stage stochastic recourse model for the double-track train timetabling problem, by defining additional time supplements to travelling times of trains and dwell times. Liebchen et al. [4] studied the construction of delay resistant periodic timetables. Carey [5] proposed heuristic methods to measure the stability of train timetables considering the probability of disturbances. Vansteenwegen and Oudheusden [6] based on the delay distributions of the arriving trains, computed the ideal buffer intervals in connections. Fischetti and Monaci [7] proposed a heuristic method to model uncertainty based on combining the robust optimization with a simplified two-stage stochastic programming approach. D'Angelo et al. [8] proposed an algorithm to ensure that, if a delay occurs, no more than a specific number of activities are affected by the propagation of such a delay. Shafia et al. [9] solved the robust train-timetabling problem by fuzzy approach. In urban railways, Jamili, and Ghannadpour [10] proposed an algorithm to compute the supplementary and buffer times.

1.2 Contribution of the Paper

The novelty of this paper is listed as follows:

(1) Proposing a new method to compute the non absorbed disruptions for classic long loop urban railway systems.
(2) Proposing a new method to compute the supplementary times based on the desired probability of non absorbed disruptions at the end of the block sections.
(3) It is demonstrated that the previous simple methods for finding the supplementary times which consider a constant percentage of travel and dwell times is not

precise, and the values of required supplementary times varies as the size of the urban railway system changes.

1.3 Outline

In this paper, after a review of urban railway operation definition in the next section, a new formula to compute the remained disruption is proposed in Sect. 3. In Sect. 4, based on the model of data uncertainty in robust approach, a new method to compute the required amount of supplementary times is proposed. In Sect. 5, the Karaj Metro Line 2 is studied and the outputs are analyzed. Finally, the concluding remarks are given at the end to summarize the contribution of this paper.

2 Urban Railway Operation Definition

Figure 3 shows a long loop urban railway system including four stations, six block sections, and two shunting areas.

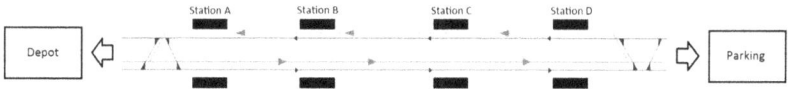

Fig. 3. Simple urban railway system

General main operational characteristics in urban railway systems are listed as follows:

1. The operation is in double track and one direction mode.
2. The timetable is periodic.
3. All trains are similar in performance.
4. To reach the required PPHPD, the headway between trains is already defined.

The operation of trains in urban railway system is categorized in four classes.

(1) Classic long-loop mode: In this mode, all trains start from the first station, e.g. station A and travel to the last station, e.g. station Z, then turn back in this station and travel from this station to the first station, and so on. In this mode, all trains are planned to stop in all stations.
(2) Classic short-loop mode: In this mode, trains follow two or more patterns. In each pattern the first station and the last station in short-loop operation differs from the long-loop one. For this purpose, instead of only two turn back at the first and last stations, more turn backs are defined along the route for short-loop operation purposes.
(3) Multi-pattern long-loop mode: In this mode, in opposite of first mode trains are planned to stop in different stations. The number of patterns is limited.
(4) Multi-pattern short-loop mode: In this mode, trains follow different patterns from two aspects: 1. different first and last stations, same as second mode, and 2. different stations which trains are planned to stop.

Figure 4 shows a simple sample of above definitions. The squares are the symbol of stations. The colored ones show the stations that trains intend to stop. The hatched ones indicate those stations that are not visited by train and the blank ones shows the stations in which trains pass and do not stop for mounting and dismounting purposes.

The scope of this paper is the first mode that is the most used one in Iran and many other countries.

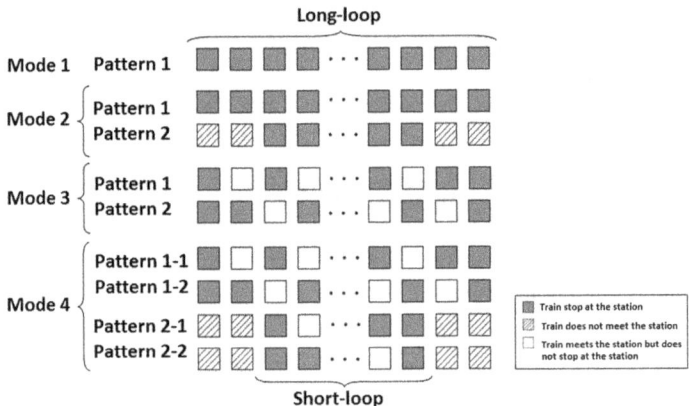

Fig. 4. Different modes in urban railway operation

3   Computation of Absorbed and Remained Disruptions

Jamili and Ghannadpour [10] proposed a method to compute the delays and applied the robustness index proposed by Shafia et al. [1] to find the required supplementary times. This method was based on considering distribution functions for all uncertain data. This method contains following difficulties:

1. Generally, fitting exact distribution functions to uncertain data is not an easy task.
2. Finding the summation of uncertain data as they may have different distribution functions is computationally intractable.

By the above explanations, in the remaining parts of this paper, to eliminate the above mentioned unwilling characteristics, a new method is proposed, where only a symmetric but unknown distribution is assigned to the uncertain data, and similar to Bertsimas and Sim robust approach [2], it is supposed that in reality only a limited number of uncertain parameters take the worst values. Table 1 shows the used notations throughout the paper.

Remark 2. For simplicity, in this paper, it is assumed that trains are numbered based on the departure time from the first station. As a result, if train i passes a block section earlier that train k, it is concluded that $i < k$.

As explained in previous sections, the travel times and dwell times are assumed to be uncertain. It is supposed that these uncertain parameters belong to a symmetric distribution $[t_j - \hat{t}_j, t_j + \hat{t}_j] \forall j \in B$, $[d_J - \hat{d}_J, d_J + \hat{d}_J] \forall J \in S$. In addition to this representing

Table 1. Used notations

Symbol	Description
i	Index for trains
i'	Index for the train which is just passed block sections before train i
j	Index for block section
j'	Index for the block section located just before block section j
J	Index for station, and refers to the station located at the beginning of block section j
n	Number of periods
H	Headway between consecutive trains
T	The set of trains
T_n	The set of trains in period n
S	The set of stations
B	The set of block sections
t_j	Travel time of trains in block section j
$\hat{t}_j$	Half length of interval related to travel time in block section j
t_{ij}	Travel time of train i in block section j
$\hat{t}_{ij}$	Half length of interval related to travel time of train i in block section j
d_J	Dwell time of trains in station J
R_{ij}	Remained disruption of train i at the end of block section j
R_{ij}^h	Horizontal remained disruption of train i at the beginning of block section j
R_{ij}^v	Vertical remained disruption of train i at the beginning of block section j
ε_{ij}	Disruption of train i in block section j
ε_{iJ}	Disruption of train i in station J
ε_j	Disruption of each individual train in block section j
ε_J	Disruption of each individual train in station J
b_j	Time interval between departure of a specific train, e.g. i, and arrival time of the previous one, e.g. i' at block section j.
s_j	Supplementary time related to travel time of each individual train at block section j.
s_J	Supplementary time related to dwell time of each individual train at station J.

method of uncertainty, one can easily define the disrupted parameters ε_j, and ε_J corresponding with t_j, and d_J, with the same symmetric distribution, with nominal value equal to 0, i.e. $[-\hat{t}_j, +\hat{t}_j] \forall j \in B$, $[-\hat{d}_J, +\hat{d}_J] \forall J \in S$, respectively.

Remark 3. Based on the mentioned characteristics of urban railway system, we have $\varepsilon_{ij} = \varepsilon_{kj}$, $t_{ij} = t_{kj}$, $\forall i, k \in T$, $\forall j \in B$ and $\varepsilon_{iJ} = \varepsilon_{kJ}$, $d_{iJ} = d_{kJ}$, $\forall i, k \in T$, $\forall J \in S$. Therefore, one can replace the symbols $\varepsilon_{ij}, \varepsilon_{iJ}, t_{ij}, d_{iJ}$, with their equivalents $\varepsilon_j, \varepsilon_J, t_j, d_J$, respectively.

The remained disruption of train i at the end of block section j, R_{ij}, shown by colored circle in Fig. 5, equals: the disruption of train i in block section j, $(\varepsilon_{ij} - s_j)$, case 1 of Fig. 5, plus the maximization of two statement: (1) The first statement is the horizontal remained disruption, R_{ij}^h, and equals $(R_{i'j} - b_j)$, case 2 of Fig. 5. (2) The second statement is the vertical remained disruption, R_{ij}^v, and equals $(R_{ij'} + \varepsilon_{iJ} - s_J)$, case 3 of Fig. 5. It is worth to mention that $(\varepsilon_{iJ} - s_J)$ equals the remained disruption of trains in station J. By this explanation, the remained disruption of train i at the end of block section j, equals Eq. 1.

$$R_{ij} = \max\{((\varepsilon_{ij} - s_j) + \max\{(R_{i'j} - b_j), (R_{ij'} + \varepsilon_{iJ} - s_J), 0\})\}, \forall i \in T, \forall j \in B. \quad (1)$$

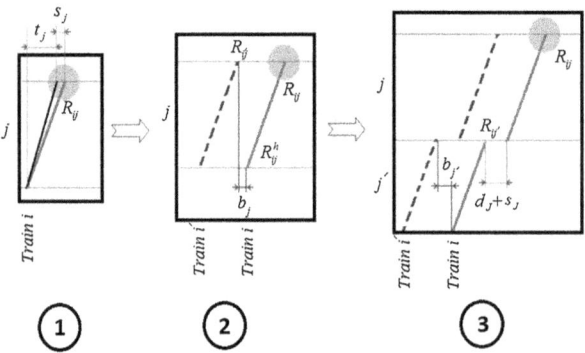

Fig. 5. Illustration of non-absorbed disruption elements

Remark 4. Considering the tradeoff effects of increasing the supplementary times, Fig. 2, and the characteristics of classic long-loop operation, one can say in optimal solution, we have:

(1) Since $\max aug\ \varepsilon_{ij} = \hat{t}_{ij}$, therefore: $s_j \leq \hat{t}_{ij}$
(2) Since $\max aug\ \varepsilon_{iJ} = \hat{d}_{iJ}$, therefore: $s_J \leq \hat{d}_{iJ}$
(3) $\max\{(R_{i'j} - b_j), (R_{ij'} + \varepsilon_{iJ} - s_J)\} \geq 0, \forall i \in T, \forall j \in B$
(4) $R_{ij} \geq 0, \forall i \in T, \forall j \in B.$

Therefore, one can easily simplify Eqs. 1–2.

$$R_{ij} = (\varepsilon_{ij} - s_j) + \max\{(R_{i'j} - b_j), (R_{ij'} + \varepsilon_{iJ} - s_J)\}, \forall i \in T, \forall j \in B. \quad (2)$$

Remark 5. As the signaling system and the position of signals is not exactly defined at the stage of generating operation plan, the travel times generated in this step does not contain the exact details of reaction time, clearance time, etc. It is assumed that these details are already considered in travel and dwell times.

Remark 6. In a railway urban system, as the headway decreases the time intervals among trains decrease as well. In the case of using track-circuit based signaling system, whenever, these time intervals in a specific block section are not enough long to absorb the potential delays, this block section will be divided in two smaller ones by defining extra track-circuits. The threshold for dividing the block section is specified in Proposition 2, as $H \geq t_j + \hat{t}_j$.

Remark 7. In the case of $H < t_j + \hat{t}_j, \forall j \in B$, for safety reasons, the block section j should be divided in two smaller block sections.

Remark 8. The travel time of a shunting operation is the summation of (1) Shunting toward changing position, (2) Cab activation and setting the points, and (3) Shunting to departure platform and setting the points. Therefore, a shunt can be assumed as three special block sections.

Remark 9. Stable operations provides the situation in which the remained disruptions are in normal amount, and are not increased from one period to another.

Proposition 1. In a stable long-loop classic urban railway system, generally, we have $R_{ij} \geq R_{i'j}, \forall i \in T_n, \forall j \in B$, and specially, when $n \to \infty$, we have $R_{ij} \geq R_{i'j} \forall i \in T_n, \forall j \in B$.

Proof. Considering the characteristics of stable long-loop classic urban railway system specified in previous sections, train i' at the end of block section j is affected by the remained disruptions generated by trains belong to set $\{1, 2, \ldots, i''\}$ passing block sections $\{1, 2, \ldots, |B|\}$ and train i' passing block sections $\{1, 2, \ldots, j'\}$. In the same way, train i is affected by the remained disruptions specified for train i' plus the remained last period, i.e. those belong to train i' at block sections $\{j, \ldots, |B|\}$, and train i at block sections $\{1, 2, \ldots, j\}$, Therefore, considering the definition of stable operation, we have $R_{ij} \geq R_{i'j}, \forall i \in T_n, \forall j \in B$, and specially, as the number of periods increases, the effect of the last period in comparison with all periods reduces linearly, and finally, when $n \to \infty$, we have $R_{ij} = R_{i'j} \forall i \in T_n, \forall j \in B$. □

Proposition 2. In a stable Long loop classic urban railway system, if $H \geq t_j + \hat{t}_j$, then $R_{ij}^h \leq R_{ij}^v \forall i \in T, \forall j \in B$.

Proof. Consider Fig. 6 as an example, and suppose that block section j is the first one in which inequality (3) is satisfied.

$$R_{kj}^h > R_{kj}^v. \tag{3}$$

Moreover, as shown in this figure, train l is the first train in daily operation plan which travels with the minimum headway and therefore, following equation is resulted.

$$R_{kj}^h = R_{lj} - b_j = R_{lj}^v + (\varepsilon_j - s_j) - b_j = R_{lj'} + (\varepsilon_j - s_j) + (\varepsilon_J - s_J) - b_j. \tag{4}$$

Substituting $R_{lj'} + (\varepsilon_j - s_j) + (\varepsilon_J - s_J) - b_j$ with R_{kj}^h in inequality (3), results:

$$R_{lj'} + (\varepsilon_j - s_j) + (\varepsilon_J - s_J) - b_j > R_{kj}^v. \tag{5}$$

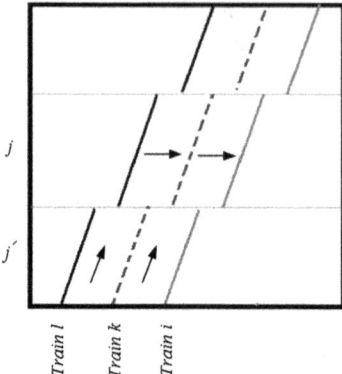

Fig. 6. A sample of classic long-loop urban railway timetable graph

Moreover, considering the results of Proposition 1, it is obvious that $R_{kj'} \geq R_{lj'}$, and as a result, $R_{kj}^v = R_{kj'} + (\varepsilon_J - s_J) \geq R_{lj'} + (\varepsilon_J - s_J)$. Therefore, inequality (5) can be rewritten as follows:

$R_{lj'} + (\varepsilon_J - s_J) \leq R_{kj}^v < R_{lj'} + (\varepsilon_j - s_j) + (\varepsilon_J - s_J) - b_j$, and therefore, we have $(\varepsilon_j - s_j) - b_j > 0$. Since $\max aug\, \varepsilon_j = \hat{t}_j$ and $s_j + b_j = H - t_j$, it is concluded that $H - t_j < \hat{t}_j$, which violates the primary assumption. □

Proposition 3. Equation (2) reduces to Eq. (6), under the assumption of $H \geq t_j + \hat{t}_j$.

$$R_{ij} = (\varepsilon_{ij} - s_j) + (R_{ij'} + \varepsilon_{iJ} - s_J). \tag{6}$$

Proof. Considering Proposition 2, $R_{ij}^h \leq R_{ij}^v \, \forall i \in T, \forall j \in B$. As a result the $\max\{(R_{i'j} - b_j), (R_{ij'} + \varepsilon_{iJ} - s_J)\} = (R_{ij'} + \varepsilon_{iJ} - s_J)$ and therefore, the proposition is proved. □

Proposition 4. The remained disruption of train i at the end of block section j equals:

$$R_{ij} = \sum_{k<i}\sum_{l\in B}(\varepsilon_{kl} - s_l) + \sum_{l\leq j}(\varepsilon_{il} - s_l) + \sum_{k<i}\sum_{m\in S}(\varepsilon_{km} - s_m) + \sum_{m\leq J}(\varepsilon_{im} - s_m), \forall i \in T, \forall j \in B. \tag{7}$$

Proof. The result immediately follows from substituting $R_{ij'}$ by its equivalent, in Eq. 6, and so on. □

4 Computation of Supplementary Times

Consider constraint $\sum_{j=1}^{n} a_j x_j \leq b$ and let J represent the set of coefficients that are subject to disruption $(\tilde{a}_j, j \in J)$. Therefore, the constraint $\sum_{j=1}^{n} a_j x_j \leq b$ can be expanded to $\sum_{j \notin J} a_j x_j + \sum_{j \in J} \tilde{a}_j x_j \leq b$. It is assumed that each uncertain coefficient $\tilde{a}_j, j \in J$ independently takes values according to a symmetric distribution with mean equal to the nominal value a_j and of half length $\hat{a}_j$. In other words, $\tilde{a}_j$ belongs to the interval $[a_j - \hat{a}_j, a_j + \hat{a}_j]$.

In robust optimization approach, the solution is immunized against all disruptions, and is called robust solution. Bertsimas and Sim, [2] supposed that it is unlikely to consider all uncertain parameters equal to their worst case bound, as a result the parameter Γ, $0 \leq \Gamma \leq |J|$, is used to adjust the conservatism level of the final solution. It means that at last only $\lfloor \Gamma \rfloor$ of parameters subjected to disruptions are allowed to change and take the worst possible values, and one coefficient a_e changes by $(\Gamma - \lfloor \Gamma \rfloor)\hat{a}_e$. Bertsimas and Sim developed an approach that if, in practice, only a subset of $\lfloor \Gamma \rfloor$ coefficients changes, then the robust solution will be feasible and even if more than $\lfloor \Gamma \rfloor$ changes, then the robust solution will be feasible with the following probability.

$$\Pr\left(\sum_j \tilde{a}_j x_j^* > b\right) \leq \frac{1}{2^n}\left\{(1-\mu)\binom{n}{\lfloor v \rfloor} + \sum_{l=\lfloor v \rfloor+1}^{n}\binom{n}{l}\right\}, \qquad (8)$$

where $n = |J|$, $v = (\Gamma + n)/2$, and $\mu = v - \lfloor v \rfloor$

By the above explanation, and considering Eq. (7), the robust condition in urban railway system is $\sum_{k<i}\sum_{l\in B}(\varepsilon_{kl}) + \sum_{l\leq j}(\varepsilon_{il}) + \sum_{k<i}\sum_{m\in S}(\varepsilon_{km}) + \sum_{m\leq J}(\varepsilon_{im}) \leq 0$, where i is the last train, and j is the last block section passed by train i during the last period. Moreover, as shown in Fig. 2, as the supplementary times increases the commercial speed reduces, therefore the urban railway operators always look for minimum supplementary times, i.e. $Min\left(\sum_i s_i + \sum_J s_J\right)$ to provide the desired level of robustness. The desired level of robustness can be measured by the probability defined by inequality (8). In the next section, the details of computing supplementary times are illustrated in Karaj Metro Line 2 case study.

5 Case Study: Karaj Metro Line 2

The Karaj Metro Line two contains 23 stations, 22 block sections, and 2 shunting areas. The general layout is shown by the colored part in Fig. 7. The minimum headway is advised to be 2.5 min, and the computed travel times and dwell times are as shown in Table 2.

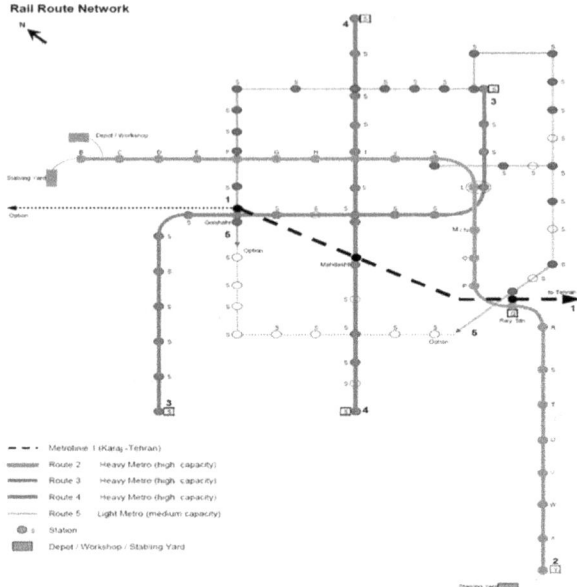

Fig. 7. Metro Karaj network

General, in order to absorb the disruptions, for each kilometer 5 s are added to the computed travel times. In this paper it is assumed that $\hat{t}_j = 0.05 \times t_j \,\forall j \in B$. Based on Eq. (7), the number of disruptions which should be considered in a complete loop equal: 92 = 23(Number of stations) × 2 + 2(Number of shunting areas) + 22(Number of block sections) × 2. The headway distribution during weekdays is computed based on the traffic studies and the capacity of trains and is depicted in Fig. 8.

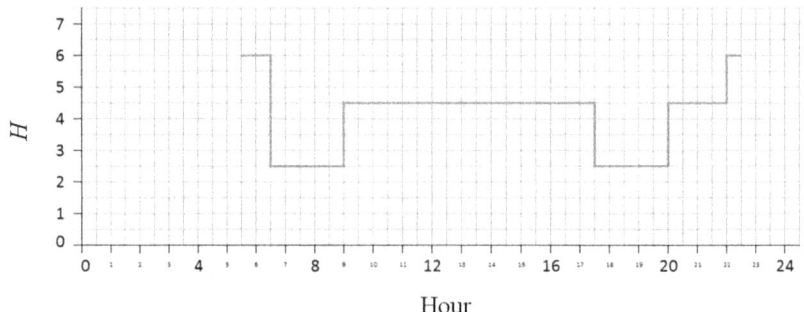

Fig. 8. Headway distribution of Metro Line 2 Karaj during week days

Based on the headway distribution, Fig. 8, the minimum headway is 2.5 min which takes 2.5 h during a working day. Considering a complete loop equal to 90 min, each train, travels 1.67 loops in 2.5 h. The probability of facing with remained disruption at

Table 2. The computed travel times and dwell times in Karaj Metro Line 2

Station	Station	Block section distance (m)	Journey time (s) Outbound direction	Return direction	Dwell time (s)
B	C	1683	110.686	110.683	
C	D	949	78.435	77.653	25
D	E	885	75.809	74.773	25
E	F	865	73.863	73.863	25
F	G	785	71.35	70.273	25
G	H	800	71.742	70.948	25
H	I	736	69.403	68.605	25
I	J	1119	86.087	85.953	25
J	K	925	77.463	75.823	25
K	M	1196	104.359	104.359	25
M	O	1201	88.993	88.933	25
O	P	1457	121.443	121.443	25
P	Q	841	76.381	76.382	25
Q	R	988	80.52	81.71	25
R	S	1642	110.6	110.8	25
S	T	1304	94.51	94.2	25
T	U	1382	97.14	97.14	25
U	V	1144	86.43	86.43	25
V	W	1188	88.41	88.41	25
W	X	1090	91.79	92.07	25
X	Y	1064	84.33	84.33	25
Y	Z	1508	93.86	96.56	

the end of 1.67 loops which consists of $92 \times 1.67 \cong 153$ disruption variables as a function of Γ is shown in Fig. 9.

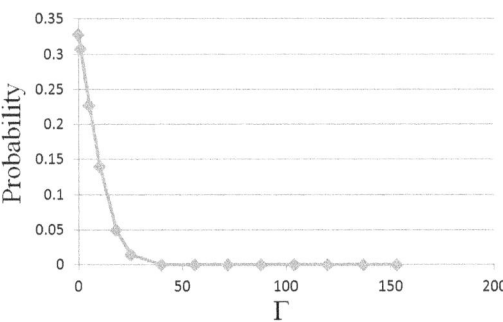

Fig. 9. The probability of facing with remained disruption at the end of 1.67 loops

Based on Fig. 9, in the case the operator interested in 5 % as the probability of facing with remained disruption at the end of the 1.67 loops, we have $\Gamma = 18$.

Therefore, considering Table (2), and the assumption, $\hat{t}_j = 0.05 \times t_j, \forall j \in B$, the summation of supplementary times equal to $\max_{\{Z|Z\subseteq (B\cup S), |Z|=18\}} \left\{ \sum_{m\in Z} (\hat{t}_m + \hat{d}_m) \right\} = 84$ s, which must be assigned to the travel and dwell times as a ratio of these times.

Moreover, in the case that the desired probability equals 2 %, we have $\Gamma = 23.5$, and the summation of supplementary times equals to 113 s.

Therefore, considering the supplementary times 84, and 113 s, in order to achieve the requested reliability, it is suggested to increase all travel and dwell times by 1.6 %, and 2.2 % respectively.

The theoretical round trip time equals 5225 s, and the number of required trains to reach the minimum headway, 150 s is $\lceil \frac{5225}{150} \rceil = 35$ sets. In the case of adding the supplementary times, the number of required train, in both cases, increases to 36 sets. The operational speed is reduced from 34.03 km/h to 33.5 km/h, and 33.32 km/h in the studied robust cases, respectively.

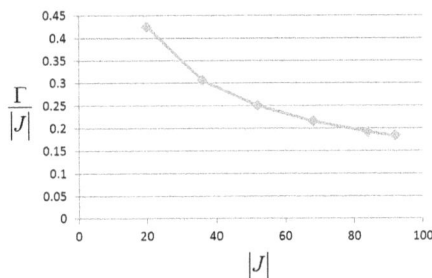

Fig. 10. The values of $\frac{\Gamma}{|J|}$ against $|J|$ in 0.05 probability.

6 Conclusion

In this paper, a new formula to compute the remained disruptions at the end of last period with minimum headway is proposed, and a new method to find the supplementary times to reach the desired robustness is proposed. Figure 10 shows that as the number of disrupted variables increases, the value of parameter Γ to reach a constant probability augmented in a descending rate. This result can be interpreted in a way that considering a fixed percentage of travel times, and dwell times as the required supplementary times, is not adequate since in practical cases this percentage is descending as the number of disruption variables increases. Moreover, the Karaj Metro Line 2 was analyzed as the case study. The result demonstrated that the number of required trains, as well as the resulted commercial speed is directly sensitive to the values of supplementary times.

References

1. Shafia, M.A., Pourseyed Aghaee, M., Sadjadi, S.J., Jamili, A.: Robust train timetabling problem: mathematical model and branch and bound algorithm. IEEE Trans. Intell. Transp. Syst. **13**(1), 307–317 (2012)

2. Bertsimas, D., Sim, M.: The price of robustness. Oper. Res. **52**(1), 35–53 (2004)
3. Khan, M.B., Zhou, X.: Stochastic optimization model and solution algorithm for robust double-track train timetabling problem. IEEE Trans. Intell. Transp. Syst. **11**(1), 81–89 (2010)
4. Liebchen, C., Chachtebeck, M., Schoebel, A., Stiller, S., Prigge, A.: Computing delay resistant railway timetables. Comput. Oper. Res. **37**(5), 857–868 (2010)
5. Carey, M.: Ex ante heuristic measures of schedule reliability. Transp. Res. Part B **33**, 473–494 (1999)
6. Vansteenwegen, P., Oudheusden, D.V.: Developing railway timetables which guarantee a better service. Eur. J. Oper. Res. **173**, 337–350 (2006)
7. Fischetti, M., Monaci, M.: Light robustness. In: Ahuja, R.K., Möhring, R.H., Zaroliagis, C. D. (eds.) Robust and Online Large-Scale Optimization. LNCS, vol. 5868, pp. 61–84. Springer, Heidelberg (2009)
8. D'Angelo, G., Di Stefano, G., Navarra, A.: Evaluation of recoverable-robust timetables on tree networks. In: Fiala, J., Kratochvíl, J., Miller, M. (eds.) IWOCA 2009. LNCS, vol. 5874, pp. 24–35. Springer, Heidelberg (2009)
9. Shafia, M.A., Sadjadi, S.J., Jamili, A., Tavakkoli-Moghaddam, R., Pourseyed Aghaee, M.: The periodicity and robustness in a single-track train scheduling problem. Appl. Soft Comput. J. **12**, 440–452 (2012)
10. Jamili, A., Ghannadpour, S.F.: Computing the supplementary times and the number of required trains in operation plan studies under stochastic perturbations. In: Proceedings of 16th International IEEE Conference on Intelligent Transportation Systems, The Netherlands (2013)

Author Index

Akiba, Masakazu 148
Bazazian, Shermin 115
Biradar, S.R. 135
Biswas, Biswajit 90

Chakrabarti, Amlan 90
Chakraborty, Aruna 20
Chatterjee, Pubali 90
Chaurasia, Brijesh Kumar 135

Das, Rik 55
Dey, Kashi Nath 90

Gavrilova, Marina 115
Ghosh, Saurav 55
Ghoshal, Somoballi 90
Gupta, Sindhu Hak 172

Horita, Tadayoshi 148

Jain, Gunjan 135
Jamili, Amin 186
Kanno, Tsuneo 148
Kar, Reshma 20
Konar, Amit 20
Kushwaha, Alok Kumar Singh 35
Nishiuchi, Nobuyuki 77
P.V.S.S.R., Chandra Mouli 3

Sharan, S.N. 172
Singh, R.K. 172
Soundrapandiyan, Rajkumar 3
Srivastava, Rajeev 35

Takahashi, Yutaka 77
Takanami, Itsuo 148
Terauchi, Mina 148
Thepade, Sudeep 55

GPSR Compliance

The European Union's (EU) General Product Safety Regulation (GPSR) is a set of rules that requires consumer products to be safe and our obligations to ensure this.

If you have any concerns about our products, you can contact us on

ProductSafety@springernature.com

In case Publisher is established outside the EU, the EU authorized representative is:

Springer Nature Customer Service Center GmbH
Europaplatz 3
69115 Heidelberg, Germany

www.ingramcontent.com/pod-product-compliance
Lightning Source LLC
Chambersburg PA
CBHW071720100426
42873CB00016B/345